DATE DUE		

Kant, Respect and Injustice

International Library of Philosophy

Editor: Ted Honderich
Professor of Philosophy, University College London

A catalogue of books already published in the
International Library of Philosophy
will be found at the end of this volume

Kant, Respect and Injustice

The Limits of Liberal Moral Theory

Victor J. Seidler

Goldsmiths' College
University of London

ROUTLEDGE & KEGAN PAUL

London, Boston and Henley

First published in 1986
by Routledge & Kegan Paul plc

14 Leicester Square, London WC2H 7PH, England

9 Park Street, Boston, Mass. 02108, USA and

Broadway House, Newtown Road,
Henley on Thames, Oxon RG9 1EN, England

Set in Times, 10 on 12pt
printed and bound in Great Britain
by Butler & Tanner Ltd
Frome and London

Library of Congress Cataloging in Publication Data

Seidler, Victor J., 1945–
Kant, respect and injustice.
(International library of philosophy)
Bibliography: p.
Includes index.
1. Kant, Immanuel, 1724–1804——Ethics. 2. Kant,
Immanuel, 1724–1804——Political and social views.
3. Social ethics. I. Title. II. Series.
B2799.E8S49 1986   170'.92'4   85–18346
British Library CIP data also available

ISBN 0–7102–0426–4

For my mother and Leo
and in memory of my father
and brother John

CONTENTS

Contents

ACKNOWLEDGMENTS

I have taken many years to bring this study to fruition. The early ideas for a study on respect, equality and dependency in Kant's moral writings were set down in 1970. By that time I had been deeply influenced by the writings of Wittgenstein in a way that helped question the separation often assumed between epistemology and politics. Some of these questions were sharpened for me as I became influenced by Marx in the late 1960s. But I remained dissatisfied with the abstractness which seemed to prevail in discussions of values and beliefs within social theory as well as in Marxist discussions of ideology and consciousness. Often they seemed too dismissive and unable to come to terms with the complexities of people's lived experience, in a class society organised around social relations of power and dependence.

During a year in Cambridge, Massachusetts in 1970, I benefited from conversations and seminars with Rogers Allbritton and Stanley Cavell. They shared an understanding of the seminal importance of Wittgenstein's work within philosophy. I also learned how hard it was to draw upon this work without imitating it. I found it hard to find my own voice. This inevitably took some time coming and involved many changes. But I was greatly helped and supported through the larger social and cultural movements of the early 1970s that were asking questions about the form and quality of personal and social relationships. There is little doubt that this study would not have its present form if it were not for the theoretical and practical challenges of the women's movement. This movement raised fundamental questions about the relationship of respect, equality and dependency in the context of what it means to be treated as a person in your own right, not as a sexual object or simply in relation to others. In learning to respect others we have to do more than acknowledge their individual rights. This helped bring into focus the depths of Kantian tradition within a liberal moral culture we took so much for granted. It also helped me understand that it was not simply a question of challenging prevailing attitudes, of learning to treat people differently, but also of transforming personal and social relations.

I had to learn the inadequacy of thinking of Kant's influence as an aspect of 'bourgeois ideology' or thinking that it articulates a tradition of individualism that can uniformly be set against a more collectivist or socialist tradition. The relationships are more complicated. A socialist moral vision has to be premised on a transformed sense of individuality and an enriched conception of individual needs. Our theory has to develop in a more dialectical relationship with a sense of the strengths of Kant's understandings of autonomy and individuality, as well as an understanding of how Kant's influence within our taken for granted liberal moral culture can leave us with an impoverished conception of the very individual which liberal theory has wanted to sustain in a language of rights. It can also make it harder for us to identify and understand the workings of social relations of power and subordination. This inevitably involves finding ways of identifying the different ways moral traditions continue to influence the ways we think and feel about ourselves. This can also involve a challenge to traditional conceptions of moral argument. It can involve a more dialectical approach which establishes through the help of different examples a growing sense of the different ways we *already* assume the influence of a broadly conceived Kantian tradition, in the ways we think and feel about our lives and our relations with others. This calls for a different awareness of ourselves and our experience. The examples often attempt to construct situations which give a sense of the fuller complexities of social life. This is different from the more restricted nature of examples often invoked in analytic philosophy and against the abstract individualism of liberal thought. This involves a more direct style of presentation in which we are encouraged to reflect upon what we so often take for granted when presented with deductive arguments. If this means it takes longer for the shape of the argument to become clear, hopefully it has been grounded in a fuller sense of what is involved in different ways of conceptualising a situation or relationship. In this way I hope that people can *notice* the living meaning of Kantianism and the different levels in which we are influenced by it. If this is different from the usual procedure of argument and counter-argument, hopefully it encourages a deeper and fuller relationship to the different aspects of Kant's continuing influence.

I have explored the relationship in Kant's writings between respect, equality and dependency to show a particular tension Kant is faced with in preserving a conception of the autonomy of morality and to argue for a fundamental shift in our moral and political theory towards a concern with respect as an issue of human needs, not simply as a defence of individual rights. It is part of the greatness of his thinking that he does not avoid this contradiction in his later writings when he seems to question some of the more formalistic notions in his moral theory. In this way he helps us to establish a broad framework within which our thinking about respect, equality and dependency has largely been organised within a liberal moral culture. This can help us explain the ease with which we often separate questions of morality from questions of politics. I focus upon the example of the relationship between rich and poor in Kant's later writings because this seems to me to present the moment at which a concern for justice calls for a language of needs, not simply of rights, and the very notion of the autonomy of morality seems to be questioned. I want to make clear some of the broader assumptions upon which the notion of the autonomy of morality so often rests. This seems to be a central feature within a liberal moral culture. I go on to illuminate the difficulties this creates in liberal moral and political theory being able to sustain an adequate sense of respect for the person in terms of a language of rights and to come to terms with the relations of power and subordination in social life. This then is also to question the difficult relationship between moral philosophy and social theory.

Many people have encouraged me in this work since my early tutorial work with Bede Rundle and John Simopoulos at Oxford. In the formative years the writing and teaching of Isaiah Berlin, Rush Rhees and Peter Winch were helpful in their different ways, connecting Wittgenstein's writings to broader questions of social theory. I had the benefit of challenging tutorials with my supervisor, Richard Wollheim, who, when we were not disagreeing about

Acknowledgments

what constitutes 'argument' in philosophy, thought my writing had
more chance as a book. Richard Norman did his best to help make
it a thesis too. For the last few years I have had the encouragement
of students studying the sociology of knowledge at Goldsmiths'
College, University of London, who have helped sharpen the focus
of many of the ideas. All along there has been the support and
friendship of Larry Blum who has constantly shared, encouraged
and stimulated my work. Others also helped me in these closing
years. They helped me believe in what I was doing and trust in
what I was trying to say. I can think of the very different and
individual kinds of support and friendship I received from Paul
Atkinson, Peter Bindley, David Boadella, Terry Cooper, Sheila
Ernst, Jo Foster, Anthony Goldstone, Lucy Goodison, Marcia
Homiak, Anna Ickowitz, Sally Inman, Bruce Landesman, Mike
Levin, Trefor Lloyd, Steve Lukes, Norman Malcolm, Alan Mon-
tefiore, Bob Moore, Paul Morrison, Caroline Ramazanoglu, Janet
Ransom, Sheila Rowbotham, Joanna Ryan, Tony Seidler, Rob
Senior, Myron Sharaf, Tony Skillen, Jim Smith, Sue Stedman
Jones, Mary Stiasny, Charles Taylor, Tom Weld, Bob Young and
the late Jerry Cohen. I want to thank Ted Honderich for his timely
encouragement, especially with the conclusion. I owe a special
thanks to Anna Ickowitz who has shared her life, joy and understanding with me through the last difficult years of re-writing in
which I was often withdrawn and morose and rarely did my full
share. And also to our son Daniel who kept smiling encouragement
when it seemed to matter.

I

INTRODUCTION: RESPECT, EQUALITY AND THE AUTONOMY OF MORALITY

We often invoke a notion of respect to express our sense of human equality. We grow up in a liberal society feeling we are owed respect because we are human beings and that we owe respect to others. Each person is owed equal respect as a human being. This helps establish a sense of human equality that we are brought up to take very much for granted. But is it possible for me to treat someone with the respect owed to them, regardless of our relative positions of wealth, power and influence in society? There is a deep liberal tradition of thought and feeling that insists it is always possible for us to abstract from these social differences, inequalities and distinctions, to treat people with the equal respect owed to them. This is deeply rooted in the notion that, as individuals, we are free to take up whatever attitude we consider appropriate in our relationships with others. In this tradition morality is very much a matter of individuals deciding what is the morally right action to take. Moral discussion and moral theory is focused upon the principles of individual action. This guarantees and legitimates prevailing notions of the autonomy of morality, the idea that we are equally capable and able to live moral lives, regardless of the inequalities of social life.[1] I want to explore some of the sources for this tradition in Kant's moral writings.

In exploring this fundamental theme through the relationship between respect, equality and dependency in the moral writings of Kant, I am inevitably touching upon the relationship between moral philosophy and social philosophy. The question of respect has usually been treated as a topic within moral philosophy, if it

1

has been considered at all. Bernard Williams's influential treatment of this theme in his article entitled 'The Idea of Equality'[2] acknowledged that the notion of respect owed to all people 'is both complex and unclear', saying 'it needs, and would repay, a good deal of investigation'. But different kinds of investigation are both possible and necessary. I think it can be crucially important to focus upon the different ways a notion of respect enters our everyday language. This can help us investigate the ways we seem to invoke a notion of respect to express our sense of human equality, while also to acknowledge inequality and even hierarchy, as in the respect we were brought up to show through standing up for teachers when they came into class at junior school. I shall explore some of the tensions in our notion of the respect for persons.

But an investigation which focuses exclusively upon the ways a notion of respect enters our everyday moral language can too easily assume what needs to be investigated. It can take for granted the very autonomy of morality and moral language that needs to be thought about. We also need a broader, more historically sensitive mode of investigation, which still stays in touch with our everyday understandings.[3] This is to question the automatic appropriateness of philosophical methods that have proved illuminating in certain questions of epistemology and the philosophy of mind, when it comes to moral and political philosophy. This is an uncomfortable and challenging idea. Especially if this demands a concern with the internal connections between moral theory, its character and implications, and issues of social organisation.

Moral traditions are often contradictory. This is no less true of the Christian tradition that maintains such a powerful influence upon our secular moral consciousness. It has often been too easily dismissed in Marxist discussion as an ideology which blinds us to realities of social inequality and the class relations of power and domination. But morality is more than the labels we give to particular instances of it. Morality has structures and is integrally part of what is social. So, for instance, in considering liberal morality it can be important to grasp how the assumptions it brings into play are continuous with, as well as in tension with, aspects of a Christian inheritance. This establishes the importance of a sense of history as something more than a set of antecedents. It has been argued with too abstractly and generally before we have learned and become sensitive to the different ways it continues to influence our secularised moral and political consciousness. Kant has had a particular importance in giving a transformed secular definition to some of these moral conceptions within a broadly conceived liberal moral culture. We cannot consider the question 'are morals autonomous or not?' purely abstractly without recognising that part of the contemporary relevance of Kant is that he continues to articulate a structure of thought that pervades contemporary structures of both common sense and philosophy.

The Italian Marxist writer Antonio Gramsci can help us focus our grasp of the historical and contradictory formation of our common-sense moral consciousness:

> Philosophy cannot be separated from the history of
> philosophy, nor can culture from the history of culture. In the
> most immediate and relevant sense, one cannot be a
> philosopher, by which I mean have a critical and coherent
> conception of the world, without having a consciousness of its
> historicity, of the phase of development which it represents and
> the fact that it contradicts other conceptions or elements of
> other conceptions. One's conception of the world is a response
> to certain specific problems posed by reality, which are quite
> specific and 'original' in their immediate relevance. ... To
> criticise one's own conception of the world means therefore to
> make it a coherent unity and to raise it to the level reached by
> the most advanced thought in the world. It therefore also
> means criticism of all previous philosophy, in so far as this has
> left stratified deposits in popular philosophy. The starting-
> point of critical elaboration is the consciousness of what one
> really is, and is 'knowing thyself' as a product of the historical
> process to date which has deposited in you an infinity of
> traces, without leaving an inventory. (*The Prison Notebooks*,
> p. 324, Notes 2 and 1)[4]

This suggests that 'knowing thyself' involves an historical and social understanding as much as a psychological awareness. These can no longer be so easily separated. It suggests that the very sense we have of ourselves and our relations with others is deeply influenced by the *moral culture* we grow up to take very much for granted. Much of our contemporary moral philosophy has been formed with a concern about the status of moral propositions, somehow separating this from issues of moral psychology, social relations and our understanding of personal identity.

These insights promise a very different kind of relationship between moral philosophy, moral psychology and social philosophy. They also call us to a deeper historical consciousness of ourselves and the society we grow up in. This has a particular pertinence for the themes we are to explore. The Christian conception which sees us all as equal in the eyes of God would encourage us to abstract ourselves from the social world, from the structures of power and inequality within which we live our everyday lives. The meaning of life lies elsewhere, in our relationship with God. The significance of everyday life is subordinated as we aspire towards salvation. Our actions are given meaning through this reference. Max Weber appreciated how important this was:

> The various different dogmatic roots of ascetic morality did no doubt die out after terrible struggles. But the original connection with those dogmas has left behind important traces in the later undogmatic ethics; moreover, only the knowledge of the original body of ideas can help us understand the connection of that morality with the idea of the afterlife which absolutely dominated the most spiritual men of that time. Without its power, overshadowing everything else, no moral awakening which seriously influenced practical life came into being in that period. (*The Protestant Ethic and the Spirit of Capitalism*, p. 97)[5]

This provides an important background against which to appreciate the ways Kant links with the Protestant ethic to give secular expression to the ideas of salvation in his notions of obedience to the moral law. Moral self-perfection became an end in itself, whose value is quite separate from the value of any particular results which one may produce in the world. The meaning of life was to lie in a realm independent of happiness and fulfilment in our everyday lives. People were to learn to act out of a sense of duty to the moral law. It was crucially our faculty of reason that gives us access to the moral law and so comes to define our very individuality. This was a powerfully democratic emphasis in Kant's writings, since it allowed him to challenge the kind of privileges often attached to a morality of intuition or emotions. Since as human beings we are equally rational, we have an equal capacity for morality. If it is solely a question of individual moral will whether we do what is morally required of us, we have equal access to discerning what is required of us by the moral law.

Bernard Williams's 'The Idea of Equality' helps identify this essentially egalitarian strain in Kant's writings:

> there is a powerful strain of thought that centres on a feeling
> of ultimate and outrageous absurdity in the idea that the
> achievement of the highest kind of moral worth should depend
> on natural capacities, unequally and fortuitously distributed as
> they are . . .. This strain of thought has found many types of
> religious expression; but in philosophy it is to be found in its
> purest form in Kant. Kant's view not only carries to the limit
> the notion that moral worth cannot depend on contingencies,
> but also emphasises, in its picture of the Kingdom of Ends, the
> idea of *respect* which is owed to each man as a rational moral
> agent – and, since men are equally such agents, is owed equally
> to all, unlike admiration and similar attitudes, which are
> commanded unequally by men in proportion to their unequal
> possession of different kinds of natural excellence. These ideas
> are intimately connected in Kant, and it is not possible to
> understand his moral theory unless as much weight is given to
> what he says about the Kingdom of Ends as is always given to
> what he says about duty. (*Problems of the Self*, pp. 234–5)

It is our rationality that gives us access to the moral law. In Kant our rationality is an independent faculty fundamentally separated from our wants and desires, feelings and emotions. In this way morality is guaranteed as an independent and autonomous realm. It is almost as if the workings of our rationality give us access to a realm completely independent of our everyday lives in society. We cannot help being tempted into seeing the moral law as somehow providing a secularised form of the will of God. This affects the respect owed to each person, since I shall show this to be fundamentally related to our respect for the moral law. Even the relations people have with each other are mediated by a relationship to the moral law.

Kant's ethical writings are central to an understanding of the formation of our liberal moral consciousness. I do not want simply to consider his arguments abstractly in their own terms, but also in relation to the persistence of a particular moral structure and the difficulties in transcending it. The tensions and and contradictions alive in the different periods of his writings reflect some of the contradictory thoughts and feelings within a liberal moral consciousness. This is especially true if we consider not only the classical Kantian formulations of the *Groundwork of the Metaphysics of Morals* (the 'Grundlegung') but also questions and doubts Kant voices in the much less systematic *Doctrine of Virtue*.[6] I will investigate the notions of respect, equality and dependency in both these works. My purpose is not to give an exhaustive interpretation of Kant's writings, though sometimes I will be concerned with the interpretation of particular passages. Sometimes I am going beyond a straightforward interpretation, while nevertheless staying within what can be called a 'Kantian tradition' or a 'Kantian way of thinking and feeling'. But sometimes I take a notion clearly beyond where Kant could have plausibly gone with it to illuminate more clearly a tendency in our own liberal moral thinking about respect, equality and dependency. I try to be clear which procedure I am following. My interest is in laying bare some of the contradictions in our liberal conceptions of equality, respect and dependency, thinking these can be more clearly illuminated through an historical awareness of the different traditions of thought and feeling that continue to influence our moral consciousness.

Bernard Williams makes clear the high price that Kant pays for the consistency of his classical formulations:

> The very considerable consistency of Kant's view is bought at what would generally be agreed to be a very high price. The detachment of moral worth from all contingencies is achieved only by making man's characteristic as a moral or rational agent a transcendental characteristic; man's capacity to will freely as a rational agent is not dependent on any empirical capacities he may have. . . . Accordingly, the respect owed equally to each man as a member of the Kingdom of Ends is not owed to him in respect of any empirical characteristics that he may possess, but solely in respect of the transcendental characteristic of being a free and rational will. (*Problems of the Self*, p. 235)

This was a position consistently held by Kant. The difficulties seemed to come from a different direction, especially in his later writings. These difficulties seem to centre around the very notion of the autonomy of morality which Kant could more easily assume to be a transcendental quality in his early writings. It seemed to him that this notion of the autonomy of morality could be guaranteed through the capacity people were assumed to have 'to will freely as a rational agent'. Kant tended to assume that individuals were free to work out their individual relationships, regardless of their positions of power and subordination within social life. This was something he was brought to the edge of questioning in his discussion of dependency in the relationship between rich and poor. This is why I give this discussion such emphasis. I think it brings out the ways Kant fundamentally assumes that people have a certain independence from each other. This is an independence which cannot so easily be guaranteed as a transcendental quality. Kant is forced to come to terms with the relations of power and dependency which exists between rich and poor. I will show how he gives an account of the ways inequalities are produced through people accepting the help of others, in order to preserve his notions of independence and moral autonomy. This is important not simply as a tension within Kant's writings, but because it relates to the deep cultural assumption of the autonomy of morals and the separation of morality from politics. Kant is brought to consider the relations of power and dependency that exist between rich and poor, as he is brought to the edge of recognising the ways this threatens his deeper assumptions of the autonomy of morality.

There are other tendencies of thought within Kant towards a radical abstraction from the inequalities and relations of social life that can allow these difficult issues to be avoided. We find this most clearly expressed in his earlier writing. This is a tendency of thought which is also an integral aspect of our liberal moral culture. It is possible within the 'common sense' of liberal culture to think we can always *abstract* from the structures of power and dependency within which people live their everyday lives. We can choose how we 'see' people, from what 'point of view'. This idea of being able to choose between different ways of regarding a person's life is well illustrated by Bernard Williams:

> We then moved, via the idea of 'respect' to the different notion
> of regarding men not merely under professional, social, or
> technical titles, but with consideration of their own views and
> purposes. This notion has at least this much to do with

equality: that the titles which it urges us to look behind are the conspicuous bearers of social, political, and technical *inequality*. ... It enjoins us not to let our fundamental attitudes to men be dictated by the criteria of technical success or social position, and not take them at the value carried by these titles and by the structures in which these titles place them. This does not mean, of course, that the more fundamental view that should be taken of men is in the case of every man the same: on the contrary. But it does mean that each man is owed the effort of understanding, and that in achieving it, each man is to be (as it were) abstracted from certain conspicuous structures of inequality in which we find him. (*Problems of the Self*, p. 237)

Williams makes the same point by saying 'that each man is owed an effort at identification: that he should not be regarded as the surface to which a certain label can be applied, but one should try to see the world (including the label) from his point of view' (*Problems of the Self*, p. 236). We can identify this as a continuing theme in our liberal social and moral consciousness. It reflects a particular way of thinking and feeling about social inequality, influenced by a Christian tradition of thought and feeling. It implies that the 'titles' are a surface we can 'look behind', and that they represent a level that should not be allowed to dictate our 'fundamental attitudes' towards people.

Williams is right to remind us that there is more to a person's life than his or her social position or technical competence. But it can also be misleading to draw such a sharp distinction as Williams does between 'the technical or professional attitude' which 'regards the man solely under that title' and what he calls 'the *human* approach, that which regards him as a *man who has* that title (among others), willingly, unwillingly, through lack of alternatives, with pride, etc.' (*Problems of the Self*, p. 236). This threatens to fragment our understanding of people's everyday lives and to separate people from what they do, from their activities and practices, as if it is almost incidental what they spend their lives doing. I shall show that this also has a deep source in Kant's moral writings.

Williams gives particular meaning to the notion of respect owed to all people through the idea that each person is 'owed an effort at identification'. This means that we show our respect by being ready to make the effort 'to see the world (including the label) from his point of view'. This will make a difference to the ways we see people, and so to the ways we relate to them. It does not, however, affect the ways in which the social relations of power and domination within social life need be organised. These social relations are not regarded as themselves possessing moral significance.

This echoes Kant's notion of morality as a matter of each individual living up to the moral law. Morality is conceived of as an individual, even private affair between a person and his conscience. This is the other side of the universalism of morality within the moral culture and consciousness of a liberal society. We hold firmly to the idea that morality is a matter of individual concern and decision. In this way morality tends to confirm the supposed social independence of individuals from each other, as we are each assumed to be working out our individual moral destinies. Kant has been fundamental in helping us think and feel that not only do we have an equal capacity to live a moral life, but that we also have an equal opportunity to live moral lives. This has meant assuming that our ability to live moral lives is only affected by the strengths of our individual determinations and moral will, not by the organisation of social life. This is the critical assumption of the autonomy of morality that I shall be questioning, showing how Kant himself came to have doubts when he thought through the relations between rich and poor. If the chances and possibilities of my living a moral life are affected by the structures of power and dependency and the character of social relations, then morality can no longer be so securely separated from politics. This was something the moral and political philosophy of Plato and Aristotle appreciates. It is something Hegel and Marx learned from them. But it is something that is radically denied in the prevailing moral consciousness of liberal society. This is why the doubts and contradictory impulses shown in Kant's later moral writings, particularly in his discussion of respect, equality and dependence in the relationship of rich and poor, are so crucially interesting.

We can find some of these contradictory impulses also uneasily echoed in Williams's 'The Idea of Equality'. Williams also feels the need to go beyond saying that 'each man is owed an effort at identification' as he acknowledges the ways in which our moral personalities, understandings and perceptions are deeply influenced by the social relations of power and subordination. He feels the

9

need to go beyond the general considerations in his conception of the relation of respect and equality, though he admits this raises much more fundamental questions. Even if he does not work through the implications of these insights for his underlying conception of respect and equality, he does recognise that they challenge 'several fundamental questions of moral philosophy'.

> But there seem to be further injunctions connected with the Kantian maxim, and with the notion of 'respect', that go beyond these considerations. There are forms of exploiting men or degrading them which would be thought to be excluded by these notions, but which cannot be excluded merely by considering how the exploited or degraded men see the situation. For it is precisely a mark of extreme exploitation or degradation that those who suffer it do *not* see themselves differently from the ways they are seen by the exploiters; either they do not see themselves as anything at all, or they acquiesce passively in the role for which they have been cast. Here we evidently need something more than the precept that one should respect and try to understand another man's consciousness of his own activities; it is also that one may not suppress or destroy that consciousness.
>
> All these I must confess to be vague and inconclusive considerations, but we are dealing with a vague notion: one, however, that we possess, and attach value to. To try to put these matters properly in order would be itself to try to reach conclusions about several fundamental questions of moral philosophy. (*Problems of the Self*, p. 237)

It is not within the framework of this study to 'put these matters properly in order'. I can only try to bring out, through an investigation of some of the tensions in Kant's moral writings, the kind of radical difficulties we face. Williams seems to accept 'the further notion that the degree of man's consciousness about such things as his role in society is itself in some part the product of social arrangements, and that it can be increased' (*Problems of the Self*, p. 238). This is an important recognition that is difficult for us to appreciate. I hope to show why it is so difficult to integrate fully such an insight into our moral theory by bringing into focus some of these 'vague and inconclusive considerations'. They are threatening because they challenge assumptions of autonomy and independence which are such integral aspects of our liberal and moral culture. Williams does not bring these assumptions into focus since he remains very broadly within a liberal framework of ideas which Kant has prepared, particularly in his sense of the possibilities of abstracting from the social relations of power and subordination.

I want to argue that *because* the notion of the autonomy of morality cannot be sustained we have to learn *how* relations of power and subordination enter into our moral theory. We cannot simply abstract from these relations on the assumption that morality can be exclusively concerned with the morality of individual action. I want to show how the autonomy of morality either depends upon such an abstraction from structures of inequality, as we find in Williams echoing one aspect of Kant's moral writings, or else depends upon an implicit social assumption about the possibility of individuals living free and independent lives. With the relations of class power and dependency which have developed with capitalist society this becomes an increasingly untenable assumption upon which to base our moral theory. The concept of respect for persons has traditionally played a crucial role in liberal moral and political theory, serving as a bridging notion which seemed to guarantee an equality between people regardless of the social relations of power and subordination. It tended to confirm the idea that people are equally able to live moral lives. It works to separate issues of morality from issues of social justice.

I want to show that Kant reached a point where these deep assumptions of his moral theory seem to have been challenged. In his discussion of the relationship between rich and poor he came face to face with moral issues of dependency and human needs. He could no longer assume that people are equally free to live out their moral lives in relationship to the moral law. He was forced to question his assumptions of independence and self-sufficiency as he recognised that some people were dependent upon others for their very means of livelihood. In the end Kant could avoid questioning the autonomy of morality as he could fall back to the familiar position of abstracting from these social relations of power and dependency, thereby avoiding the moral issues they seemed to be confronting him with. But he does not deny the contradictions completely as he consistently denies equal political rights to those who are dependent upon the will of others.

11

Before I reach examples which relate directly to issues of dependency in Chapter VI, I have to make clear the different assumptions upon which Kant's conception of the autonomy of morality is built. In particular I explore the ways in which they relate to notions of the person and individuality. I try to show the ways in which they work to undermine the fuller conception of respect and individuality which we find heralded in the idea that people should never be treated merely as means towards the ends of others, but should always be treated as ends in themselves. This is something that Kant never fully develops though it continues to have deep resonance with a liberal sense of the dignity of human life. It is no accident that Kant could never develop this fuller sense of individuality since the very assumptions upon which the autonomy of morality were grounded tended to undermine it. It left Kant with an increasingly attenuated conception of the person. This is all the more important to establish since Kant's moral writings tend to be treasured for the ways in which they guarantee the separateness and integrity of individuality. This is taken to be a strength in contrast to utilitarian moral theory which has also been enormously significant in shaping liberal moral and political theory. This study shows the problematic character of these assumptions for a liberal moral and political theory of rights. In this way I want to question the autonomy of morality and hopefully leave suggestions for developing a moral language of needs which could fully identify and articulate the moral nature of relations of power and subordination. This calls for a different kind of moral theory which will inevitably develop in critical relationship with the moral traditions which have formed and sustained our liberal moral consciousness.

Kant's moral imperative to treat everyone as an end in him/herself is undermined by his rationalism and individualism because the denial of wants and feelings is in some way a denial of what is particular in people's lives and because there are structures of power and morality that lie beyond that language of individualism. So Kant's terms prevent him thinking about what it might actually mean to treat a person as an end rather than as a means. I also argue that Kant's assumptions undermine his attempts to guarantee dignity to people, while showing at another level how his conception of dignity is itself inadequate in that it assumes a connection between fairness, abstraction and people being instances of the moral law. If this does not prevent Kant sometimes glimpsing, especially in the later writings, the depths to which individuals can be hurt and humiliated in a position of subordination and dependency, it prevents him illuminating the moral realities. But at least he does not assume, as later liberal moral and political theory has tended to, that the moral issues can be side-stepped if we are ready to abstract from structures of inequality. But it would have questioned too many of his deepest assumptions to develop a moral language which could identify and express the moral issues of dependency and subordination.

I go on to show that weaknesses of a liberal theory of individual rights also go back, at least in part, to the particular form of rationalism and individualism it adopts uncritically from Kant. This is as true in its different ways of the socially concerned liberalism of John Rawls and Ronald Dworkin as it is of the conservative libertarianism of Robert Nozick. This is not to deny the critical importance of the differences that exist between them. As a conclusion I show the different ways liberal political philosophy has been tied into the very assumptions Kant is struggling with in his discussion of the relations between rich and poor. More specifically they tend to inherit a conception of respect and of moral personality, expressed in the language of rights, which would render individual autonomy and fundamental aspects of the self somehow invulnerable and beyond the reach of social relations of power and dependency. They operate within polarities which often have their source in Kant's distinction between the intelligible and the sensible world. This is mirrored in the key idea of deontological liberalism that the right can always be established prior to and independent of people's conceptions of the good. As morality is defined within a Kantian tradition as identified with reason so within a liberal tradition is a conception of justice often identified with rights impartially conceived. This establishes a framework of moral and political discussion in terms of a language of individual rights that precludes the asking of questions about respect in terms of the fulfilment of human needs, as well as generating an impoverished sense of individual experience. It also generates an inability to address issues of substantive justice, namely questions about the justice or otherwise of social relationships.

It becomes difficult for liberal theory to illuminate the moral issues involved in learning how to treat people more equally in an unequal society, since it sees social relations as a kind of constant within which we are individually free to relate to others as we choose. This makes it easy to identify justice with the law being brought in impartially to settle competing claims. I suggest a different framework which brings moral and political theory into much closer relation with social theory, wherein the connections between what is individual – what individuals choose to do in particular contingent circumstances – and what is structural or social is necessarily a moral one. I also point concretely to the positive contribution of emotional life to the development of a sense of justice. I show that it is false to see relativism as the only alternative to a liberalism that focuses on the absolute character of rights impartially conceived.

If our autonomy and independence can no longer be guaranteed within an independent moral realm, we are forced to consider the concrete social relations through which it is either undermined and fragmented or nourished and sustained. We have to develop a moral language of needs which connects a sense of autonomy and independence to the fulfilment of individual needs. In a society characterised by relationships of power and subordination we cannot assume, as liberal theory has wanted to, that it can be secured with the guarantee of equal legal and political rights. Rather we have to be concerned with the nature of the control people have in the different areas of their lives, knowing that we can only exist as persons in our own right through the ways we express our individual and collective identities. It is part of challenging the fixity and abstraction of a liberal conception of self to realise that our autonomy and independence can no longer be simply theoretically substantiated. We renew the moral significance of a relation between theory and practice, as we recognise that our autonomy and independence have to be realised in our everyday activities and relationships. As we gradually learn that respect for our activities, needs, desires and emotional lives can be an integral part of defining our individuality and deepening our respect for others, we are renewing our moral language in critical relation with our inherited moral traditions. This calls for a transformation of our moral and political theories as an integral part of transforming social relations of power and subordination.

II

RESPECT AND HUMAN NATURE

Kant expressed his newly discovered sense of human equality by saying that he has learned to respect human nature, instead of despising people for their ignorance. His sense of respect for human nature has helped establish our liberal conception of equality. However, I want to show that Kant's respect for human nature is a respect for a particular conception of the nature of people. It involves a particular conception of human freedom and moral action. Kant's respect for a person is respect for the rational noumenal self. In his desire to restore people to a sense of what is 'essential and permanent' in human nature Kant identifies our morality with our rationality. Even though this is supposed to assert our freedom and independence from our emotions, feelings and desires which would otherwise determine our behaviour, I argue that a systematic denial of important aspects of our experience can undermine the very independence and autonomy which Kant cherishes.

In the second section I show how it is the rationality we share that defines our humanity and which for Kant allows us to escape the determinations of the sensible world. But this is done at the cost of fragmenting our conception of the person. Our sense of ourselves is not only fragmented between the 'sensible world' and the 'intelligible world' but involves a subordination of our emotions, feelings, wants and desires which remain part of our unfreedom. I argue that in giving them no place in helping us discover and define our individualities Kant is unwittingly undermining our very autonomy and independence. Our equality as moral beings equally able to live moral lives is guaranteed to us at the cost of

15

separating us from our activities and relationships. Our 'moral worth' and 'dignity' are taken to have essentially 'inner' sources and are thereby radically separated from our everyday social lives. So living a moral life can have little reference to the fulfilment of our wants and needs in our everyday lives.

1 LEARNING TO RESPECT HUMAN NATURE

When Kant was forty he registered his debt to the writings of Rousseau. It had been Rousseau who had helped him to a different conception of the nature and meaning of philosophy:

> I am myself by inclination a seeker after truth. I feel a
> consuming thirst for knowledge and a restless passion to
> advance in it, as well as satisfaction in every forward step.
> There was a time when I thought that this alone could
> constitute the honour of mankind, and I despised the common
> man who knows nothing. Rousseau set me right. This blind
> prejudice vanished; I learnt to respect human nature, and I
> should consider myself far more useless than the ordinary
> working man if I did not believe that this view could give
> worth to all others to establish the rights of man. ('Fragmente
> aus Kant's Nachlass' (ed. Hartenstein, Bd VIII), 624, quoted in
> Ernst Cassirer, *Rousseau, Kant, Goethe*, p. 1)[1]

Kant saw Rousseau as 'the restorer of the rights of humanity' who had helped him learn to respect human nature. This was the source for whatever democratic impulse informs Kant's writings. It also helped him articulate his sense of human equality. But this also marked a profound change in his understanding of the importance of the growth of knowledge and his understanding of human life. As Cassirer says, 'His naive confidence that the cultivation of the mind and its steady progress would suffice to make men better, freer and happier is shaken' (Rousseau, Kant, Goethe, p. 6). This helps him question some of the enlightenment notions which would see the growth of knowledge as a guarantee of human happiness.

Kant thought that it was a respect for human nature which would 'give worth to all others to establish the rights of man'. This was certainly something that changed his attitude towards 'the common man' whom he no longer despised for his ignorance.

16

Respect and human nature

When Kant talks about the respect he learns to have for human nature, he distinguishes himself from a tradition of thought and feeling which would identify a predisposition towards the good within human nature. In this way he still wants to distinguish himself from Rousseau. He sets himself against such an optimistic belief.

> More modern, though far less prevalent, is the contrasted optimistic belief ... that the world steadily (though almost imperceptibly) forges in the other direction, to wit, from bad to better: at least that the predisposition to such a movement is discoverable in human nature. If this belief, however, is meant to apply to *moral* goodness and badness (not simply to the process of civilization), it has certainly not been deduced from experience; the history of all times cries too loudly against it. The belief, we may presume, is a well-intentioned assumption of the moralists, from Seneca to Rousseau, designed to encourage the sedulous cultivation of that seed of goodness which perhaps lies in us – if, indeed, we can count on any such natural basis of goodness in man. (*Religion Within the Limits of Reason Alone*, pp. 15–16)[2]

We have to be careful about the particular definition Kant gives of 'human nature'. There remains an implicit opposition between the 'human' which is identified with such notions as 'freedom', 'rationality' and the 'will' and Kant's understanding of 'nature'. When Kant talks about 'human nature' he is careful to warn us that he is talking about a particular 'nature of man':

> Lest difficulty at once be encountered in the expression *nature*, which, if it meant (as it usually does) the opposite of *freedom* as a basis of action, would flatly contradict the predicate *morally* good or evil, let it be noted that by 'nature of man' we here intend only the subjective ground of the exercise (under objective moral laws) of man's freedom in general; this ground – whatever its character – is the necessary antecedent of every act apparent to the senses. But this subjective ground, again, must itself always be an expression of freedom. ... (*Religion Within the Limits of Reason Alone*, p. 16)

So when Kant talks about learning 'to respect human nature', he is learning to respect a particular conception of the 'nature of man'.

17

It is the freedom we have as moral beings, which is part of the 'nature of man', that allows us to rise above a 'nature' we are assumed to share with animals. It is this quality of a free moral being that Kant learns to identify in his respect of 'human nature'.

Rousseau initially challenged the eighteenth-century faith in reason and science. He challenges the idea that the growth of knowledge and understanding would inevitably bring human happiness. This is what Rousseau says about whether the restoration of the sciences and arts tended to purify morals:

> Civilised peoples, cultivate talents: happy slaves, you owe to
> them that delicate and refined taste on which you pride
> yourselves; that softness of character and urbanity of customs
> which make relations among you so amiable and easy; in a
> word, the semblance of all the virtues without the possession
> of any. (*The First and Second Discourses*, ed. Roger Masters,
> p. 36)[3]

This idea deeply influenced Kant, as did the notion that the growth of science and letters stifles in people 'the sense of that original liberty for which they seemed to have been born' (Masters, p. 36). Kant wanted to restore to people this sense of 'original liberty' which he tended to identify with moral freedom. He wanted to help people to a sense of themselves as moral beings. This would involve people in learning to respect human nature, as Kant had learned for himself.

Kant wants his moral philosophy to bring us back to a sense of ourselves, to a deeper understanding of our nature. Kant has a clear understanding of the importance of the task he has set himself:

> If there is any science man really needs it is the one I teach, of
> how to occupy properly that place in creation that is assigned
> to man, and how to learn from it what one must be in order
> to be a man. Granted that he may have become acquainted
> with the deceptive allurements above him or below him, which
> have unconsciously enticed him away from his distinctive
> station, then this teaching will lead him back to the human
> level, and however small or deficient he may regard himself, he
> will suit his assigned station, because he will be just what he
> should be. (quoted in Ernst Cassirer, *Rousseau, Kant, Goethe*,
> p. 23)

So Kant wants his writings to help us 'back again to the human level'. In order to be secure in this position, we have got to know these 'deceptive allurements' which are both 'above' and 'below' us. This means becoming aware of the enduring qualities within human nature, as well as 'the proper place of man in creation'.

It is on the investigation of these essential qualities that the deeper critique of social life implicitly rests. If Kant is right, he prepares the way for a much deeper level of social and cultural critique. According to Cassirer this is what Kant learns from Rousseau:

> And Kant credits Rousseau the ethical philosopher with having discerned the 'real man' beneath all the distortions and concealments, beneath all the masks that man has created for himself and worn in the course of its history. ... We know that this was the enterprise he made central in his academic teaching during the 'sixties'. 'Since in Ethics I always undertake an historical and philosophic consideration of what occurs before I point out what should occur,' Kant states in announcing his lectures for the year 1765-66, 'I shall set forth the method by which we must study man – man not only in the varying forms in which his accidental circumstances have moulded him, in the distorted forms in which even philosophers have almost misconstrued him, but what is enduring in human nature, and the proper place of man in creation' (Werke, II, 326). According to Kant it is precisely the empirical philosophers, those who derive their doctrine from experience and aim to base a knowledge of human nature on the history of man's previous development, who have failed to face this task. They have seen only the changing and accidental, not the essential and permanent. (*Rousseau, Kant, Goethe*, pp. 20-1)

Kant learns from Rousseau about all the different ways people can be influenced by society.[4] He tends to think our emotions, feelings, desires and needs can easily be manipulated, and it is only through our independent faculty of reason that we can become aware this is happening. Kant is very aware of how 'deceptive allurements' can unconsciously entice us away from our true nature. But, rather than identifying this return 'to the human level' with a different, more critically informed, sense of our needs, wants, desires and

19

aspirations, he tends to see our 'inclinations' as an aspect of a 'natural instinct' which has to be irredeemably conditioned. In order to understand why Kant devalues our 'natural' feelings and desires in this way, we need to look at his more general distinction between the sensible world and the intelligible world.

2 THE SENSIBLE WORLD AND THE INTELLIGIBLE WORLD

Respect for human nature is given a particular definition within Kant's moral philosophy. I want to show how it involves respect for a particular understanding of the nature of people and so for an increasingly attenuated conception of our individuality. This is in tension with other strands of Kant's thought which would promise a fuller notion of an autonomous individual. Initially we discover that respect for a person is respect for a particular 'nature of man' which becomes respect for persons 'as belonging to the intelligible world'. Kant invokes a fundamental dichotomy between the 'animal' and the 'human', which mirrors a distinction between the 'empirical' and the 'rational'. It is the rational faculty which fundamentally defines our humanity for Kant and which guarantees the possibility of our freedom.

In voicing this distinction Kant is situating himself within a deep tradition of Christian thought which would draw a sharp distinction between the 'earthly' and the 'spiritual'. This still fundamentally affects our consciousness and experience of ourselves, even if these notions have been secularised. It has created a deep suspicion, even fear, of the body and bodily experience, since this is identified with the 'animal' and the 'lower'. This is related to a conception of our natural selves as fundamentally controlled and determined. Kant imagines that our feelings and emotions are always threatening to control us and determine our behaviour. This is the area of our experience which we share with animals. It is fundamentally the sphere of unfreedom. It is only the external intervention of the faculty of rationality that can give us 'a lofty sense of the dignity of human nature', as Kant says in his sketch of the melancholoy disposition.[5] This allows Kant to identify our capacity to live moral lives with our faculty of reason. This is the only source of our realm of human freedom. I need to say a little more about this,

20

because it fundamentally affects our inherited cultural sense of the respect owed to people.

In Kant's *Groundwork of the Metaphysic of Morals*, he shows the ways he conceives of us living in different worlds. He draws a fundamental distinction between the 'sensible world' and the 'intelligible world'. But in establishing the plausibility of this distinction, Kant does rely upon our being able to register its validity within our own experience:

> Now man actually finds in himself a power which distinguishes him from all other things – and even from himself so far as he is affected by objects. This power is *reason*. ... Because of this a rational being must regard himself *qua intelligence* (and accordingly not on the side of his lower faculties) as belonging to the intelligible world, not to the sensible one. He has therefore two points of view from which he can regard himself and from which he can know laws governing the employment of his powers and consequently governing all his actions. He can consider himself *first* – so far as he belongs to the sensible world – to be under the laws of nature (heteronomy); and *secondly* – so far as he belongs to the intelligible world – to be under laws which, being independent of nature, are not empirical but have their ground in reason alone ....
>
> We see now that when we think of ourselves as free, we transfer ourselves into the intelligible world as members and recognise the autonomy of the will together with its consequence – morality; whereas when we think of ourselves as under obligation, we look upon ourselves as belonging to the sensible world and yet to the intelligible world at the same time. (*Groundwork of the Metaphysic of Morals*, 452, 453)

This helps us identify the ways Kant thinks of morality as a consequence of the will and as an aspect of 'the intelligible world'. It also helps us mark a distinction between 'the sensible world' as the realm of nature which is 'external' in the sense of being 'affected by objects', and 'the intelligible world' relating to the 'inner' and the essential autonomy of the will. This can help us think about 'moral worth' and 'dignity' as essentially 'inner', and thereby separated from our everyday empirical lives.

It is our will which is to guarantee our freedom. This allows us to escape the determination of our nature and 'elevates man

above himself as part of the world of sense'. It is our moral disposition and our capacities to legislate for ourselves that give us
our dignity. This is what makes every rational creature an end in
itself:

> The moral law is holy (inviolable). Man is certainly unholy
> enough, but humanity in his person must be holy to him.
> Everything in creation which he wishes and over which he has
> power can be used merely as a means; only man, and, with
> him, every rational creature, is an end in itself. He is the
> subject of the moral law which is holy, because of the
> autonomy of his freedom. Because of the latter, every will,
> even the private will of each person directed to himself, is
> restricted to the condition of agreement with the autonomy of
> the rational being, namely, that it is subjected to no purpose
> which is not possible by a law which could arise from the will
> of the passive subject itself. This condition thus requires that
> the person never be used as a means except when he is at the
> same time an end . . . (*Critique of Practical Reason*, p. 90)

It is the autonomy of a person's freedom which makes a person
subject to the moral law. This is an abiding theme for Kant.[6] In
the *Grundlegung* Kant was clear about the source of people being
ends in themselves, when he warns us that 'the will of a rational
being must always be regarded as *making universal law*, because
otherwise he could not be conceived of as *an end in himself*'. This
relates to the fundamental 'Idea of the *dignity* of a rational being
who obeys no law other than that which he at the same time enacts
himself' (*Grundlegung*, 434).

Kant also points out that 'The practical necessity of acting on
this principle – that is, duty, – is in no way based on feelings,
impulses, and inclinations, but only on the relation of rational
beings to one another' (*Grundlegung*, 434). There is a deep assumption that our feelings and desires inevitably want to control and
determine our behaviour, while it is only the workings of our will
which can guarantee us freedom in our independence from these
influences. It is crucial for Kant to insist upon this autonomy, since
it means that each individual can work out his individual moral
destiny. This is why it becomes so threatening to him when this
very freedom and autonomy seems to be challenged from another
source, which he was only to acknowledge in the *Doctrine of Virtue*,

namely the social relations of power and dependency. In the *Grundlegung* he does not have to face these difficulties:

> What else then can freedom of will be but autonomy – that is, the property which will has of being a law to itself? The proposition 'Will is in all its actions a law to itself' expresses, however, only the principle of acting on no maxim other than the one which can have for its object itself as at the same time a universal law. This is precisely the formula of the categorical imperative and the principle of morality. Thus a free will and a will under moral laws are one and the same. (*Groundwork of the Metaphysic of Morals*, 47)

This identification of 'a free will' with 'a will under moral laws' has had a crucial significance in the moral and political theory of liberalism.[7] Our freedom exists in the sense that we legislate for ourselves and make a choice to subordinate ourselves. This notion would not see us as any less 'free', since we have 'chosen' the form of our subordination.

Freedom understood in this way has little to do with the empirical world. Rather it involves taking up a position of superiority towards this everyday empirical world. As Kant says, 'This better person he believes himself to be when he transfers himself to the standpoint of a member of the intelligible world.' This involves withdrawing ourselves from the necessities of the sensible world, which is also taken to be the animal world and the world of determination. Our freedom comes from our rationality, which has little to do with this world. Rather, as Kant says, 'having a will free from sensuous impulses he transfers himself in thought into an order of things quite different from that of his desires in the field of sensibility'. This is the way that we discover 'of not being dependent on *determination* by causes in the sensible world'. It is because our freedom seems to be guaranteed in a higher realm that we do not have to worry about the kind of determinations we are subject to in the sensible world, even if this involves the satisfaction of our wants and desires. We are to automatically identify our 'selves' with our rationality and so with our wills. This is easier to do the more aware we are that it is our rationality which is also the source of our dignity, since it allows us to escape a destiny of determination we would otherwise share with the animal world.

Kant's moral thinking is fundamentally influenced by the division between the 'sensible world' and the 'intelligible world'. This echoes the deeply held Christian distinction which opposes the 'worldly' to the 'spiritual', and which automatically understands the 'worldly' to mean turned away from God.[8] Kant sees our wants, desires, feelings and emotions as essentially part of this 'sensible world'. It is the rationality we share that allows us to escape the determinations of this sensible world. But this also profoundly affects Kant's discussion of human dignity and moral worth. This provides the grounds for his sense of respect and equality. Living a moral life can have little reference to the fulfilment of our wants and needs in our everyday earthly lives. As Kant warns us, it cannot 'satisfy any of his actual or even conceivable inclinations'. It is given its reference and meaning in a different realm.

III

RESPECT AND DIGNITY

Kant argues that morality, and humanity so far as it is capable of morality, is the only thing which has dignity. The sensible world as a world of determination becomes the world of equivalence and price. It is denied as a source of dignity and moral worth. This is intended to guarantee the autonomy of morality and our dignity as moral beings through withdrawing the notion of 'dignity' from our emotional and bodily selves as well as from our activities and relations. Within this framework they are not only denied any dignity and moral worth, but they can no longer be expressive of our individualities which have been so closely identified with our rational noumenal selves. Kant assumes that our 'earthly activities' have to be done for some kind of advantage or profit. He is caught within a distinction between the 'outer' and the 'inner' where it is only the 'inner' which can express our freedom and choice. This guarantee of our 'dignity' as 'an absolute inner worth' can strengthen our sense of self, but it can also blind us to the different ways in which our feelings and emotions can themselves be a source of self-respect.

I go on to show in the following section that this builds a sense of hierarchy and subordination into our very conception of the person. It is only to the extent that we are moral beings that we are owed equal respect with all other rational beings and are to be recognised as ends in ourselves. This gives a particular form and meaning to our sense of dignity and self-esteem since our 'dignity as a moral man' is heightened in a comparison with our 'insignificance as a natural man'. This encourages us to subordinate our emotions and feelings, wants and desires. We are encouraged to identify ourselves with what is required of us by the moral law regardless of the costs in terms of our needs, wants and desires. Kant wants to separate these as sources of our happiness from any connection with our dignity and self-esteem. I argue against this, suggesting a conception of respect which involves challenging this fragmented conception of people's experience, showing that Kant can offer us only an increasingly attenuated conception of a person.

1 DIGNITY AND NATURAL INCLINATIONS

Kant articulates a particular sense of the value and dignity of people's lives. He helps us express in his moral theory our inherited cultural sense of the intrinsic value of human life.[1] This remains a central theme and grounds what he says about respect and equality. He relies upon a fundamental distinction between something having either a price or a dignity. In his earlier writings he relates this directly to a discussion of the kingdom of ends:

> In the kingdom of ends everything has either a *price* or a *dignity*. If it has a price, something else can be put in its place as an *equivalent*; if it is exalted above all price and so admits of no equivalence, then it has a dignity.
>
> What is relative to universal human inclinations and needs has a *market price*; what, even without presupposing a need, accords with a certain taste – that is, with satisfaction in the mere purposeless play of our mental powers – has a *fancy price* (*Affektionspreis*); but that which constitutes the sole condition under which anything can be an end in itself has not merely a relative value – that is, a price – but has an intrinsic value – that is, *dignity*.
>
> Now morality is the only condition under which a rational being can be an end in himself; for only through this is it possible to be a law-making member in a kingdom of ends. Therefore morality, and humanity so far as it is capable of morality, is the only thing which has dignity. Skill and diligence in work have a market price; wit, lively imagination, and humour have a fancy price; but fidelity to promises and

kindness based on principle (not on instinct) have an intrinsic worth. (*Groundwork of the Metaphysic of Morals*, 435)

Kant thinks of price in terms of a 'relative value' and in terms of 'equivalence'. If something 'is exalted above all price and so admits of no equivalence, then it has a dignity'. This resonates with a deeply held moral sense within liberalism that people are not commodities and should not be exchangeable for each other. We are encouraged to feel that an individual's life is unique and that at some fundamental level people are not replaceable. Sometimes we can experience this in terms of the equal respect which is owed to each person's individual experience. It is this recognition of the value of each person's life and experience that has been recognised as an enduring strength of Kant's moral writing. It is less often appreciated how partial Kant's acknowledgment of the individuality and meaning of people's experience often is. This is something I want to show.

So, for instance, I can continually learn that Paul gets a great deal from listening to modern jazz while I find it hard to appreciate. Paul might be annoyed at some dismissive remark I make about jazz, saying 'How many times do I have to say to you that I really like that music?' I have to remind myself not to be so insensitive and to appreciate this experience. Often it is as we get to know people more closely and intimately that we have a fuller sense of the individuality of their needs and wants. Though the example initially seems to enable us to make sense of what Kant is saying, it immediately begins to raise doubts about Kant's position. For what it points to is the way in which our sense of people as irreplaceable and therefore non-exchangeable derives from our awareness of the particularity of their empirical inclinations, from their empirical rather than their noumenal selves. But this can make it difficult for us to agree readily with Kant that 'What is relative to universal human inclinations and needs has a *market price*'. Is it so clear to us that 'skill and diligence in work have a market price'? If we think about a carpenter who makes chairs we can say that the chairs he makes can be sold on the market, but this is different from saying that the skill and diligence with which he works should be thought of in this way.

Why does Kant, contrary to what our example would suggest, see people's non-exchangeability and therefore their dignity as deriving from the noumenal self rather than from their empirical particularities? This is because he is again invoking the distinction between the sensible world and the intelligible world which we considered in the previous chapter, seeing the sensible world as a world of determination. This becomes the world of equivalence and price. This is what allows Kant to say that 'morality is the only condition under which a rational being can be an end in himself'. He tries to make this clearer when he is explaining why 'fidelity to promises and kindness based on principle' 'have an intrinsic worth':

> In default of these, nature and art alike contain nothing to put in their place; for their worth consists, not in the effects which result from them, nor in the advantage and profit they produce, but in the attitudes of mind – that is, in the maxims of the will – which are ready in this way to manifest themselves in action even if they are not favoured by success. Such actions too need no recommendation from any subjective disposition or taste in order to meet with immediate favour and approval; they need no immediate propensity or feeling for themselves; they exhibit the will which performs them as an object of immediate reverence. .... This assessment reveals as dignity the value of such a mental attitude and puts it infinitely above all price, with which it cannot be brought into reckoning or comparison without, as it were, a profanity of its sanctity.
> (*Groundwork of the Metaphysic of Morals*, 435)

This carries with it a particular conception of the ways things are carried out in the sensible world. People are imagined to do things for 'the effects which result from them' or for 'the advantage or profit they produce'. This is not taken as characterising the social relations of a particular kind of society, which fosters individual competitiveness and acquisitiveness, but to be defining the very character of the sensible world.[2] But this is to withdraw the notion of 'dignity' from the ways people live and the character of the activities and relations people are involved in. It automatically becomes an 'inner quality' that has a direct reference to the 'intelligible world'. It leaves little promise and hope for the transformation of social relations and the social world.

When Kant says that 'fidelity to promises and kindness based on principle' have 'an intrinsic worth', this is partly because 'nature and art alike contain nothing to put in their place' and because

Respect and dignity

their worth consists 'in the attitudes of mind'. This is to rely upon a distinction between the 'inner' and the 'outer'. But this works to deny dignity to the activities of people themselves. Rather it tends to sever any connection between our understanding of people and the significance of what they do, so that it becomes difficult to appreciate the sense of what we do as an *expression* of our individualities. Kant tends to assume an instrumental interpretation of human action, where we often do things to prove ourselves individually. He does not leave much space for an investigation of the different kinds of relationship we can have to our activities and relationships, where our activities have a purely instrumental significance, and where our activities are intrinsically rewarding and fulfilling. This makes it difficult to investigate the nature of human inclinations and needs, or for them to have any bearing upon our sense of respect and equality. It makes it difficult to acknowledge the needs we have for particular kinds of activities and relations within which we can express ourselves, and for personal and social relationships in which we can be nourished and fulfilled through having our needs met. I argue that this could promise a conception of respect and equality which is grounded in a fuller sense of individuality than Kant can articulate within his rationalistic assumptions.

When Kant thinks of 'human inclinations and needs' he is thinking of people 'in the system of nature'. He tends to see us as determined by these needs for hunger, clothing and sexuality. Kant thinks of these as needs we share with other creatures. There is little sense of the ways these needs become transformed as they become articulated and expressed as human needs. Sometimes it seems as if we can only see our 'animal nature', as long as we dwell at the level of these needs. There is no way we can give these needs a dignity, since the source of dignity comes from another realm, for, as Kant says, 'morality, and humanity as far as it is capable of morality, is the only thing which has dignity'. This conception has a powerful influence on our liberal moral consciousness, though it remains in contradiction with traditions of moral thought which, for instance, allow us to recognise the dignity of human labour. For Kant a man or a woman regarded as a worker is still regarded as part of the 'system of nature', and so cannot be thought of as having dignity.[3] For, as Kant says, 'morality is the only condition under which a rational being can be an end in himself'. This is when someone can be 'regarded as a person'. This shows the special meaning Kant gives to what it means to be a person. This is still clear when he is exploring similar themes in the later *Doctrine of Virtue* under the general heading 'On Servility':

> Man in the system of nature (homo phaenomenon, animal rationale) is a being of slight importance and shares with the rest of the animals, as offspring of the earth, a common value (pretium vulgare). Although man has, in his reason, something more than they and can set his own ends, even this gives him only an *extrinsic* value in terms of his usefulness (pretium usus). This extrinsic value is the value of one man above another – that is, his *price* as a ware that can be exchanged for these other animals, as things. But, so conceived, man still has a lower value than the universal medium of exchange, the value of which can therefore be called pre-eminent (pretium eminens).
>
> But man regarded as a *person* – that is, as the subject of morally practical reason – is exalted above any price; for as such (homo noumenon) he is not to be valued as a mere means to the ends of others or even to his own ends, but as an end in himself. He possesses, in other words, a *dignity* (an absolute inner worth) by which he exacts *respect* for himself from all other rational beings in the world: he can measure himself with every other being of this kind and value himself on a footing of equality with them. (*The Doctrine of Virtue*, 434)

This draws a sharp distinction between 'man regarded as a person' and 'man in the system of nature'. Within this passage even our power to reason is not enough to give us more than an 'extrinsic value'. At some level it seems Kant recognises the ways people become exchangeable on the market as labour. What is more, he seems to recognise the market as a place where values are created. The fact that people are able to reason, think things out for themselves and set their own ends, only makes them into more expensive forms of labour. It only makes people more useful to others than they might otherwise be. In this way the skills people have can be compared with each other on the market, and are priced according to their scarcity. Some skills are more in demand than others and this allows people to command more of a return on the market. This is what allows Kant to say that 'This extrinsic value is the value of one man above another – that is, his *price* as a ware that can be exchanged.' This means that, when Kant talks of 'useful-ness', he is implicitly accepting the criteria of the market economy.[4] But Kant is not only talking about the value of labour on the market; he is talking more generally about the value of 'man in the system of nature'. Again Kant treats as a characteristic of human nature what is really a characteristic of specific kinds of social relations. His assumptions leave him no room to investigate this.

This profoundly affects Kant's conception of human equality since it systematically denies any dignity to our earthly lives, to our social relations. It legitimates the idea that our earthly lives can have only 'extrinsic value'. It is almost as if morality has little to do with the organisation of our earthly lives, only with making sure we act out of a sense of duty in our relations with others. Morality has to do with the demands of the 'intelligible world', since this is the only possible realm of freedom. We cannot hope for this kind of freedom in the organisation of our earthly lives, since here we seem to be inevitably determined by the forces of nature. Kant seems to think that 'skill and diligence in work' are 'relative to universal human inclinations and needs' and so have a market price. This can easily blind us to important moral distinc-tions that need to be made.

To see the need for such distinctions, consider the following example. It can help us question some of these guiding assumptions to show the importance of expressing our individualities through the activities we engage in. Pete is a carpenter who applies himself to his carpentry. He has spent a great deal of time and effort improving and developing his craft. He feels a great deal of satis-faction that he has eventually discovered what he really wants to be doing with himself and what gives him genuine satisfaction. At the same time he is forced to acknowledge that it is not easy to get a job as a carpenter which will use the skills he has developed, which will give him the kind of 'intrinsic satisfaction' he wants to have from a job. He has to come to terms with the fact that, with the price of wood so high, few can afford to buy hand-made things, especially when so many factory-produced goods are available in the shops. This does not stop Pete feeling a need to have 'intrinsic satisfaction' from the work he does, or from feeling frustrated and denied at the kind of work available on the market, especially when it does not make the demands on the skills that give him satisfac-tion. Pete often feels the wrongfulness of work which 'gives him

31

only an *extrinsic* value in terms of his usefulness'. Often he feels
that he is being used by his firm to make goods he does not have
any faith in. It is not simply a question of wanting to raise 'his
price' through being paid more. He wants to feel that *his work* has
dignity, in the sense that it draws upon his skills and is an expression of himself.

Pete is expressing his difficulties in finding the kind of work he
needs as a carpenter, given the kind of work available. Sometimes
it seems as if Kant is arguing that he should not want more than
an 'extrinsic value' from the work he does, so that he should be
ready to adapt himself to the prevailing market conditions of work.
He certainly does not help us develop clear criteria to critique the
social organisation of work insofar as it fails to give us 'intrinsic
value'. It is as if Kant assumes that all our 'earthly activities' have
to be done for some kind of advantage, profit, or effects. This is
taken to be a feature of their very 'externality', in contrast to the
'absolute inner worth' of such a 'mental attitude' as, say, fidelity to
promises. It is almost as if Pete is misguided in looking for dignity
and intrinsic satisfaction in the work he is doing, since for Kant it
has to have a completely different source. It is as if one's skill and
one's ability to get satisfaction from one's work cannot be the
source of one's essential dignity as a person if they depend on
adventitious external circumstances. If this allows Kant to secure
our sense that Pete should not lose any of his human dignity if, for
instance, he suffered permanent injury to his hands, it does this at
the cost of minimising the importance of maintaining a sense of
our human dignity through involving ourselves in activities which
enable us to express our individualities. This makes it all the more
important to bring into existence circumstances in which dignity
can be sustained since it can also be undermined, though this is
again something Kant has trouble acknowledging.

It is because people are 'subject to morally practical reason' that
our lives have such a different kind of value. The fact that we are
subject to the moral law has a central significance for Kant. This
is the source of our redemption. This is what it means for Kant to
be able to say 'But man regarded as a *person* – that is, as the
subject of morally practical reason – is exalted above any price.'
This helps us grasp the special meaning Kant gives to regarding
someone 'as a *person*'. It is only when a person seeks 'to judge
himself and his actions from this point of view' (*Grundlegung*, 433)

that a person 'is exalted above any price' and 'is not to be valued
as a mere means to the ends of others or even to his own ends, but
as an end in himself'.[5] It is as if it is only 'man regarded as a
person' but *not* 'man in the system of nature' who can be regarded
as having 'a *dignity* (an absolute inner worth)'. Crucial questions
remain about the consequences of seeing people 'from this point of
view' for the organisation of relationships that exist in the 'sensible
world'. Surely the recognition that people should regulate their
behaviour towards each other according to the moral law must
also influence the character of social relations that exist in the
everyday social world. Again it is unclear what force to give to
Kant's discussion of the kingdom of ends which he admits himself
is 'only an Ideal':

> For rational beings all stand under the *law* that each of them
> should treat himself and all others, *never merely as a means,
> but always at the same time as an end in himself.* But by so
> doing there arises a systematic union of rational beings under
> objective laws – that is, a kingdom. Since these laws are
> directed precisely to the relation of such beings to one another
> as ends and means, this kingdom can be called a kingdom of
> ends (which is admittedly only an Ideal). (*Groundwork of the
> Metaphysic of Morals*, 433)

Kant seems to allow in the *Grundlegung* that at least in the 'sensible
world' someone can be treated as a means, as long as they are not
treated 'merely' as a means. Kant stresses that, while they might
be used as a means, they must 'at the same time' be treated as an
end in themselves. Though Kant mentions this a number of times,
his underlying assumptions make it impossible for him to develop
this into a stronger sense of respect and individuality. In *The Doctrine of Virtue* it is only as a homo noumenon that someone can be
'regarded as a person', and then 'he is not to be valued as a mere
means to the end of others or even to his own ends, but as an end
in himself'. This is centrally related to Kant's fuller understanding
of individual autonomy, of what it means to have a dignity which
allows someone to 'value himself on a footing of equality' with
every other being of this kind. It is this dignity which allows someone to 'exact respect for himself from all other rational beings in
the world'. But at the same time it is crucial that this 'dignity' is
conceived of as 'an absolute inner worth'.

It is because we share this quality of 'an absolute inner worth' with all other people that we can feel 'on a footing of equality with them'. It is not only that we are 'equal before God', but Kant also helps us establish a real sense in which we can regard ourselves as equal to each other. Kant helps us articulate a sense in which we deserve the respect of others and can value ourselves 'on a footing of equality with them'. What is more, we can be assured by this notion of dignity as 'an absolute inner worth', since it is not something that we can be dispossessed of. This respect is not something we have to earn, but is something we are owed. But this should not blind us to a recognition of the difficulties we face in sustaining this sense of dignity and self-respect. It is partly because people can feel they are owed this dignity that they feel strength to demand conditions which realise it in their everyday lives. This is part of what Pete was searching for in our example.

But we have already highlighted something deeply problematic in this notion of dignity which Kant was himself to face in his later writings. It is the very guarantee of our dignity as 'an absolute inner worth'[6] that can make us insensitive to the different ways in which our dignity can be *undermined* by social relations, and the different ways that people can *fail* to treat us as people in our own right. This is something we shall go on to explore. This kind of insensitivity seems to be built into the very notion Kant has of 'the concept of every rational being', as involving an abstraction from what he calls 'the personal differences between rational beings, and also from all the content of their private ends'. It seems as if 'man regarded as a *person*' involves making these kind of abstractions:

> The concept of every rational being as one who must regard
> himself as making universal law by all the maxims of his will,
> and must seek to judge himself and his actions from this point
> of view ... since laws determine ends as regards their universal
> validity, we shall be able – if we abstract from the personal
> differences between rational beings, and also from all the
> content of their private ends – to conceive a whole of all ends
> in systematic conjunction ... (*Groundwork of the Metaphysic of
> Morals*, 433)

It is partly because this 'absolute inner worth' is guaranteed to us that Kant wants to stress that it is owed to us, as is respect, regardless of the organisation of social life. But this tends to separate

these notions of 'respect' and 'dignity' from the everyday organisation of social life. But 'man regarded as a person' cannot be so
drastically divorced from considerations of people as workers,
neighbours, friends, lovers, and sisters. I try to suggest a conception
of respect which can escape these oppositions, mainly through
showing how Kant's conceptions can mystify us. This is especially
important if we are to connect with the challenge presented when,
for instance, a woman can feel she is not being treated as a person
but as a sexual object, or is not being given the respect owed her,
or being treated as an equal, not simply in the attitudes others are
taking up but in the ways they are relating. Otherwise there is a
pervasive moral and cultural tendency that our lives are to be
fundamentally separated into an 'earthly realm' and a 'spiritual
realm' where we can excuse different ways in which people are
exploited and oppressed in the 'earthly realm', secure in the knowledge that they have dignity and respect guaranteed to them in the
'spiritual realm'. This is not Kant's intention, but it is important
to learn the source of moral traditions which implicitly prepare us
to pay lip service to treating people with 'dignity' and 'respect'
while sometimes unknowingly legitimating forms of exploitation
and oppression.

2 DIGNITY AND SELF-ESTEEM

Kant's conception of an individual is fundamentally fragmented.
We are divided within ourselves. In learning to respect ourselves
we are implicitly elevating certain aspects of ourselves and subordinating others. We take this for granted so it is difficult to recognise how it affects our culturally inherited sense of respect. This
hierarchy within ourselves in which aspects of our natures are to
be subordinated is clearly illustrated in a quotation from *The Doctrine of Virtue*:

> Humanity in his own person is the object of respect, and he
> can demand this respect from every other man; but he must,
> also, do nothing by which he would forfeit this respect. Hence
> he can and should value himself by a low as well as by a high
> standard, depending on whether he views himself as a being of
> the sensible world (in terms of his animal nature) or as an

35

intelligible being (in terms of his moral disposition). When, as he must, he regards himself not merely as a person as such but also as a man – that is, as a person who has duties laid upon him by his own reason – his insignificance as a *natural man* cannot detract from his consciousness of his dignity as a *moral man*, and he should not disavow his moral self-esteem regarding the latter; he should seek his end, which is in itself a duty, not abjectly, not in a *servile spirit* (animo servili) as if he were seeking a favour, not disavowing his dignity, but always with consciousness of his sublime moral disposition (which is already contained in the concept of virtue). And this *self-esteem* is a duty of man to himself. (*The Doctrine of Virtue*, 434)

We are warned not to regard ourselves 'merely' as a person, but 'as a person who has duties laid upon him by his own reason'. We should be constantly aware of our dignity as moral beings, whilst also being aware of our 'insignificance' as a 'natural man'. It is as if we cannot have any 'dignity' when we think of ourselves as 'beings of the sensible world'. But cannot our feelings have a certain 'dignity'? Am I to regard my feelings of anger, concern, love, caring, compassion, fear, as if they are 'insignificant'? Am I to learn that these feelings do not 'matter', since what is really important is what I think or what I am prepared to do? Is a person's 'consciousness of his dignity as a *moral man*' supposed to be heightened in an implicit comparison with his 'insignificance as a *natural man*'? Kant is less clear about this than he is about 'the strict comparison of ourselves with the moral law':

True humility follows inevitably from our sincere and strict comparison of ourselves with the moral law (its holiness and strictness). But along with it comes exaltation and the highest self-esteem, as the feeling of inner worth (valor), when we realize that we are capable of this inner legislation, and the (natural) man feels himself compelled to reverence the (moral) man in his own person. By virtue of this worth we are not for sale at any price (pretium) and possess an inalienable dignity (dignitas interna) which instills in us reverence (reverentia) for ourselves. (*The Doctrine of Virtue*, p. 101)

So a sense of our 'inner worth' is drawn from a realisation that 'we are capable of this inner legislation'. This gives a particular form

36

to our 'self-esteem', since it does not develop in relation to what we can call a 'trusting of our experience'.[7] Rather it is compatible with feelings of doubt in relation to our feelings and desires and a sense of worthlessness in what we are individually capable of achieving.

It is because we are 'capable of this inner legislation' that 'we are not for sale at any price'. This is the reason that we 'possess an inalienable dignity'. In this way Kant is helping develop a tradition of moral thought that insists upon fundamentally segmenting our experience. This has a profound effect upon the formation of moral character which we can barely conceptualise in a moral theory that focuses upon the worth and correctness of individual actions. Not only are we to be fundamentally divided within ourselves, but 'the (natural) man feels himself compelled to reverence the (moral) man in his own person'. So when Kant says that 'Humanity in his own person is the object of respect' he is talking about our capacity for morality. We are not to feel the same kind of respect for our emotions, feelings, needs, wants and desires. Rather we should 'value' them by a low standard, since this is to view ourselves as being of the 'sensible world'.

We are given an education within a Kantian moral tradition that makes the subordination of our individual wants, needs, desires, emotions and feelings that much easier, since we are taught they are 'insignificant'. This can make it easy to be mystified about the emotional and psychological costs, as we are brought up to feel that our individual needs, wants and desires should not be given moral significance and importance.

An example can help bring out how our respect for others is affected by the low estimation we are encouraged to give to aspects of our experience. John wants his father to accept him as he is, not to make him feel he has to prove himself before he is to be respected. This can make John feel he can only be respected by his father if he does well at school, while at another level feeling his father cannot really recognise him as a person in his own right at all, because he cannot consider his individual feelings or what he wants and needs for himself. John might feel he is just not interested in doing well at school. He wants to be a dancer. This is the way he feels he can express himself most fully and deeply. But this is not something Kant can acknowledge, since he tends to assume that wants and desires have to do with furthering our individual ends and purposes. This is one reason why Kant thinks it is only morality that can give us 'dignity'. Kant would allow that John has 'dignity' only insofar as he does his duty, whereas we may feel that he has dignity and self-respect precisely insofar as he ignores his 'duty' and is true to his feelings.

John's father thinks that his dancing is just a matter of self-indulgence. Kantian morality can help his father feel John should apply himself to his studies, even if he does not want to. This is the only way he can prove himself in his father's eyes. Otherwise his father thinks he is a 'lazy good for nothing' who is only indulging in his individual desires. This leaves John feeling he has to become someone he is not, in order to win the respect of his father. He would be encouraged to see his dancing as a form of self-indulgence. His father will not respect the choices he has made for himself. Kant can be enormously strengthening to John in his notion that he knows what he wants to do with his life and that his father cannot know better than he does. But I would argue that he is *also undermining* of this *very process of self-affirmation* in the way he brings us systematically to *distrust* our wants, desires, emotions and feelings. It becomes easy for John to feel he is only satisfying his 'animal nature' and that this kind of decision can have no 'moral worth', since John is simply following his inclinations. Rather a Kantian tradition in ethics works to separate us from our very emotions, desires and needs. Rather than helping us recognise the ways they are integral to a clarification and expression of identity and individuality, we learn to subordinate them in our search to identify ourselves with what we 'ought to do'. Life can become very much a matter of proving ourselves. At a deeper level Kantian morality, through its separation of dignity and moral worth from the expression of our individualities in our activities and relationships, prepares the moral ground for the very 'estrangement' that Marx was to begin to analyse in his *Economic and Philosophical Manuscripts* in 1844.[8]

Within a Kantian tradition we are brought up to subordinate our needs, wants and desires to the ends we have set ourselves. Our dignity and self-esteem are to be grounded in our moral dispositions. This is not to say that Kant does not recognise the end of happiness in our lives, but it does say that our wants, needs and desires cannot be a source of dignity or self-esteem. At some level we cannot *trust* our emotions, feelings, wants and desires. They are changeable and unreliable. They distract us from the moral law and our duties, but also from the ends we set ourselves. This is why we can only really depend upon our reason. This is why the goals and ends we set for ourselves have to be set through the workings of our reason. In this way Kant's rationalism affects his particular conception of respect and equality. But our dignity and self-esteem cannot simply come from the workings of our reason. We have to acknowledge the higher purposes we have because of our moral disposition. This is what makes us superior to animals, but also to the animal nature within ourselves. This is what we have to learn to separate from in ourselves in order to claim our 'humanity'.

> Man is a being of needs, so far as he belongs to the world of sense, and to this extent his reason certainly has an inescapable responsibility from the side of his sensuous nature to attend to its interests and to form practical maxims with a view to the happiness of this and, where possible, of a future life. But still he is not so completely an animal as to be indifferent to everything that reason says on its own and to use it merely as a tool for satisfying his needs as a sensuous being. That he has reason does not in the least raise him in worth above mere animality if reason only serves the purposes which, among animals, are taken care of by instinct; if this were so, reason would be only a specific way nature has made use of to equip man for the same purpose for which animals are qualified, without fitting him for any higher purpose. No doubt, as a result of this unique arrangement, he needs reason, to consider at all times his weal and woe. But he has reason for a yet higher purpose, namely to consider also what is in itself good or evil, which pure and sensuously disinterested reason alone can judge. . . . (*Critique of Practical Reason*, p. 64)[9]

So Kant echoes his idea that 'reason does not in the least raise him in worth above mere animality'. Are we to understand all our needs, desires, emotions and feelings as aspects of this 'mere animality'? Are our individual needs and wants to be subordinated because we have a 'higher purpose'? Are we to identify ourselves with this 'higher purpose' on the assumption that it has nothing to do with our individual happiness and fulfilment? It is clear that when Kant talks about 'happiness' he wants to remind us 'where possible, of a future life'. This shows how important is an implicit notion of salvation. This is what can make the satisfaction or fulfilment of our individual needs and desires seem so 'insignificant' when set against the need for salvation and 'a future life'.

If Kant helps us become conscious of our 'dignity' and 'self-esteem', he does this at the cost of making us aware of our 'insignificance as a *natural man*'. We are told that this self-recognition 'cannot distract from his consciousness of his dignity as a *moral man*', but we are given little sense of the workings of this moral psychology and social practice. Our 'self-esteem' and 'dignity' is to be drawn solely from our moral disposition not from our needs, wants and desires. In making us experience our 'insignificance' when we think of our needs, desires, wants and feelings, this can work to *undermine* whatever 'esteem' and 'dignity' we might, within a different tradition, be able to draw from these sources. It can so easily reproduce a morality of self-denial as we negate the significance and meaningfulness of our needs and wants, emotions and feelings. We learn that we have to 'value' ourselves by a 'low standard' when we view ourselves 'as a being of the sensible world'.

Within a Kantian tradition we cannot accept our needs and desires, our emotions and feelings as aspects of our humanity. They exist at a level beneath our humanity which has independent sources of its own. The fundamental demarcation between the 'natural man' and the 'moral man' can work to undermine our 'self-esteem', in the very ways that it declares as 'unacceptable' the different feelings of anger, resentment, rage, frustration, passion, dislike and fear. It becomes easy to feel that these feelings only prove our 'animal nature'. They simply confirm our low estimation of ourselves. This can make us feel even more unworthy, worthless and inadequate. This will tend to fuel a morality in which we are anxious to prove ourselves, be it in relation to the moral law, or in terms of individual ends and achievements. At another level we are likely to be plagued by these feelings of inadequacy and worthlessness. This can produce the very kind of moral self-righteousness Kant is critical of. Because these emotions and feelings are so easily judged as 'unacceptable', we do our best to negate them. We banish these feelings to our unconscious, barely wanting to become aware of them. This blinds us to the ways they can continue to influence our behaviour and relationships. The consequences of Kant's treatment of our emotions for the ways we relate to ourselves as well as others can be brought out in considering an example of Roger, a married man who feels attracted to another woman. He might not want to acknowledge these feelings even to himself. He might think that 'he shouldn't feel this way if he loves his wife'. This is the way in which our moral conceptions of what is 'right' can have a real influence upon the organisation of our emotions and feelings. Within this kind of morality a man is concerned to act properly towards his wife. But in its own way this is to deny his experience, since he cannot easily deny these feelings of attraction. For some people it might be a large step to acknowledge that they have these feelings at all, since the strength of morality might be such that someone was shocked even to admit these kinds of feelings to themselves. It becomes easy to place a severe judgement upon these feelings as 'disgusting', 'dirty', 'disloyal', rather than to acknowledge their existence and reality. This acknowledgment can make it easier to recognise the gap between acknowledging our feelings and the decision to act upon these feelings. This distinction can be very full of tension and uneasiness just because the feelings are not acknowledged in the first place.

Perhaps the depths of the moral psychology and social implications of Kantian ethics can only be appreciated with a full grasp of the importance of Freud's work. I can only suggest how the subordination of our 'animal nature' can itself work towards impersonalising our relationships. Very briefly, for example, as Roger denies his feelings for other women he is likely to have a guilty conscience in relation to his wife Ann. Not only is he aware that he is not sharing these feelings, he knows that a certain distance is created between them, through the silences he is responsible for. Roger might feel that if he acknowledges these feelings to her, she is bound to feel the worse about him. Given the moral culture they share, he can hardly help feeling bad about himself, feeling that he is little better than an animal. This is bound to make a difference to the quality of their relationship. It would be very different if he could accept these feelings as 'natural', even if they might reflect upon what is happening in their marriage.

Within a Kantian tradition Roger might be ashamed of feeling the way he does. He wishes that he did not feel this way. It makes him sacrifice his self-respect. When Kant says that 'Humanity in his own person is the object of respect' and that he must 'do nothing by which he would forfeit this respect', Roger might feel that he has already forfeited his respect in allowing himself to feel the way he does about another woman. At another level Kant recognises that we cannot really help what we feel, because we do not have perfect control over our feelings. It is partly because he recognises the importance of what we do, as opposed to what we feel, that he advises Roger that 'he can and should value himself by a low as well as a high standard', so that Roger should not give the slightest significance to these feelings knowing they derive from his 'animal nature'. This can help Roger deny the significance of these feelings, thinking they should not have the slightest bearing upon what he chooses to do.

But at another level denying the very existence of these feelings can mean that Roger is not being very honest with himself, nor with Ann. Kant has little room for this kind of consideration, but it is important to acknowledge it, since it bears upon the tensions in our everyday language of respect and self-esteem. Within a different moral tradition Roger might not have to put any kind of 'value' upon these feelings, but just *acknowledge* their reality as an aspect of his experience. Rather than feel that he would be forfeiting respect in acknowledging these feelings and in sharing them with Ann, he could feel that he owes it to her to work out these feelings with her. Rather than his sense of his 'sublime moral disposition' leading him to deny these feelings, it would encourage him to share them. Sharing these feelings might make him feel more honest in the relationship and could even lessen the emotional distance between them.

This is not simply a matter of acting according to a maxim that people ought to be honest and open in their relationships. It contains a deeper challenge. I think it helps to put into question the very duality which Kant assumes between the 'sensible world' and the 'intelligible world'. This suggests we cannot separate questions of morality from our emotions, feelings, wants and desires. Rather there is a sense in which respecting someone involves a recognition of the validity of someone's experience, their emotions and feelings as much as their moral actions. Sharing our emotions and feelings, desires and wants is an integral aspect of sharing our experience. In the sense that this can help people acknowledge their emotions and feelings, rather than avoid and deny them as they judge them as showing an animal nature, it can help people feel better about themselves. In this way it can help people's self-esteem. I would argue that to the extent that we deny our emotions and feelings we are choosing to deny important aspects of our experience. But this is deeply contradictory within the moral culture. Kant speaks clearly for a tradition which carries a particular interpretation of dignity, respect and self-esteem which relates them directly to our moral disposition. If this tradition can be questioned for denying integrity, dignity and significance to important aspects of our experience, it has also found a way of powerfully guaranteeing a sense of equality and respect.

Kant's notions of dignity and self-esteem play a fundamental role in his discussions of respect and equality. They are crucial in establishing our sense of how people can be equally capable of living moral lives, regardless of inequalities of social life. The particular interpretations we assume within a liberal moral culture tend to be in tension with traditions that build upon a notion of respect which involves a fuller and more complete validating of a person's experience. This is difficult for a Kantian tradition to do, for all its recognition of the conditions of individual autonomy. It tends to inevitably make a somewhat abstract recognition of people's needs and inclinations. This becomes even clearer in Kant's discussion of the moral law when we see that our respect for people is really a respect for the moral law which becomes the very source of our 'humanity'.

IV

RESPECT, IMPARTIALITY AND THE MORAL LAW

In this chapter I want to show further limitations within Kant's fundamentally rationalistic conception of respect and equality. We shall discover that Kant's respect for a person involves an even more attenuated conception of the individual, as respect for the rational self becomes respect for the moral law which the rational self exemplifies. The moral law is established as the source of all moral worth. Our sense of equality with others becomes an equal subordination before the moral law, even though Kant wants to conceive of the moral law as something which we legislate for ourselves. The sense of respect as hierarchy is made an integral aspect of our sense of respect for others, since it is mediated through our relationship with the moral law. This is only reinforced through Kant's sense that acting out of a sense of duty involves a systematic subordination of our inclinations.

In the second section I go on to show that if rationality can ensure universality and impartiality, it often does this at the cost of abstracting from social, sexual and cultural characteristics which could otherwise help us to a fuller sense of our individualities. Often it encourages us to abstract from importance aspects of our experience, just as we have already seen that it encourages us to discount our emotions and desires. Kant's rationalism can only establish a sense of human respect and equality through offering us an increasingly attenuated vision of individuality. It is this which makes it difficult for Kant to develop the fuller sense of individual dignity and autonomy which he sometimes promises us. This remains a deep tension within his moral theory.

44

1 RESPECT AND THE MORAL LAW

As we have seen, Kant reproduces a deep distrust of human nature. As we subordinate ourselves to the moral law, even if this is a law we supposedly legislate for ourselves, we learn to distrust our needs, wants and desires as simple forms of 'self-love'. This not only affects the sense we have of ourselves, it also deeply influences the character of our relations with others. *We learn that the respect we owe to others is really a respect for the moral law:*

> The only object of respect is the law, and indeed only the law which we impose on ourselves and yet recognise as necessary in itself. As a law, we are subject to it without consulting self-love; as imposed on us by ourselves, it is a consequence of our will. In the former respect it is analogous to fear and in the latter to inclination. All respect for a person is only respect for the law (of righteousness, etc.) of which the person provides an example. Because we see the improvement of our talents as a duty we think of a person of talent as the example of a law, as it were (the law that we should by practice become like him in his talents), and that constitutes our respect. All so-called moral interest consists solely in respect for the law.
> (*Groundwork of the Metaphysic of Morals*, footnote to 401)

I want to begin with identifying some of the positive aspects of Kant's position, especially as they have become integral aspects of liberal moral culture. I will then go on to explore negative aspects they are tied to. When Kant says that 'All respect for a person is only respect for a law', he is implying that we do not have to humble ourselves before others in the respect we feel for them. We can all equally have the same relationship to the moral law, so we do not have to put ourselves down in relation to others. This is what sustains Kant's sense that we are equally capable of living moral lives. This can be seen as an aspect of the democratic strain in Kant's writings. Even if it brings home that we each have to subordinate ourselves to the moral law, at least we all have to subordinate ourselves and no one can escape from this relationship to the moral law.[1]

In this way Kant is confirming the position of the moral law in all our lives, while making us feel that it is quite appropriate for us to subordinate ourselves to the moral law, since we are not subordinating ourselves to other people, to whom we can still feel equal. This reminder can teach us our own humility, insofar as it denies us grounds for thinking that we are better than other people. Rather than putting ourselves down or judging ourselves inferior or inadequate in comparing ourselves with 'a person of talent', we should simply see this person 'as the example of a law' which we are equally subordinated to. This produces a sense of human equality through reminding us that we are equally subordinate to the moral law.

This can also serve to teach us that the moral law is the source of all goodness, so we should never overestimate our own achievements in the world. It is only because we are creatures who can hear the voice of the moral law that we have been able to achieve any worth and dignity in our lives. This teaches us humility and can give us a sense of fitting into a larger order of things. It limits whatever personal ambitions we have for ourselves, as it makes us aware of just how dependent our moral worth and dignity is upon the moral law. This shared subordination to the moral law is made all the more acceptable, since it is thought of as something that we have created for ourselves.

While Kant is reminding us of the necessity to subordinate ourselves to the moral law, he is also making us aware of what we are capable of achieving ourselves. Rather than feeling down about ourselves, for instance, when we see someone who has taught herself to play the guitar, we are supposed to be reminded of what we are capable of ourselves through the moral law that 'we should by practice become like her in her talents'. Being reminded of the very universalism of the law is supposed to give us confidence, rather than remind us of our own lack of abilities. A recognition of this moral law is supposed to reflect back upon us and remind us of the duty we have to improve our own talents. In showing that when we respect someone, we are really respecting a particular law, we are also reminding ourselves of something we are capable of doing ourselves. If we cannot learn to play the guitar, there is bound to be something else we can be working on to improve ourselves. We do not have to feel down about ourselves. Rather we can be awakened to new possibilities and opportunities we might otherwise be blind to. This is another way in which an awareness of the moral law can stop us valuing others more than ourselves, and can remind us of an equality in the respect owed to us, since we are equally capable of living according to the moral law. There is no way for people to gain advantage over us in their relationship to the moral law. They can simply remind us of what we are capable of ourselves. In helping us retain a sense of our equality with others and in encouraging us to develop our own capacities and potentialities the idea that respect for persons is respect for law has had positive and emancipatory implications within a liberal moral culture.

I want to go on to consider negative aspects of the idea that respect for persons is respect for the law since they are related within our moral inheritance. At some level we can feel that the respect owed to people is never really given to them. In Kant's more formal writings it is as if our respect for people is only for their 'humanity so far as it is capable of morality', since this 'is the only thing which has dignity'. Not only are our desires and inclinations unreliable but they are assumed to be uniquely individual. This encourages Kant to separate the human self from an 'animal nature'. This idea is shared by those who assume that emotions and desires are necessarily partial so that morality has to be identified with rationality. But if rationality can ensure universality and impartiality, it often does this at the cost of fully understanding the moral significance of individual personal experience. This was a danger that Adorno recognised in Kant's writings.

> In inveighing against psychology, Kant expresses not only the fear of losing the laboriously caught scrap of the intelligible world; he expresses also the authentic insight that the moral categories of the individual are more than strictly individual. What manifests itself in them as universal, after Kant's concept of the law, is secretly social. For all the oscillation of the concept of humanity in Kant's Critique of Practical Reason, one of its major functions is that pure reason, being general, is valid for all rational beings; this is a point of indifference in Kant's philosophy. The concept of generality was obtained from the multiplicity of subjects and then made independent as the logical objectivity of reason, in which all single subjects – as well as, seemingly, subjectivity as such – will disappear ... (*Negative Dialectics*, pp. 281–2)[2]

The very self-conception of ourselves as 'rational beings' subject to the moral law presupposes the identification of 'self' with our 'rationality' and implicitly the subordination of our wants and de-sires. But this can make it difficult to give people the respect due to them, if all the time we are really 'seeing through them' to give respect to the moral law. In this case the things that people do are experienced as indications of the moral law, rather than as express-ive of the individuality of the person we are relating to. This has an influence upon the sense we culturally develop of what it means to respect others. It is as if we *cannot* relate to the person himself or herself, but only to the moral law which we see present in the things they do. This remains true despite all the talk about the independence and autonomy of individuals. This is something Max Scheler helps us think about. The analytical tradition has often been too ready to accept this self-definition of people as 'rational beings', without thinking about the consequences this has for the form and character of our moral theory.

> It is no terminological accident that formal ethics designates
> the person first as *'rational* person' ... with this one expression,
> formalism reveals its implicit material assumption that the
> person is basically nothing but a logical subject of rational
> acts, i.e. acts that follow these ideal laws. Or, in a word, the
> person is the X of some kind of rational activity; the moral
> person, therefore, the X of volitional activity conforming to
> the moral law ... the above definition of the person as rational
> leads first to the consequence that every concretization of the
> idea of the person in a concrete person coincides at once with
> a depersonalization. For that which is here called 'person',
> namely, that 'something' which is the subject of rational
> activity, must be attributed to concrete persons – indeed to *all
> men* (*and women*) – in the same way as something *identical* in
> all men (and women). Hence people are not distinguishable by
> virtue of their personal being alone. Indeed, the concept of an
> 'individual person' becomes, strictly speaking, a contradictio in
> adjecto. (*Formalism in Ethics and a Non-Formal Ethics of
> Values*, p. 371)[3]

Though Kant goes beyond this conception of a person especially in the strand of thought when he recognises people 'as ends in themselves', this can help us identify certain implicit processes of *depersonalisation*. In Kant this is related to the fundamentally reli-gious inspiration which allows him to see through what people do, to 'signs' of the presence of God in the world. This is particularly significant since Kant's moral theory is often taken as guaranteeing the separateness and distinctness of individuals. It is less often appreciated how this is one of the centrally contradictory aspects of his moral theory. Sometimes he seems to be unwittingly undermining the very notions of autonomous individuality he is trying to articulate.

Scheler helps us think about one of the basic claims of Kantian ethics, that it alone can confer upon a person a 'dignity' which is beyond any 'price'. Even though he agrees with Kant that you cannot measure the goodness of a person in terms of the degree to which they achieve certain goods or realise certain purposes, he still thinks that:

> it is another matter to ask whether a formalistic and rational ethics of laws does not *de*grade the person (although in a different manner from that of the ethics of goods and purposes) by virtue of its subordination of the person to an impersonal nomos under whose domination he can become a person only through obedience. ... In other words, the being of the person is never exhausted in being a subject of rational acts of a certain lawfulness – no matter how this being must otherwise be more precisely conceived, and no matter how wrong it is to conceive of this being as a thing or a substance. The person could not even be 'obedient' to the moral law if, as its executor, he were created, as it were, by this law. For the being of the person is also the foundation of any obedience.
> (*Formalism in Ethics and a Non-Formal Ethics of Values*, pp. 370, 372)

If some of these formulations remain unfamiliar within a more analytical tradition, the question retains its challenge.[4] This can help us identify a difficulty about the kind of validation and acknowledgment we can give to the experience of people themselves, in the equal respect people are due within a moral culture so deeply influenced by Kantian moral traditions. Not only does this help us identify the ways in which we tend to understand the separateness and individuality of people, it also helps us identify inadequacies in the way we are brought up to conceptualise people's experience, deeply influenced within a rationalistic tradition we take very much for granted.

When Kant says that 'All respect for a person is only respect for the law of which the person provides an example' this turns our attention towards the moral law which remains the source of a person's 'dignity' and 'worth'. So when we respect Jane, for instance, for having taught herself to play the guitar, we see her as an 'example' of a law that 'we should by practice become like her in her talents'. We are reminded not only of what Jane has been able to do, but of what we are capable of ourselves. If this restores a sense of equality, it can make it harder to appreciate fully what Jane has managed to do. Rather than appreciating how much Jane has been able to learn herself, especially if, say, she is learning after a hard day at work, we tend to see her as an 'example' of what is possible and of what we can achieve ourselves. Jane might feel that in our respect for her we are not really appreciating what she has done individually. She might feel we are simply seeing her as someone who has taught herself the guitar, without appreciating how she has always wanted to express her individuality in learning to play the guitar. This is to see what she had done less as an achievement that fulfils a certain law, but more as an expression of her individuality. It would seem that this is something that cannot be acknowledged within Kant's conception of respect. It fails to identify some of the crucial aspects in our respect for others.

Kant might object that it simply illustrates a different concept of 'respect' from the one he is concerned with. He might argue that what we feel for Jane is respect in the sense of admiration, and this may indeed be a response to her particular individual qualities. If this is supposed to be quite different from the moral respect which should not be dependent on particular individual qualities but should be accorded to all human beings in virtue of what is human in them, it does not allow us to feel moral respect for what she has achieved individually or to acknowledge the moral qualities she has shown. The admiration we might feel for her playing should not prevent us from being able to acknowledge our respect for her because of what she has achieved rather than having to see her as an example of a law. This relates to other tensions in Kant's notions of respect, equality and individuality.

2 INDIVIDUALITY, IMPARTIALITY AND EQUALITY

When Kant says that 'All respect for a person is only respect for the law' this is easily accepted as a way of guaranteeing impartiality. We do not want to judge people according to our likes and dislikes, favouring people because we happen to like them. This is an important strain in Kant's writings which has been historically significant in challenging social privilege and favouritism. It is part of the strength of the rationalist tradition in ethics.

In this way our sense of equality is related to 'universality' and 'rationality'. It is in our relationship to the moral law that we can be regarded as 'equal'. This is what encourages us to identify ourselves with our 'intelligible selves', since this is the source of our equality with others. In contrast to this we are encouraged to assume that the more we relate to our needs and desires, our emotions and feelings, the more *unequal* we have to consider ourselves. As Max Scheler realised, this is related to the ways Kant 'identifies everything good that is merely *individually* valid with the merely "subjective", i.e. with what is merely fancied as good' (*Formalism in Ethics*, p. 510).

The fact that our acknowledgment of others can become purely *formal* relates to the notion of abstract rights which are so central to a liberal conception of an individual's relationship to social life. Rather than existing as individual men and women who have individual wants, needs and desires, we exist as the abstract bearers of these rights.[5] Our individuality is defined very much in these terms. We are encouraged to abstract from the personal qualities that people have, in the respect we owe them as human beings. We do not want to know too much about them, since this respect is due to them regardless of the particularities of their history, experience and background. Knowing more will serve as a temptation to discriminate, and can easily be interpreted as a form of interference. It is as if saying that it is the 'individual' who is owed respect is *already* to abstract someone from their personal, sexual and class histories. This is something that Sartre notices in *Anti-Semite and Jew*, where he talks of the implications of liberal moral and political theory upon our thinking about history and collectivities:

He has no eyes for the concrete syntheses with which history confronts him. He recognises neither Jew, nor Arab, nor

Negro, nor bourgeois, nor worker, but only man – man always
the same in all times and in all places. He resolves all
collectivities into individual elements. . . . And by individual he
means the incarnation in a single example of the individual
traits which make up human nature. (*Anti-Semite and Jew*,
p. 55)[6]

It is this conception of an 'individual' which has a powerful influence upon liberal social thought. It can serve to *depersonalise* our
conception of others whom we implicitly see as clusters of abilities,
qualities or capacities. This has had far-reaching effects upon our
sense of equal treatment for people. It becomes easy to assume that
we relate to people equally if we treat them the same regardless of
the differences in their circumstances. This often underlies our sense
that people are equally capable of living moral lives as long as they
are left alone to do so. Again this has been very important in
formulating our liberal conviction that we do not want to discriminate or show favouritism in our treatment of people, but want
to be able to treat people equally.

This is illustrated if we think for a moment about the experience
of a primary school teacher who has been taught to treat all the
pupils in her class equally. She does not want to discriminate on
the basis of people's class, sexual or racial backgrounds, so she is
anxious to 'abstract' from these differences in her relationships with
the children. She might express this through a particular language
of individualism, saying that she wants to treat each pupil as an
individual in his or her own right. So she is concerned to see each
one of them as a pupil struggling to learn. In this way we can think
of them as 'examples' of a law that we should learn as much as we
can. In this situation 'treating them as individuals' comes to mean
'abstracting' them from their social and class backgrounds. She is
scrupulous in treating all the pupils in the same way regardless of
the background they come from. When she sets them an exam she
is careful to judge each script only as a sign of the individual
abilities of a student. She is careful not even to look at the names
so that they cannot influence her. In this way she treats each pupil
as a set of abstract abilities, as far as the exams are concerned.

A similar situation is depicted in *Letter to a Teacher* in which
the school children of a small school in Southern Italy offered a
challenge to the very notion of 'impartiality' by drawing up a graph

which showed the relation between school promotion and father's profession:

When a test gets a 4.
When the instructors saw this graph of school promotion and fathers' profession, they called it an insult to their fairness as impartial judges.

The fiercest of them all protested that she had never sought or received any information about the students' families: 'When a test is worth a 4, I will mark it with a 4'. She could not understand, poor soul, that this is exactly the charge against her. Nothing is more unjust than to share equally among unequals. (*Letter to a Teacher*, p. 50)[7]

It is partly because we are encouraged by Kantian moral traditions implicitly to regard people as providing an example of a law that we will also find this hard to understand. It deeply challenges our conceptions of 'fairness' which make us think we are being fair through abstracting individuals from all the social differences of class, race and sexuality in order to be able to treat people 'as equals'. This hardly touches the issue of what makes 'a test worth 4', when it is done by children with very different backgrounds and preparations. If we are not 'to share equally among unequals' we need to begin by understanding how easy it is within our inherited moral culture to do so unknowingly, while thinking and feeling we are being fair and just in our treatment of others.[8]

Sometimes to make sure that we are not discriminating between people we often prefer to know little about them. In our example a teacher thinks she is showing respect to the pupils in the class by being careful not to be too aware of their backgrounds. She is anxious to relate to them equally. But this does not necessarily help the pupils to a sense of their own individual identities and histories. It can make our sense of people even more attenuated. It can encourage children to discount their class, cultural and sexual backgrounds, secure in the knowledge that these will not count against them within the social relations of schooling. So pupils are encouraged to think of themselves simply as individuals with particular abilities and talents. This is what it means to define our individuality within the liberal school. It provides us with the ways in which we can prove ourselves as individuals. In its own way this can unwittingly work to make children of, say, Jewish or Black

53

background feel uneasy, almost ashamed of their background, even though this is no part of the conscious intention of the schooling. Even if the school openly encourages pupils to be proud of the background they come from, the social relations of schooling can work in a way that makes people *discount* their culture and history. At least it becomes no part of a person's recognised identity and sense of self. It can easily become threatening to the sense of individuality which is encouraged within the school. As an individual with a discrete set of abilities, it is taken to be almost contingent that I happen to have a certain cultural background. Since this is not supposed to affect the ways others relate to us, since they would be discriminating, so it is not supposed to influence the ways we think and feel about ourselves and our 'identities'. Our individual identities are to be given to us by the inner qualities and abilities we have. This can encourage a Jew to discount his jewishness, as Sartre clearly understood:

> The democrat, like the scientist, fails to see the particular case; to him the individual is only an ensemble of universal traits. It follows that his defence of the Jew saves the latter as a man and annihilates him as a Jew ... he fears that the Jew will acquire a consciousness of the Jewish collectivity – just as he fears that a 'class consciousness' may awaken in the worker. His defence is to persuade individuals that they exist in an isolated state ... wishes to destroy him as a Jew and leave nothing to him, but the man, the abstract and universal subject of the rights of man and the rights of the citizen.
>
> Thus here may be detected in the most liberal democrat a tinge of anti-Semitism; he is hostile to the Jew to the extent that the latter thinks of himself as a Jew (*Anti-Semite and Jew*, p. 57)

So our individuality is thought of in terms of 'the abstract and universal subject of the rights of man and the rights of the citizen'. Learning to think and feel about ourselves in this way is taken as a sign of cultural maturity. In this way, for example, a person's jewishness can only be a matter of the individual beliefs he or she happens to hold. It can be no part of his or her individuality. So in claiming that individuality, people learn to renounce tacitly their jewishness. It is this very universalism which is taken as a sign of moral maturity. This is embedded in the ways Kant conceives us to be individually subject to the moral law. This is partly why the 'defence of the Jew saves the latter as a man and annihilates him as a Jew'. In learning to prove ourselves individually, we learn to distance ourselves from a cultural and historical heritage. Since this is no part of our individuality, it cannot be anything that we draw our strength and identity from. It is an individual's relationship to the moral law which, in Kant, works 'to persuade individuals that they exist in an isolated state'.

Even though Marx was critical of this tradition of abstract rights and the notion of the universal subject of the rights of man, this has also remained a very powerful influence within the Marxist tradition. It has been too easy to dismiss abstract notions of 'bourgeois individuality' in contrast to notions of class solidarity and collectivity. Often these oppositions just show that the critique has not gone deep enough. This has been a feature of otherwise very different traditions such as the Hegel-influenced Lukács and the anti-Hegelian rationalist tradition encouraged by the writings of Louis Althusser.[9] Crucial issues about the notions of individuality which have taken into consideration notions of class, ethnic and sexual formation have barely been thought about. This is hardly something that we can do justice to within this work. Hopefully, however, our discussion of Kant will throw some light on the broader issues involved.

V

RESPECT, INDEPENDENCE
AND SELF-SUFFICIENCY

In this chapter I want to focus upon a further aspect of the individualism in Kant's conception of respect and equality. This is the notion of respect as non-interference, the idea that we show our respect for others by leaving them alone to pursue ends and goals they have chosen for themselves. It is easy to feel that this is all that can be expected from us in our relations with others. I shall attempt to show that this notion of 'respect' gives us little sense of our need for relations with others, of ways others can sometimes help us to clarify our goals and define our individualities.

I go on to show how our moral lives are assumed to be very much a matter of our proving ourselves individually. Kant assumes that people can live fundamentally independent and self-sufficient lives.

1 RESPECT AND NON-INTERFERENCE

When Kant attempts to give a definition of respect it is striking that he takes his bearings by relating himself to legal thought on the one hand and Christian ideas on the other. These different comparisons are brought together in his sense of respect as a negative duty.

> The duty of free respect to others, since it is actually only
> negative (Not to exalt oneself over others) and is thus
> analogous to the juridical duty (Not to encroach upon their

56

rights), can, although it is merely a duty of virtue, be regarded
as a strict duty in comparison with the broad duty to love
one's fellow men. (*The Doctrine of Virtue*, Section 25, 448)[1]

The universalism of Christian thought was a great and lasting influence upon Kant's thought. In formulating his sense of our moral
duties the broader conceptions of Christianity were never far from
his mind. Often it seems as if this presents a perfection that we
cannot expect from ordinary people. This is why it becomes so
important to develop a clear sense of what people can expect from
each other. This is partly why Kant thinks of our moral duty to
respect others as 'analogous' to the juridical duty 'not to encroach
upon their rights'. Since this is taken to have a perfectly clear
definition within the law, this can provide a reliable bench mark
against which to think about the meaning of respect.

The idea that we should not encroach upon the rights of others
is central within Kant's moral and political universe. He seems to
see little need for a discussion of the nature and character of 'rights'
which are implicitly taken to be fundamental. If Kant does not say
much to explain the meaning of the notion 'Not to exalt oneself
over others', this is perhaps because he is assuming that reference
to the juridical duty stands as some kind of explanation itself.
There seems to be something much closer than an 'analogy' here.
It is as if for Kant the moral duty almost comes to be *identified
with* the juridical duty.

Our duty to respect others is explained as the negative duty 'Not
to exalt oneself over others'. This is like the juridical duty of not
encroaching upon another's rights in that they are both 'negative',
telling us what we should not do, not what we should do towards
others. This connects to our sense of respect as taking up a certain
attitude towards others, one that largely recognises that we should
keep our distance from others so they can live lives of their own.
This becomes a deep assumption of liberal moral and political
theory.

Kant presupposes in his moral writings that people are fundamentally independent of each other. This is easy for him to maintain as long as he is imagining each individual working out his or
her relationship to the moral law, through proving himself or herself. This makes it easier for him to sustain the 'analogy' between
morality and law and to think of 'not exalting oneself over others'

as being more or less 'analogous' to 'not encroaching upon their rights'. It is this very vision of people standing alone before the moral law that makes it easier to think of this 'independence' as something that can be guaranteed through 'abstracting' from the social and historical relations people find themselves in, so it is not compromised and brought into question through the structures of power and dependency reproduced through the development of society. The very notion of not 'encroaching upon their rights' seems to presuppose that individuals have their own individual rights which can be thought about completely independently of the situation of others. He wants to think of 'not exalting oneself over others' in these kinds of terms. This becomes something we very much have a choice about, since we are assumed to be free to relate to others in any way we choose. It is only later in *The Doctrine of Virtue* that Kant has to question this, as he discovers there are forms of human dependency which grow out of the very organisation of social life, and which would seem to question the notion of the 'autonomy of morals' Kant so much wants to preserve.

The respect Kant discusses is limited to not interfering in the lives of others. It does not mean that we have to 'venerate others' or show 'positive reverence to them'. Rather it means we should allow others the freedom to work out their own individual lives in relation to the moral law, without the interference of others. This is why respect is called a negative duty. In this way it has become fundamental to liberal social and political theory:

> under the preceding title, virtues are not so much praised, as rather, vices opposed to them are censured. But this is already implied by the concept of respect, which, as we are obliged to manifest towards others, is only a negative duty. I am not bound to venerate others (regarded merely as men) i.e. to show them positive reverence. . . . (*The Doctrine of Virtue*, section 44, 467)

At a fundamental level Kant believes that people should be free to pursue their own ends. People are assumed to find satisfaction and fulfilment as long as they are left free to pursue goals and ends they have set for themselves. For Kant the finite rational will always has an end (Zweck) or object (Object, Gegenstand). It is for this reason, as Allen Wood points out, that Kant calls the will a 'faculty of desire' (Begehrungsvermogen) or 'faculty of ends'

58

(Zweckenvermogen). As Wood says, 'Human action, from a practical point of view, is thus both *motivated* and *purposive*' (*Kant's Moral Religion*, p. 41). He then goes on to show that the finite rational will involves both duty and inclination:

> The finite rational will is subject to the moral law as an imperative only because *both* duty and inclination are naturally adopted into his maxim, and form a necessary part of the practical concepts of finite rational action. This is what Kant means when he says that happiness 'is necessarily the desire of every rational but finite being, and thus it is an unavoidable determinant of its faculty of desire' (*Critique of Practical Reason* 25 g 24 e). The difference between good and evil in the human will thus cannot consist in the presence or absence of any incentive (for in this case man would always be *both* good and evil); rather it consists in the *subordination* of one incentive to another, 'i.e. which of the two incentives he makes the condition of the other'. (*Kant's Moral Religion*, p. 42)[2]

Kant distinguishes different kinds of maxims for rational action. The form of a maxim is always given in its generality as a principle or rule. So the maxims upon which we act show both our freedom, but also our subjection to our needs and desires, our sensibility. To the extent that our action is thought of as 'human', it is taken to be rational. We are assumed to set goals for ourselves and to find our happiness in the achievement of these goals. But with this Kant draws a significant distinction:

> A *maxim* is a subjective principle of action and must be distinguished from an *objective principle* – namely, a practical law. The former contains a practical rule determined by reason in accordance with the conditions of the subject (often his ignorance or his inclinations): it is thus a principle on which the subject *acts*. A law, on the other hand, is an objective principle on which we *ought to act* – that is, an imperative. (*Groundwork of the Metaphysic of Morals*, 416)

So even when Kant is talking about a 'subjective principle of action' he is talking about an end or goal we set ourselves. In this way our happiness is assumed to come from the fulfilment of the goals we have set ourselves. This is already to pose a deep contrast with a notion of happiness that talks in terms of the fulfilment of our bodily needs and desires, or which recognises our needs for certain kinds of close and loving relationships with others. Rather Kant articulates a tradition which sees the individual pursuing goals he or she fundamentally sets for himself or herself. This tends to assume that others are likely to be a 'distraction' or 'interference' in achieving the goals or ends we have set ourselves. Our happiness is assumed to be fundamentally individualistic and to require that we be left alone, protected from the interference of others. This is why Kant remains so easy with the notion that we should not encroach upon the rights of others. Each person is imagined to be surrounded by a ring of rights which serve to ward off others. This reveals the deeper connection between our respect for others and acknowledging the rights of others which are not to be infringed. At a fundamental moral level for Kant, people do not really need others. Rather we need to be left alone to work out our individual relationship to the moral law. But to say that Kant has an individualistic view of our relationship to the moral law is quite different from saying that he sees our needs and desires in individualistic terms, and as not including any need for relationships with others. It is this second claim that we still need to say more about.

This is related to the deep assumption that whatever meaning or 'worth' our lives come to have is given in working out our own individual relationship to the moral law. Life is very much a struggle for salvation, for winning approval in the eyes of God. As this has become secularised, the basic structure has remained much the same, as we feel the need to prove ourselves to others as well as ourselves. This makes the quality of our social relations with others more or less secondary to proving ourselves in the eyes of God. This is why we are fundamentally interested in the protection we can get from the interference of others. It prepares us to live in a world in which we take for granted the ways our relations with others can only have a secondary importance in our lives. We do not really need other people, in the sense that they cannot affect the core meaning of our lives which is worked out in our individual relationship to God, in the ways we prove ourselves. We might be able to enjoy ourselves with other people so that we do not feel lonely or bored, but this itself can only be a moment of ease and recovery in what has to be the real meaning of our lives. Our lives can only have meaning 'as individuals'. This helps explain at a deeper level why some of the implications of Kant's moral thinking within our culture encourage us to take up *instrumental* attitudes towards people. Within this deeper framework we do not expect to find meaning or 'worth' in our relations with others, though they might afford us different opportunities to prove ourselves as moral individuals. We might be called upon to help others in a way that will confirm our moral worth.

This is related to the ways we set 'ends' or 'goals' for ourselves so that our behaviour is assumed to be fundamentally 'purposive'. This is so readily identified with our 'rationality', and so with our 'humanity', that it is barely questioned. The assumption of Kant's moral theory can make it difficult to grasp how the very *'subordination* of one incentive to another', of duty being given priority over inclination, *does not* leave the structure of our needs, wants, desires, emotions and feelings untouched. Rather we are educated into feeling that it would almost be better if we did not have these desires and emotions, since they only interfere with the 'goals' we set ourselves. We look for the meaning in our lives in these very 'goals', which come to be set almost independently of our 'animal natures'. The deeper implications within a capitalist moral culture are clearly drawn when we think of the ways we are brought up to identify ourselves with 'individual achievement' and 'making money'. These become ends in themselves. It is then very easy for our relationships with people to be implicitly subordinated to these 'goals', though we might be hardly aware this is happening.

Since we identify ourselves so strongly with the 'goals' we set ourselves, the costs this involves in terms of our individual happiness and fulfilment and the satisfaction of our needs and desires is barely visible. Since we redefine our happiness as the 'fulfilment of these goals', and since we remain aware at some level that we have set these goals for ourselves, having little understanding of how the social relations we take for granted encourage us to adopt these goals, we are barely aware of these 'costs'. This is something Max Weber appreciated, recognising the ways this very 'irrationality' has come to seem 'rational', if not 'obvious' to us:

> In fact the summum bonum of this ethic, the earning of more
> and more money, combined with the strict avoidance of all
> spontaneous enjoyment of life, is above all completely devoid
> of any eudaemonistic, not to say, hedonistic, admixture. It is
> thought of so purely as an end in itself, that from the point of

view of the happiness of, or utility to, the single individual, it
appears entirely transcendental and absolutely irrational. Man
is dominated by the making of money, by acquisition as the
ultimate purpose of his life. Economic acquisition is no longer
subordinated to man as the means for the satisfaction of his
material needs. This reversal of what we should call the natural
relationship, so irrational from a naive point of view, is
evidently as definitely a leading principle of capitalism as it is
foreign to all peoples not under capitalistic influence. (*The
Protestant Ethic and the Spirit of Capitalism*, p. 53)

If this morality has come to have much more of a 'hedonistic
admixture', we can still recognise ourselves in it. Certainly if we
think about the notion of 'individual achievement' and the need to
'prove ourselves', we can recognise what an enduring and generally
unacknowledged role the Protestant ethic still has within our moral
culture.[3]

2 INDEPENDENCE AND SELF-SUFFICIENCY

Kant assumes that our lives have 'moral worth' through the individual relationship we work out with the moral law. We have to
acknowledge in our relationships with others that this is an individual quest, so we show our respect to others by keeping ourselves
within our own bounds:

When I exercise a duty of love towards someone, I at the same
time obligate that person; I make myself deserve well from
him. But when I observe the duty of respect, I obligate only
myself and keep myself within my own bounds in order not to
deprive another of any of the value which he as a human being
is entitled to put upon himself. (*The Doctrine of Virtue*, 448)

We do not want to deprive others of 'the value which he as a
human being is entitled to put upon himself'. This assumes that
individuals are proving their individual worth, and that therefore
they will want to be left alone to pursue the goals they have set for
themselves.

In the above quotation the notion of respect is illuminated by a
comparison with the duty of love. When I do something out of a

sense of love for someone, I obligate that person to do something for me, or at least to think well of me. In contrast I show my respect for someone by keeping myself 'within my own bounds', by making sure that others are left alone to pursue lives they have chosen for themselves. It is assumed that we want to be left alone to pursue these goals. Not only do we not welcome the help of others, but this takes away from whatever 'worth' we might have gained from the activity. It is as if only doing something on my own can be morally praiseworthy, since otherwise I shall have to share the praise. Again it is assumed that the moral life concerns our being able to prove ourselves individually.[4] This relates to the 'value which he as a human being is entitled to put upon himself', and to the ways in which we have been able to prove ourselves individually, through acting according to the moral law. It is as if we are each involved in accumulating as much moral credit as possible and that we need to guard jealously our opportunities to do so. Only if I have done something on my own am I going to be able to feel good about what I have done.

This implicitly presents an ideal of 'self-sufficiency', as latent within the ways we live and think about ourselves. This can be a persuasive picture, but it can also mislead us when we think more generally about our relationships with others. An example can help bring out some of the assumptions we implicitly make about our need for relations with others. If someone helps me with a maths puzzle I might feel a little disappointed that I had not been left alone to work it out myself. It would have given me a greater sense of achievement. But if a friend of mine has a sick child whom he has to stay at home to look after, he might be very grateful if I go round to help him out, even if it is just a matter of keeping him company. He might feel that 'I shouldn't have bothered to come', but at another level feel very grateful that I have come to keep him company. I am not sure whether he would feel it would have been much better if he had been able to manage on his own. Suppose he is not used to looking after kids, since his wife usually does it. He might want to reach a stage where he is able to look after them on his own without needing the help of others. At the same time he might think it is really good sharing childcare with a number of people, since otherwise it is quite a lonely activity. This is very different from a Kantian ethic that encourages us to think it is somehow more morally praiseworthy to do this on his own, since he thereby accumulates more individual moral worth. Again it is unclear whether Kant is recommending this moral ideal, or whether he is saying that our conception of moral worth already invokes such a conception and has to be built around it.[5]

It is only if we accept this ideal of self-sufficiency that we are bound to regard the help that others give us as unwelcome – as inevitably taking away from the moral worth of our individual achievement, since somehow this worth has now to be shared. Does this involve an implicit conception of what is involved in putting 'value' upon ourselves? If it looks as if Kant is not legislating about the different ways we can 'value' ourselves, this is because the grounds of his discussion remain largely hidden. If self-sufficiency can be assumed in our relationships towards the moral law, then it does not have to be argued for. If we already presuppose these conceptions in our social relations, then asking for the help of others or admitting that we need help is *already* to admit some kind of moral weakness. I can only think less of myself. If this is a shared understanding in the community we live in, then we only have to be reminded to keep within our bounds, if we do not want to make others think less of themselves.

By making such an implicit notion of moral self-sufficiency a presupposition of our very sense of the 'moral', it becomes almost a matter of common sense that we will want to live within our bounds. It gains plausibility from the important fact that often individuals have to discover for themselves the sources of their own happiness and duty. Sometimes we can be guided by others, but often we have to learn what satisfies us through our own mistakes, and through our own individual experience. I have to discover the sources of my individual happiness. I might discover that I do not enjoy playing with the mechanical toys my father has got for me, but prefer listening to music. I might even feel a little surprised to discover this about myself, since this makes me different from my brothers and from the family's expectations. I might be constantly surprised to discover the kinds of things that make me happy, and how different individuals can be in what they want out of life. This is a deep insight in Kant that has been valuably developed within liberal social theory. It is the basis for the ways Kant's notion of respect becomes grounded as a *territorial* notion. It has a long history in the sense we develop of ourselves within liberal moral and social theory. We become anxious not to interfere in the lives of others, we even become wary of offering others help, since we do not want this to be misinterpreted as an attempt to interfere in the course of their lives. In this way respecting others becomes a form of non-interference in the lives of others.[6]

The important recognition that individuals have to make discoveries for themselves about the kind of life they want to live is easily compromised by a sense that these 'ends' or 'goals' are somehow already given in our inner lives. We need to distinguish the idea that morality is 'inner' from the idea that our ends are 'inner' because for Kant morality is clearly *not* a matter of ends and goals. So from the fact that he sees morality in terms of individual self-sufficiency, it does not at all follow that he sees ends and goals in terms of individual self-sufficiency. Kant employs a fragmented conception which sees our desires, wants, emotions and feelings as being the result of external influences upon us. In this sense they *cannot* be an expression of our 'freedom' which is taken to be essentially 'inner'. Rather they are an expression of the ways we are influenced and determined by forces which are essentially 'external'. In contrast to this our 'ends' or 'goals' are imagined to be chosen by us, to be an expression of our freedom. They have their source in our inner lives. This kind of dichotomy makes it extremely difficult to understand the influence of social relations of power and subordination within a class society upon the very formation of our wants and desires, as well as upon the ends and goals we set for ourselves. But to become aware of the ways this builds tensions into the very core of people's experience is not to negate the important realisation that individuals have to make crucial choices and decisions for themselves.

An example can help us question this implicit contrast, helping us to a fuller sense of the personal and social context in which we often have to make decisions. It can help us to recognise the limitations of Kant's view, especially in ways it denies the importance of others in helping us clarify our ends and goals. The fact that relations of dependency can also mislead and influence us away from ourselves does not make this less true. So, for instance, Tom might find it difficult to make his decision to become a nursery school teacher because he knows it is women who usually do this kind of work. One part of him is saying that men do not usually do this kind of work, so there must almost be something wrong with him if this is what he wants to do. It might have been difficult

65

for him to realise that this is what he wants to do, given the kind of pressures from family and college that this would be 'wasting his life', and that he could be doing something more worthwhile for himself, since he is a person with many talents. This shows the kind of pressures Tom is up against, not only within himself, but in the way the society is organised. This is also related to the very poor pay and conditions he is going to get if he makes this kind of career decision. These kinds of 'goals' are not set in some kind of social vacuum. Tom knows that it is going to be difficult to live on the kind of money he is going to get, and he is not impressed with the argument that if he really wants to be a nursery teacher this is not going to matter to him. He does not feel he should be expected to make this kind of sacrifice. It is in these kinds of complicated situations that we often have to make decisions. Even if Tom makes this decision he knows that, with the number of unemployed teachers, he is not guaranteed to get a job and that it means working in poor conditions, since so little money is being given to nursery education.

At one level Tom might be aware that he has to make this decision for himself. He knows that it very much depends on his acknowledging how much joy and fulfilment he gets from working with children. This involves listening to this part of himself, rather than to the powerful cultural forces which say that this is not something which 'real men' should be doing. It is not simply a question of believing in himself, since it is hard for him to trust his own feelings, given the ways he is treated by others, including initially mothers who often expect to leave their children with women teachers, since this is how it has usually been in the past. In trusting his own feelings Tom knows he is challenging established notions of masculinity. But Tom also knows he needs the support of others to make these changes. He is aware of the difficulties of going against the social stream, and knows he will only be strong enough if he has the support of others involved in making similar changes in their lives. Tom acknowledges he needs to make these decisions with the help of others, even if he knows he has to take responsibility for the decision he eventually makes.

So Tom might experience the advice his parents give as a kind of 'interference', when they say that he could 'do something better', while finding that he needs the support of his friends to talk through the situation. Tom might feel that his parents are 'interfering' because they do not really want to listen to what he has discovered about himself and what he wants to do with his life. They seem to be coming with a ready-made judgement about what it would be 'better for him to do'. They think they know best. In some sense they do seem to be 'exalting themselves' above him, using what they assume to be their superior knowledge about how the society works. They cannot help feeling that he would be 'wasting his life' if he makes this decision to become a nursery teacher. Within a Kantian tradition it is difficult to acknowledge that the help and advice of others does not have to be like this. Since it assumes that the goals or ends we set are an expression of an inner quality, it does not appreciate the ways we might need others to define and clarify these goals and ends with us. But it is also because Kant assumes that if we make these decisions for ourselves then more moral worth will accrue to us, that we are more or less inevitably compromised by the help of others.

It is also because of the sensitivity within Kant's moral theory to the ease with which we can influence others for our own ends that we so readily listen to a notion of respect which guarantees to people the space within which they can live their own lives. Kant recognises the ease with which we can encroach upon the rights of others to make decisions for themselves, even if he does not fully realise the social relations which encourage us to exalt ourselves over others, to prove that we are better than others. Certainly within a competitive society it is partly because it is so easy for us to fall into securing a firmer sense of ourselves through showing that we are better than others, that Kant's warnings have a deep resonance for us.

VI

OBLIGATION AND
INEQUALITY

In this chapter I want to indicate further inadequacies in Kant's notion of respect as 'non-interference' and as respect for people's independence and self-sufficiency. In the previous chapter I have shown how this idea fails to do justice to the way in which we may need the support of others. In this chapter I will show how it fails to take account of the way in which our moral activity may be affected and distorted by the social relations of power and subordination. I shall be looking at the two cases of such relations which Kant himself discusses, that of relations between the sexes, and that of relations between rich and poor.

1 AN OBLIGATION TO HELP A POOR PERSON

In *The Doctrine of Virtue*, when Kant is talking about the duties of love and respect in the beginning of Part 2 which addresses itself to our duties to others, he immediately draws conclusions about our obligations to help a poor person. He is continually drawn to this example as if he is deeply troubled by it. It seems to offer a special challenge to some of the more deeply held assumptions of his moral theory:

> But in their ground in the law love and respect are always joined together in a duty, only in such a way that now one duty and now the other is the subject's principle, with the other joined to it as an accessory. Thus we shall recognise an

obligation to help a poor man; but since our favour humbles
him making his welfare dependent on our generosity, it is our
duty to behave as if our help is either what is merely due to
him or but a slight service of love, and so to spare him
humiliation and maintain his self-respect. (*The Doctrine of
Virtue*, trans. M. Gregor, 448)[1]

Kant is aware of the dangers of making someone's 'welfare dependent on our generosity'. He thinks that this threatens a person's
'self-respect' and that it can humiliate someone. So Kant says that
it is our duty to act towards someone as if the obligation towards
us does not really exist – 'to behave as if our help is either what is
merely due to him or but a slight service of love'. It is not clear
whether this is an issue of charity or justice for Kant. This raises
issues which are threatening to the very framework Kant has established for himself. It is difficult for Kant to think about the character of the obligation to the poor and oppressed, because he does
not want to acknowledge that someone's welfare is 'dependent on
our generosity'. To do so would be to compromise the independence of people, which is so crucial to the presupposition that
individuals are equally capable of living moral lives. It also
threatens the fundamental conception of individual responsibility
for morality and justice. It threatens the idea that as individuals we
are equally free to prove ourselves before the moral law.

Sometimes it seems as if Kant is calling us to 'ignore' or 'over-
look' the ways in which someone's welfare has become 'dependent
upon our generosity'. There seems to be little thought that the
situation itself should be transformed. It is as if the social relations
of inequality and dependency are to remain unquestioned, and so
not a proper object of moral assessment. Our duty for Kant seems
to lie in minimising the degree of help we are offering someone. At
one level it seems important to develop this sensitivity and understanding of others, so we realise that the ways we treat this situation of inequality and dependency can make a difference to the
ways people feel about themselves. It is important to appreciate
that this situation gives us the power to humiliate others and make
them feel small. Kant is forced to recognise this aspect of the moral
dimensions of relations of power and dependency, but he resists a
fuller recognition of their moral nature that would challenge some
of his deeply held moral assumptions.

At one level Kant is acutely aware that the ways we treat others can affect the ways in which they think and feel about themselves! So it is important to think about *how* people are to relate to situations of dependency and inequality. Kant needs to be able to think that people are owed an equal respect of their relationship to the moral law, regardless of the social relations of power and dependency. Kant is keenly supported in our sense that it makes a difference *how* we relate to others whom we have power over, or who are less fortunate. It can make a real difference how we give to others, if we are fully alive to the recognition that they are human beings like ourselves. It can be difficult to maintain this sense, especially within a competitive and acquisitive society in which we are brought up to affirm ourselves through thinking that we are 'better' or 'superior' to others. Kant reminds us of an important sense in which we remain equal as human beings, whatever our individual talents and abilities. If Kant underestimates the difficulties of maintaining this sense of human equality within hierarchically organised societies, he does make us fully aware of the need to make the effort. It is important to understand how people behave towards others, when it would be so easy for them to take others for granted. It might be so much more important in an unequal society to learn how to give to others in a way that does not humiliate them:

> Doctor Kafka is a fine man. He is quite different from the
> others. You can see that even in the way that he gives you
> something. The others hand it to you in such a way that it
> almost burns you to take it. They don't give – they humiliate
> and insult you. One would often like to throw their tips away.
> But Doctor Kafka gives, really gives, in such a way that it's a
> pleasure. For instance, a bunch of grapes which he has not
> eaten that morning. They are left-overs. You know what they
> usually look like – with most people. But Doctor Kafka never
> leaves them looking like a tasteless lump. He leaves the grapes
> or the fruit nicely arranged on the plate. And when it comes
> into the office, he says, by the way could I possibly make use
> of them. Yes, Doctor Kafka does not treat me like an old
> chair. He is a fine man. (from a conversation with Frau Svatek
> included in Gustav Janouch's *Conversations with Kafka*, p. 99)

If we learn to follow this example this involves an inner change in

70

our sense of others, rather than simply adopting a maxim in our relations with others. However we think the quality of our giving to others is to change, this makes relations more pleasant, more bearable, more human, but it does not transform the relations of power which exist between people. Kant focuses upon the behaviour of the giver, so he is inevitably less concerned with thinking about *why* someone like Frau Svatek should be at the mercy of the ways others in the office choose to treat her. It is difficult for her to protest at the ways some people treat her 'like an old chair', since it would be regarded as 'rude' or 'out of character', or 'out of place' for her to talk directly to people in this way. It is not for her to take initiatives in relationships. This is part of what it means to be in a situation of subordination.

Kant did not fully acknowledge this as a social relationship of subordination, but simply as a relationship between two individuals which very much reflected their qualities as individuals. He did not want to acknowledge a relationship of dependency that extended beyond a particular interaction. If he was not to challenge his assumption of the autonomy of morality he had to assume that people were living fundamentally independent lives. This helps explain why it is important for Kant to relate to others 'as if our help is either what is merely due to him or but a slight service of love', since this can mean that, although a poor person is dependent on the generosity of others, this does not have to compromise the independence he or she has as a moral agent. But sometimes this theoretical challenge is avoided only by almost pretending that this dependency has not been produced. This is to avoid the crucially important moral issues that are raised by issues of power, inequality and dependency. Not only do we have to investigate the different forms of this dependency, but we have to learn to think about the implications this has for our understanding of the autonomy of morals, and for our understanding of what it means for someone to be a person in his or her own right. These issues have been sharply raised in a contemporary context in both theory and practice through the experience of the women's liberation movement.

The thinking that Kant does about the relationships between rich and poor uncovers some of the deeper assumptions he makes about human dignity and dependency. In its own way the women's movement has raised questions about dependency and autonomy.

Women in the movement have shown the difficulties of relating to others in a way that sidesteps or ignores the relations of subordination. They have been saying that, although men have thought that they have been relating to them as equals, the very relations of power and subordination between the sexes have served to undermine women so that they do not exist as people in their own right, with their own independent lives, but only in relation to men and children.[2] Not only is this stance accused of being patronising, but it denies women the insight and understanding of their own situation, through presenting it in a way which mystifies the workings of the relations of dependency and subordination. This gives a peculiarly contemporary relevance to Kant's suggestion that 'it is our duty to behave as if our help is either what is merely due to him or but a slight service of love'.

This is not the way Kant conceived the relations between the sexes. He accepted the relations of subordination as necessary, if not desirable. He tends to invoke the quality of 'rationality' to legitimate the subordination of women. In a strange way his discussion 'On the Character of the Sexes' invokes the notion of machines with unequal force, which seems to be the way he thought about the differences between men and women:

Any machine that is supposed to accomplish just as much as another machine, but with less force, implies *art*. So we can already presuppose that nature's foresight put more art in the make-up of the female than of the male: for it provided the man with greater strength than the woman in order to bring them together into the most intimate *physical* union, which, insofar as they are still *rational* beings too, it orders to the end most important to it, the preservation of the species. Moreover it provides them, in this capacity of theirs (as rational animals), with social inclinations to stabilise their sexual union in domestic union.

If a union is to be harmonious and indissoluble, it is not enough for two people to associate as they please; one party must be *subject* to the other and, reciprocally, one must be *superior* to the other in some way, in order to be able to rule and govern him. For if two people who cannot dispense with each other make *equal* claims, self-love produces nothing but wrangling. As *culture* advances, each party must be superior in

72

his own particular way: the man must be superior to the
woman by his physical strength and courage; the woman to
the man, however, by her natural talent for gaining mastery
over his desire for her. In a still uncivilised state, on the
contrary, all superiority is on the man's side. (*Anthropology
from a Pragmatic Point of View*, 303)[3]

Kant accepts the necessity for the relationship between the sexes to
be a relationship of subordination. But he also seems uneasy about
this subordination, or at least about giving it public recognition. It
is almost as if an unbalanced 'superiority' can only be a feature of
'a still uncivilised state' but 'As *culture* advances, each party must
be superior in his own particular way.' This tends to mystify us
about the realities of sexual power and subordination. It encourages us to see Kant's talk of man's superiority in his physical
strength and courage as somehow equivalent to 'her natural talent
for gaining mastery over his desire for her'. Later Kant even describes the ways in which woman 'disarms him by tears of exasper-
ation as she reproaches him with his lack of generosity'.

Kant's belief that 'each party must be superior in his own particular way' blinds him to the ways in which women are *undermined*
through these social relations of power and subordination. He
tends to think about the rivalry of women amongst themselves,
without thinking about how the form and character of this rivalry
is mediated through the social relations of power that exist between
men and women. He recognises that certain features would be
wrongly regarded as part of the 'character' of women, though significantly he has less sensitivity to the relations of power than when
he thinks about the relations between rich and poor. He does not
want to concede that similar issues of moral autonomy and dependency are concerned:

The fact that the female sex is constantly feuding with itself
while remaining on very good terms with the other sex might
rather be considered as its character, were this not merely the
natural *result* of women's rivalry among themselves, in which
one tries to get the better of others in the favour and devotion
of men. For inclination to dominate is woman's real aim, while
pleasing in public, insofar as it widens the field of her charm, is
only the means for giving effect to that inclination.
(*Anthropology from a Pragmatic Point of View*, 305)

73

Why do women have 'to get the better of others in the favour and devotion of men'? What creates this rivalry amongst women? Sometimes it seems as if Kant does not escape attributing this to the 'character' of women, for instance when he says that 'The man has taste *on his own*: the woman makes herself the object of *every-one*'s taste.' It is as if this is to be taken for granted as 'natural', as if the requirements of autonomy and the conditions which allow us to exist as people in our own right barely relate to the experience of women. But the force of Kant's critical notions of autonomy and the need for people to be treated not merely as means but as ends in themselves can be used to criticise the very patriarchal assumptions of Kant's moral discussion of the relations between the sexes. At a deeper level we have to learn to criticise the fragmentation of reason and emotion which Kant's discussion of sexual relations mirrors, particularly when he says that 'the woman should *reign* and the man *govern*; for inclination reigns and understanding governs'. Within this it is all-important that our rationality sets the ends we have to organise our activities around, since this already presupposes the subordination of women. This is clear in the same passage of the *Anthropology* when Kant asks pointedly

> Who, then, should have command in the household? – for
> there can be only one person who co-ordinates all occupations
> in accordance with one end, which is his ... The husband's
> behaviour must show that his wife's welfare is the thing closest
> to his heart. But since the man must know best how his affairs
> stand and how far he can go, he will be like a minister to his
> monarch who thinks only of amusement. (*Anthropology*, 310)

Again we are confronted with the importance of manipulating the realm of appearances. We are not supposed to remind the poor person that his welfare is 'dependent on our generosity'. In this way we allow a person to maintain 'his self-respect'. In a not too dissimilar way the husband is supposed to 'show that his wife's welfare is the thing closest to his heart' while all the time being confident in the knowledge that he 'must know best how his affairs stand and how far he can go'. It is not surprising that when Kant thinks of woman he chooses the analogy of the 'monarch who thinks only of amusement', since women are identified in his mind with the inferior realms of emotions and feelings which are hardly to be taken seriously. It is the minister who has a secure grasp of the realities of life.

Kant was to be more deeply challenged in his thinking about the relations between rich and poor. He could not just assume that riches and power do not make it easier for some people to live a moral life. He had to face the reality of the ways a person's dignity and self-respect are compromised by the social relations of power and subordination, even if he could not face the social relations of power between the sexes. Kant was aware of the ways in which people having needs which required others to fulfil them challenge the very independence which he took for granted. It means that you can no longer assume that people are equally capable of living their lives according to their own individual conception of happiness. Kant had to face the ways this conception threatened to become a mystification, where some people have control and power over the lives of others. He was forced to face the realities of human dependency though he never learned to think about this systematically. He barely faces the nature of the assumptions he makes about 'independence', 'moral autonomy' and 'self-sufficiency', even though he is aware of the ways these very presuppositions seem to be questioned when people are forced to be dependent upon others.

Kant acknowledges that the most 'natural' maxim for people to adopt is 'Every man for himself: God for us all.' But he feels the need to question this kind of rampant individualism especially when he thinks about the needs of the poor. He does not help us understand the 'naturalness' of this maxim, but he knows that it has to be questioned even if 'It is not self-evident that any such law is to be found in reason':

> But how can it be required, as a duty, that we go beyond
> *benevolence* in our wishes regarding others (which costs us
> nothing) and make this benevolence practical, so that everyone
> who has the means should be *beneficent* to the needy? –
> Benevolence is satisfaction in another's happiness (well-being);
> but beneficence is the maxim of making another's happiness
> one's end, and the duty of benevolence is the necessitation that
> reason exercises on the agent to adopt this maxim as universal
> law.
>   It is not self-evident that any such law is to be found in

75

reason; on the contrary, the maxim 'Every man for himself:
God (fortune) for us all' seems to be the most natural one.
(*The Doctrine of Virtue*, 452)

It is significant that Kant says that it is 'everyone who has the
means' who 'should be beneficent to the needy'. He is not talking
here about the duties we all have towards others as human beings.
For the duty of benevolence to become 'practical' and 'active' Kant
has to begin talking about those who have the means and those
who are needy. He has to recognise the significance of differences
in the relative social positions of wealth and poverty that people
find themselves in. He can no longer talk about the universal duties
people have towards others. Different kinds of considerations seem
to have become morally relevant. The idea of universal respect for
others is compromised as soon as we begin to think about the
relations of power and dependency which are created between rich
and poor. We cannot simply assume that others are free to get on
with their own individual lives, if they are without control of their
very means of livelihood. It seems inadequate for us to assume that
we show our respect for others in this situation simply by leaving
people alone, thinking that this is none of our concern. Nor is it
enough for us to feel an identification with the poor 'which costs
us nothing'. Rather we have to adopt the maxim 'of making another's happiness one's end'.

Kant appeals to the workings of the categorical imperative to
show that this maxim of beneficence should be adopted. It seems
to come down to the realisation that we would not want others to
deny us help if we were the ones in need. But this leaves open the
question of what kind of help we can be expected to give to others.
It also makes it seem unnecessary for us to think about the sources
of these inequalities as long as we are aware of our individual
duties:

> It is every man's duty to be beneficent – that is, to promote,
> according to his means, the happiness of others who are in
> need, and this without hope of gaining anything by it.
>
> For every man who finds himself in need wishes to be helped
> by other men. But if he lets his maxim of not willing to help
> others in turn when they are in need become public, i.e. make
> this a universal permissive law, then everyone would likewise
> deny him assistance when he needs it, or at least would be

entitled. Hence the maxim of self-interest contradicts itself
when it is made universal law – that is, it is contrary to duty.
Consequently the maxim of common interest – of beneficence
towards the needy – is a universal duty of men, and indeed for
this reason: that men are to be considered as fellow-men – that
is, rational beings with needs, united by nature in one dwelling
place for the purpose of helping one another. (*The Doctrine of
Virtue*, 452)

Crucial significance is given by Kant to avoiding self-interest con-
tradicting itself. This is partly what encourages Kant to talk about
beneficence as 'the maxim of common interest'. But it is possible
to feel a tension in the passage with the recognition of the less
individualistic sentiments in the close, especially the more generous
notion that we are beings 'united by nature in one dwelling place
for the purpose of helping one another'. This seems to promise the
acknowledgment of the naturalness of forms of human community,
of people helping each other. This seems at odds with Kant's earlier
writings, when it is very easy to think that helping others has to be
an unwelcome if necessary task, since it inevitably distracts us from
following the goals and ends we have set ourselves individually.

When Kant talks about us as 'fellow-men – that is, rational
beings with needs' – it is possible to think that it is the somewhat
surprising acknowledgement on Kant's part or the needs we share
that makes us 'fellow-men'. When he says that we are 'united by
nature in one dwelling place for the purpose of helping one another', this suggests that we help others through recognising the
needs they have. Kant seems to be acknowledging the ways some
of our needs are shared. This is also significantly related to the
ways we have to give help to people because they are in need. It is
the way in which the *needs* of others obligate us towards them
that partly makes this passage so striking. Kant gives importance
to the recognition that 'every man who finds himself in need wishes
to be helped by other men'. This makes us crucially aware of at
least one source of human interdependency. It helps us give more
significance to questions of the satisfaction, fulfilment and nourish-
ment of our needs than is usual within a Kantian moral tradition.
It can also make us aware of the importance of the frustration,
denial and invalidation of our needs.

This gives a slightly different emphasis to Kant's saying that the

77

maxim of beneficence 'is the maxim of making another's happiness one's end'. Kant often thinks about happiness as a uniquely individual vision that has to do with the goals and ends individuals set. Often it is a conception that profoundly separates people off from each other, as we are encouraged to assume that we only need to be left alone to pursue the goals we set for ourselves. Liberal social theory often recognises the truth of this realisation, at the expense of acknowledging the importance of our relations with others and the needs we share with others. This is why it is striking when Kant finds this note in his own writing. He even seems to acknowledge that promoting the happiness of others can involve recognising the needs they have. Some of these needs we will share with others. Some of them might even relate to the needs for certain kinds of relationships with others.

2 FOR THE RICH BENEFICENCE IS NOT MERITORIOUS

It can be easy for us to recognise our duty to help others as the duty of charity. There is a strand within our moral culture which would argue that the poor should be thankful for our generosity, since there is no reason why we are obliged to give support to them. This is in line with a deeply embedded individualistic tradition which would see poverty as a sign of moral inadequacy or individual failure. This assumes that people are individually responsible for the social situation they find themselves in. They only have themselves to blame. Kant shows different sentiments, especially in *The Doctrine of Virtue*. As far as he is concerned a rich man is obliged to give to the poor. He must not expect to be thanked for what he gives, nor must he regard this as a reason to think well of himself:

> The *rich* man (the man supplied abundantly with means for the happiness of others – that is, beyond his own needs) should hardly ever regard his beneficence as meritorious duty, even though in practising it he does put others under obligation. The satisfaction he derives from his beneficence, which costs him no sacrifice, is a kind of revelling in moral feeling ... (*The Doctrine of Virtue*), 453)

Kant is quite clear that for the person who has 'beyond his own needs' giving to others 'costs him no sacrifice'. The ways Kant has talked about us as 'fellow-men – that is, rational beings with needs' could imply some sense of shared human needs. This would help us question the rich man who says that he simply has far greater needs than others so that he cannot spare anything for others. There are real difficulties in the ways we define our needs and acknowledge the different needs people have. I do not want to minimise these difficulties. But the crucial point for Kant is that we can recognise within society people who have more than they need, while others have clearly less than they need. The moral questions emerge with this situation of social inequality, as soon as we acknowledge the claims that people having less than they need make on others who have beyond their needs.

At the same time Kant realises that when the rich man gives to the poor 'he does put others under obligation'. Kant recognises this, even though he realises that it is the duty of the rich to give. Kant recognises that obligations are created through giving, however much people want to minimise the acknowledgment of this obligation. The fact that the rich person is only doing his duty and, in some sense, the poor person is only receiving what is 'owed to him' does not prevent the production of obligation. Kant recognises the way dependency has been set up and a situation of power created, though he does not conceptualise it in these terms. This is signalled in the ways people are put under obligation. Even though Kant is very sensitive to *the ways* the rich should give to the poor to minimise the harm done to self-respect, the obligation remains. He was always sensitive to the ways individual dignity can be compromised in relationships involving dependency. If you cannot avoid the creation of obligation, you can at least minimise the pain and humiliation this inevitably causes.

Kant does not help people understand the relationships of dependency they enter into through accepting the help of others. He assumes that people are already too painfully aware of this. If Kant's suggestions threaten to mystify the social realities of inequality, he was concerned to leave people feeling as good about themselves as possible. This is also an important reality. But this is to accept the legitimacy of the relations of wealth and power. In acknowledging the 'obligations' that are produced, Kant is undermining any sense he might otherwise have that people are receiving only what is due to them. This is very much within the ethos of charity rather than justice. Kant is teaching the rich tact and sensitivity:

> He must also carefully avoid any appearance of intending to put the other under obligation, for if he showed such an intention (thereby humbling the other in his own eyes) he would not be extending true beneficence. Rather, he must make it felt that he is himself obliged by the other's acceptance or honoured by it, hence that the duty is merely something that he owed. But it is still better if he can practice his beneficence in complete secrecy. This virtue is greater when the benefactor's means are limited and he is strong enough quietly to take on himself the hardship he spares the other. Then he can really be considered morally rich. (*The Doctrine of Virtue*, 453)

If the richer person is giving to the poor over and above what they need for themselves why does this create an 'obligation'? Kant is aware that this 'costs him no sacrifice'. Is he saying that the fact that this 'costs him no sacrifice' does not mean it is a sacrifice he has to make? But what does this mean about our duty to be beneficent?

Kant helps us challenge a view that the poor should be grateful for whatever they receive. He recognises the ways this humbles 'the other in his own eyes' He does his best to instruct the rich to give in a way that avoids these consequences. But he remains deeply ambiguous. Even though he instructs the rich to 'avoid any appearance of intending to put the other under obligation', he recognises that obligations are inevitably produced. And when he says that 'he must make it felt ... that the duty is merely something that he owes', it is no longer clear whether this is simply an appearance we have to create to help maintain a person's self-respect, or whether it is something owed because we cannot justify having more than we need while others so manifestly have less than they need. This remains one of the raw nerves of liberal moral and political theory.

If Kant had consistently thought that dignity was an 'inner quality', he could have argued that this is something people retain, regardless of the social relations they enter and regardless of the obligations created within relationships. In this strand of Kant's thinking nothing can humble people, since nothing can interfere with a person's sense of moral worth. This would be to separate systematically conceptions of 'individual dignity', 'moral worth' and 'respect' from the social relations people find themselves in. This forms a continuing strand in liberal moral thinking. It encourages us to think that the different situations people are in just afford different opportunities for people to prove their inner qualities. It makes people invulnerable to the social world.

Kant questions this assumption as he becomes acutely aware, especially in *The Doctrine of Virtue*, of the ways in which people can be undermined and humbled in their own eyes. Kant knows that the rich have to be very careful about the ways in which they give help to the poor if they are not to humiliate them and make them feel bad about themselves. So Kant seems to become at least partially aware in his discussion of the relationship between rich and poor, of ways in which 'individual dignity' and 'worth' can be *maintained* or *undermined* through the relations of power and dependency created through social relations. This is no longer simply a matter of individual moral strength and will, but also of the ways others treat us. It makes us aware of the vulnerability of such notions as 'dignity' and 'self-respect', which can no longer be completely isolated from the relations of power and dominance we discover in social life. This makes it difficult for people to abstract themselves completely from the social relations of wealth and power. This is to question an important strand in the Christian notion of human equality.

But we also need to dig a little deeper into Kant's presuppositions to think about the character of the obligation created when rich help poor. Why are people assumed to be so sensitive and compromised by the help and support they receive from others who have more than they need? This brings out how central it is for Kant to believe that people are 'self-sufficient', able to live without the help and support of others. This needs to be thought about carefully since it is not simply that people are brought up to value 'independence' and 'self-sufficiency'. It would be misleading simply to see these as 'bourgeois values' which people in a particular society happen to care about deeply. This is often the error of sociological accounts of values, often reproduced in different forms within Marxist writings.[4] At one level it is certainly illuminating to realise that Kant takes very much for granted a connection between 'dignity', 'independence' and 'self-sufficiency', without realising how he is articulating the historical values built into the social relations of a particular society. It is partly because of the ways people are brought up to be self-sufficient that they often feel that needing others has to be an admission of individual weakness or inadequacy. If Kant is in danger of presenting the values of a particular historical period as if they are universal, this is partly because he recognises the need to illuminate the ways dependency in different societies and periods also gives others power over our lives, so that in a very real sense we are compromised in our capacity to live lives of our own.

When Kant says that people should not be treated as means for the purposes of others, he is helping us to a sense of the value of an individual's human life. This does not have to be a transcendental acknowledgement, even if it is often so for Kant. If he is less clear about the material relations which allow people to live free and independent lives, he does make us more aware of the terms of criticism we need to evaluate different social relations. It is when Kant goes on to think about the sources of wealth that he is forced to think about the moral legitimacy of property relations, not simply the tact with which the poor are to be helped. But it always remained difficult for Kant to consider fully social relations of inequality as proper objects of moral assessment without questioning the autonomy of morality. This is something he was only once forced to the edge of considering.

3 THE SOURCES OF WEALTH

Kant seems to doubt whether the help the rich give to the poor should be regarded as beneficence at all. It is not clear how much this has to do with his understanding of the sources of this wealth production, or whether it is simply to do with Kant's sense of the wrongness of some people having more than they need, while others have less. For at least a moment in *The Doctrine of Virtue*, he is not convinced by the idea that social inequality is created because some people have more natural talents than others, or because they have worked harder. Kant saw the inequalities of wealth as the natural outcome of an unjust distribution of property and favours:

> The ability to practice beneficence, which depends on property,
> follows largely from the injustice of the government, which

favours certain men and so introduces an inequality of wealth
that makes others need help. This being the case, does the rich
man's help to the needy, on which he so readily prides himself
as something meritorious, really deserve to be called
beneficence at all? (*The Doctrine of Virtue*, 453)

This shifts the whole terms of discussion. Does this remove the
basis of the obligation created when the rich person helps the poor?
Does this reveal the difficulties of separating considerations of our
moral duties to help others from questions about the justice of a
particular system of property relations? Does this show a deeper
connection between morality and politics than we often assume
when we take for granted the legitimacy of the prevailing property
relations?

Kant is saying that the inequality of wealth that makes some
people poor grows out of an unjust organisation of social relations,
related to the unjust distribution of property. This undermines and
questions that whole tradition of individualistic moral theory which
would say that some people need the help of others only because
of individual weaknesses and inadequacies. Rather Kant seems to
be saying that it is the organisation of property relations in the
whole society which makes some people need the help of others.
This acknowledges a form of social interdependence, since we can
no longer simply assume that individuals are free to work out
whatever situation in society they deserve. This makes it necessary
to find a way of identifying moral issues presented within particular
forms of social inequality. It must also mean that people can no
longer assume an unquestioned right to the wealth they have accumulated. A source of uneasiness is created and questions have to
be asked about the sources of wealth and thus about the basis of
social inequality.

Does this mean that people should feel that it is 'morally wrong'
for such inequalities of wealth to persist, especially if they make
some people dependent upon the goodwill of others for the very
means of their livelihood? Kant's moral conceptions are too deeply
tied to a notion of the individual redeeming himself or herself to
be able to develop this insight fully. It is almost as if Kant wants
to limit the power of this insight challenging the love and respect
people are to show to each other, and wants to believe that if
certain readjustments are made in the forms of beneficence, then

people will not have to question the moral legitimacy of property relations. In a similar way he avoided the moral issue of autonomy and independence raised about sexual relations of power and subordination between men and women. This shows the need for a moral theory which can identify the different kinds of moral issues which different forms of social inequality present us with.

This might be one reason why the rich have to be so very careful in the tact they show in the help they give to the poor, lest they bring into question the very basis and legitimacy of the inequalities of wealth and power in society. So Kant almost hopes that help can be given in such a way that people hardly notice that it has been given at all. Even though Kant does continue in his conviction that giving help to others puts them under obligation, he wants to think that people can continue to relate to each other *as if* they are equal. There are different reasons why Kant has to believe this. He wants to minimise the moral value of beneficence when it is exercised by the rich, making it a matter of duty, because he does not want to acknowledge that wealth can give a rich person more chance to live a moral life. In order to maintain his notion of individual dignity, it is very important to believe that rich and poor, powerful and powerless, are somehow equally capable of living moral lives. If he is forced to acknowledge that it is easier for the rich and powerful to live moral lives, then this would challenge the very basis of the autonomy of morals. We would be forced to think seriously about the moral consequences of relations of power and dominance, no longer able to believe that an individual is equally able to prove his or her own moral worth, depending upon their individual moral qualities. This would be to challenge a basic assumption of liberal moral and political theory.

This connects to the fundamental question Kant raises about whether the rich are entitled to have more than they need, while the poor have less than they need. This concern has raised itself at different moments within the Christian tradition. Charles Gore introduced a collection in 1913 entitled *Property: Its Duties and Rights* with a recognition of this central tension when he refers to:

the disappointing fact, when Christianity became the
established religion, it did so little to impress its ideal of
property upon the law and custom of the later Empire. But
certainly the church bore the strongest witness to the idea of

property as a trust for the common good. And in no way is
this more strikingly shown than in its identification of 'charity'
– that is, charity in the narrowest sense of almsgiving – with
justice. The needy can claim our alms as a matter of justice: to
retain more property than we strictly need is a violation of
justice, and not merely a failure to perform a work of
superogation. Lord Hugh Cecil has recently drawn a strong
distinction between charity and justice. He says 'originally the
relief of the poor was based on the duty of Christian charity,
and not on any supposed right of justice' (*Conservatism*,
Williams and Norgate, p. 172). As far as Early Christianity is
concerned the distinction here drawn would be repudiated. To
withhold charity is to refuse justice. (*Property: Its Duties and
Rights*, Foreword, p. 14)[5]

When Kant raises questions about the very sources of wealth and
power in society, he is raising deep questions about the relationship
of morality to social justice. These issues can only remain separable, and the notion of the autonomy of morals preserved, if we
think this is simply a matter of how to give to others so that we do
not compromise their self-respect. This means that the inequalities of wealth simply become a 'problem' we have to learn to get
around through being more sensitive to others. This involves tact
and consideration within the processes of interpersonal relationships,
rather than the social transformation of relations of power and
wealth. This makes it seem that if only we have sufficient tact and
understanding we can avoid compromising a person's self-respect.

It has been important for liberal moral and political theory to
be able to believe that, even though there are dangers of humbling
someone in giving them help, it is possible to give help 'as if our
help is either what is merely due to him or but a slight service of
love'. This would be a way of reading Kant which stresses that it
is quite possible to treat people *as if* we are equal to them, even
though some kind of obligation might have been created. This
connects up with the sense that we show our respect to others by
our very willingness to *abstract* from social relations of power and
inequality. This means that we are ready to treat others as if we
are equals, which means we do not draw attention to what differences of power and wealth separate us. We somehow affirm that
what we share in common as human beings has to be so much

more important than what separates us. In this way the wealth and power that separates people does not have to interfere with the respect people can give each other, or even with the ways people feel about themselves. We can make sure that we treat others *as if* we are equals, so that we do not give any kind of weight to the differences created and maintained through social life. In this way we are supposed to make sure that a person's dignity and self-respect need not be compromised. This would be a way of arguing that social inequality does not have to present us with moral issues nor do we have to reconsider the nature of our moral theory to take account of them.

At the same time it is significant that Kant, at least in *The Doctrine of Virtue*, shows signs of being uneasy with this position. He refuses the option of completely abstracting from the inequalities and dependencies created. Rather he feels the need to think through some of the concrete difficulties which exist within the relationships of power and dominance themselves. He is forced to think about the moral character of these relations, and so answers himself those who would deny that social relations of inequality are a proper object of moral assessment. This is clearly sharpened in Kant's awareness of the ease with which we compromise people just because of the power we assume over their lives. This means it is not simply a matter of the motives with which we help others. Kant is very aware of the ease with which we can help others according to *our* conceptions of what their lives are, of what they need, of what would bring them happiness. This is to raise deep issues about the nature of human subordination and dependency, though he continues to think about this very much in terms of the relationships between individuals, so he does not have to involve himself in a fuller moral critique of forms of social inequality. At the same time he seems to be aware that he is not simply talking about the relationship between rich and poor, but is talking more generally about relationships of subordination, between 'master and bondsman'. This is one of his Casuistical Questions:

What of the man who deprives another of his *freedom*, but,
in exercising over him the supreme authority permitted by the
law of the land, does so according to his own idea of how to
make that person happy (of how to do good to his bondsman)?
Can this man consider himself beneficent for taking paternal

care of his bondsman in keeping with *his own* concept of happiness? Or is not the injustice of depriving someone of his freedom a thing so opposed to juridical duty as such that the man who freely consents to submit to this condition, counting on his master's beneficence, commits the supreme rejection of his own humanity, and the master's utmost concern for this man would not really be beneficent at all? Or could the service which the master renders him be so great as to outweigh man's right? – I cannot do good to anyone according to my conception of happiness (except to young children and the insane), but only according to that of the one I intend to benefit; and I am not really being kind to someone if I force a gift on him. (*The Doctrine of Virtue*, 453)

Kant is clear that nothing we could do for others could be 'so great as to outweigh man's right'. We have to be careful to help others according to their own 'concept of happiness'. So it is not simply a question of the rich giving to the poor, of the redistribution of wealth. We also have to be aware of the forms of power and dependency which are built into the very form and quality of human relations. But at the same time Kant does not want to acknowledge that the very condition of poverty and hunger can force people into subordinating themselves to others. It is important for Kant to assume that people, in some sense, *choose* to renounce their freedom, not simply that it is denied to them through the social and material circumstances and relations they find themselves in. So Kant considers the bondsman 'who freely consents to submit to this condition', and wants to think that the inequality is somehow *created*, as a result of the rich giving to the poor, of the master helping the bondsman, of the powerful giving to the powerless, or because the bondsman is prepared to 'give up his freedom'. This can make it possible for us to assume that, if individuals had decided to act differently, these situations of subordination would not be created. In a crucial sense this is to mystify us about the sources of power within relationships, especially when this is thought about as an issue of the interaction between individuals, rather than as a relationship of subordination. It is as if we are to assume that the rich have no power in relationship to the poor in society, only what is created through the help the rich give to the poor. So it can be argued that the fact that one person is richer than another may mean they can afford to buy more things for themselves, but it does not give them any recognisable social power. Others might regard them as being more 'successful' or more 'able' because they have accumulated such wealth. But as long as people can be assumed to be independent of each other, in having their own means of livelihood, it does not matter how rich others are. Even though Kant discusses the sources of wealth, he usually wants to assume that, as long as people can do without the help and support of others, they can be thought of as fundamentally equal and independent.

This makes it difficult to understand the difficulties involved in treating someone 'according to his own idea of happiness'. Often it seems as if we are implicitly talking about the realm of personal relations, as if it is clearly separable from the other areas of people's lives. So, for instance what does this mean for the large employer in a small town thinking about what workers to employ? Does he not automatically think about the needs of production? How are we to think about the nature of his power in relation to people who are looking for work, especially if there are very few alternatives in the town? We cannot simply understand this as a series of personal relations since the power which the employer has is a power that he has in relation to all the people seeking work, not something comprehensible in terms of individual qualities. The employer might think he is helping others since without him they would not have a job at all. Somehow we have to understand the nature of the power he has in relation to the people who work for him. If this is to be thought about as a situation of *structured dependency*, it can throw into focus the kind of material preconditions Kant takes very much for granted. It is also another argument for developing a moral theory of social relations of inequality. If people are poor, they are assumed to have their own means of subsistence, so that it is possible for them to live their own lives without needing the help and support of others. It is as if Kant was presupposing the kind of situation that de Tocqueville discovered in the early years of the American Republic. This seems to be the situation he would like to see, if he did not already assume its existence in our moral relations:

Among people whose ranks are nearly equal, no ostensible
bond connects men together or keeps them settled in their own

88

station. None of them have either a permanent right or power to command, none are forced by their condition to obey; but every man, finding himself possessed of some education and some resources, may choose his own path and proceed apart from all his fellow men. The same causes that make the members of the community independent of each other continually impel them on to new and restless desires and constantly spur them onwards ... (*Democracy in America*, p. 256)[6]

It is important for Kant to think that if people accept to be subordinate to others, then someone 'freely consents to submit to this condition'. This is not something that is in any sense 'forced' upon people because of the relations of power and dominance within the larger society. So there is always a temptation for Kant to think that people can maintain a sense of freedom, as some kind of inner state of mind, unless they 'choose' to give it up. There is a tendency for him to blame someone for committing 'the supreme rejection of his own humanity'. If there are different ways in which people reconcile themselves to situations of subordination, this does not help us grasp the *difficulties* people face in retaining a sense of their individual lives, when they are in a relationship of subordination. It becomes difficult to appreciate the ways the social situation is *working to undermine* whatever independent sense people have of themselves and their individual worth. It is always possible for Kant to fall back into thinking that the exigencies and humiliations of social life are of little consequence as soon as the individual turns towards God. There is always a temptation for Kant to accept the radical denial of the social world, especially when the relations of power and subordination seem to challenge the very notion of the autonomy of morality. If people accept their superiors' definitions of their own happiness as more or less a direct consequence of being in a situation of subordination, then the very basis upon which we are to respect others equally as human beings becomes threatened.

It is difficult for Kant to hold firm to the insight that people in relations of subordination can sometimes no longer have a vision of their own happiness, but tend to take on definitions of themselves held by those who have power over their lives. Is this simply a consequence of certain relations of dependency? Are we saying that they inevitably work in this way? Does this mean that it is much harder for us to maintain a sense of our own concept of happiness, of our individual wants and needs, if we are living within this kind of relationship? Kant recognises 'women's rivalry among themselves, in which one tries to get the better of others in the favour and devotion of men' (*Anthropology*, 305), but he does not see this as very much a consequence of a relationship of power between the sexes, in which the very notion of 'femininity' involves the idea of women being attractive *to* men. This can encourage woman to deny their own individual strength and intelligence out of fear of being accused of being 'masculine'. This can make it difficult for a woman to develop her own 'concept of happiness', since it becomes hard for her to believe she can find happiness and satisfaction without having a relationship with a man. On her own she is made to feel incomplete. In learning to trust what she wants for herself individually, she is challenging the very relations of sexual power that exist in society. The modern feminist movement gives us some understanding of the depths of *invalidation* which a patriarchal society produces, even without realising it. It also gives us a chance to grasp the difficulty of holding to our conception of our own individual needs and wants within a competitive society in which both men and woman, in different ways, have to prove themselves to others.

Often it is simply an aspect of these relations of power that we assume that we know what is best for others. An example can help bring out the kind of moral issues which can come to the surface to reveal the working of social inequality within a relationship which would often within liberal theory be seen as a relationship between equals. So, for instance, David gets tickets for the family holiday on the assumption that they are all going away together. It comes as very much of a shock to him that Karen has decided that she wants some space for herself this year, so that she wants him to go away with the kids on his own. He finds it hard to hear this. He can only say 'I'm sure that we'll all have a good time if we go away together'. Karen feels that he is taking her for granted again. He is assuming that he knows what is best for her, even though she has said she wants to go away on her own. David cannot help thinking that this means there is something wrong with their relationship since this is just not 'normal'. He cannot help worrying about what his friends are going to think. One part of him feels deeply resentful. He finds it hard to accept that she has wants and needs of her own. Somehow he has always expected her 'to put the family first'. Of course he has always acknowledged that she has a mind of her own and can make decisions for herself, but the workings of the relations within the family have somehow denied this very acknowledgment in practice. This had made it harder for Karen to appreciate the different ways she has been undermined in the family. She automatically seems to think about her husband and children, and finds it much harder for her to define what she needs and wants for herself individually. Her confidence in herself has been undermined. She does not really understand how this has happened, but she knows that the relations in the family have worked to produce this result. It does not help Karen to know that she chose this kind of relationship, and that at some level she and David have always tried to work things out pretty equally amongst themselves.

The notion of freedom that Kant invokes, when he says that the bondsman has freely consented 'to submit to this condition', has deep roots within liberal moral and political theory which puts such store upon the contracts people make with each other. So it is important for people to be able to feel, say, that an employee 'has freely chosen the job he has taken and that if he didn't want it, he didn't have to accept it'. This is to place the responsibility firmly on the shoulders of the individual employee. The implicit notion of 'freedom' works to make us think and feel that this is somehow a contract between equals, which has to be honoured as such. This can make it difficult to investigate the relations of power and dominance involved. Accordingly Kant is tempted into presenting the situation instrumentally as bondsman choosing to give up his freedom, so that he can gain the beneficence of his master. This presents it almost as a matter of individual exchange in which the bondsman is guilty of 'the supreme rejection of his own humanity'. It makes it seem as if this exchange is almost incidental within the relationship between master and bondsman. It is not understood as a consequence which grows out of our understanding of a relationship of subordination. This is a way of avoiding giving central importance to the crucial issue of how being in a situation of relative dependency and powerlessness *works* to make you accept the definitions of those who have power over your life. This would make us more aware of the *difficulties* of maintain-

91

ing our individual sense of what we want and need, within the context of this kind of relationship. It would put the whole issue of 'freedom' and 'choice' in a very different kind of context. It is in recognising the significance of these issues that we discover that social relations of inequality need to find a central place within our moral theory.

Kant can make us think that it is simply a question of individuals being ready to sell their freedom in exchange for a pot of gold. This makes it very much a matter of the personal relationship between two individuals. This gives us little sense of the sources of social power that someone has as a 'master' in relation to a 'bondsman'. It gives us little sense of the processes of the relationship, which make it so important for the bondsman to win approval and legitimation in the eyes of his master. This also gives us little sense of how the processes of identification work within such a relationship of power. De Tocqueville gives us a glimpse of this when he talks about the situation of servants:

> Servants ... sometimes identify themselves with the person of the master, so that they become an appendage to him in their own eyes as well as his ... In this predicament the servant ultimately detaches his notion of interest from his own person; he deserts himself as it were, or rather he transports himself into the character of the master and thus assumes an imaginary personality. He complacently invests himself with the wealth of those who command him; he shares their fame, exalts himself by their rank, and feeds his mind with borrowed greatness, to which he attaches more importance than those who really and fully possess it. There is something touching and at the same time ridiculous about this strange confusion of two different states of being ... (*Democracy in America*, p. 190)

This gives us some sense of the ways in which someone 'deserts himself as it were', as an aspect of the *workings* of subordination. It is difficult to be clear about the sense in which someone can have 'chosen' this situation. At the same time this *identification* of the servant with his master enables him to think well of himself. This is not totally dissimilar from the situation feminists have described, of the ways women are often encouraged to identify with the achievements of their husbands, since this very much reflects upon the status they themselves are given in the wider society.

Kant is critical of someone who thinks 'himself beneficent for taking paternal care of his bondsman in keeping with *his own* concept of happiness'. He makes us aware of the wrongness of treating others according to our own 'idea of how to make that person happy'. But he also tends to assume that it is easier for the bondsman, or the person in a situation of relative powerlessness, to maintain a sense of his or her own concept of happiness. He tends to think that the person has made some kind of free choice in making 'the supreme rejection of his own humanity', rather than recognising the ways in which a person's sense of individual identity and worth are *undermined* within the context of these relations of power and subordination. This is much more challenging to the notions of freedom we assume within liberal moral theory, and argues for a moral theory which can identify these features of social relations of inequality. This makes people much more vulnerable to the social relations they are involved in than we would otherwise assume.

Kant can always fall back upon a notion, that it depends very much upon a person's will and inner qualities whether they allow themselves to be undermined in this way through the relation of subordination. He assumes that people have much more consciousness and awareness of what is happening for them within these relationships, while we have implied that these processes work to undermine people's sense of their individual lives, without people being fully aware of what is happening to them. Of course it makes a difference if people have a strong and confident sense of themselves, so they do not feel so dependent upon the approval of others. But we still need to grasp the ways relations of subordination are continually working to undermine this confidence and sense of self.

If we acknowledge the ways people's very sense of self is undermined through relationships of subordination, then it becomes so much more difficult to treat people according to their *own* conception of happiness. The development of capitalism has developed relations of class power and dependency that undermine the very presupposition of 'independence' and 'self-sufficiency' that Kant makes for his moral theory. This is something that Bernard Williams glimpses in an important insight in his article on 'The Idea of Equality:

For it is precisely a mark of extreme exploitation or

93

degradation that those who suffer it do *not* see themselves
different from the way that they are seen by their exploiters;
either they do not see themselves as anything at all, or they
acquiesce passively in the role for which they have been cast.
(*Problems of the Self*, p. 237)

As Williams admits, 'Here we evidently need something more than
the precept that one should respect and try to understand man's
consciousness of his own activities; it is also that one may not
suppress or destroy that consciousness.' But we are forced to intro-
duce different kinds of considerations if we acknowledge that this
is not simply a matter of what one individual does to another, but
also very much depends upon the character of the social
relationship of power and subordination within which individuals
relate to each other, say as master and bondsman, employer and
employee, husband and wife. This is to challenge the idea that these
are 'roles' that individuals play, as if they are different perform-
ances we give. It is this very conception that we often find in liberal
social theory.

If it is the workings of a relationship, rather than simply the acts
of an individual, which work to undermine our sense of self, then
it is important to rethink the character of these relationships. If
'one may not suppress or destroy that consciousness', this will not
only involve that we relate differently towards others, but will involve the *transformation* of this relationship of subordination itself.
If the workings of the very relationship between master and servant
work to 'suppress or destroy that consciousness', then this makes
it hard for us to settle for the precept 'that one should respect and
try to understand another man's consciousness of his own activities'. Often this is a conclusion that we avoid, because it is too
challenging to our deeply held individualistic moral assumptions,
which encourage us to assume that we are free to relate to others
in any way that we choose. It was crucially the ways Kant thought
about the relationship of dependence and gratitude, in his thinking
about the sources of social inequality, that allowed him to protect
his assumption of the autonomy of morals.

VII

LIBERALISM, INEQUALITY
AND SOCIAL DEPENDENCE

In this chapter I show the difficulties that Kant has with structured relations of dependency. His moral theory tends to assume that people can live independent and self-sufficient lives until they call upon the help and support of others. I argue that specific kinds of social relations tend to create but also conceal situations of dependency and subordination. Kant's concepts of respect and equality fail to illuminate relations of structured dependency which go beyond individual interactions and do not simply depend upon the qualities of individuals. But if Kant does not want relations of subordination and dependency to threaten his sense of equality of people before the moral law, he is consistent enough to deny people full rights of citizenship. At least he does not pretend that people have an independence and autonomy which they do not enjoy in their everyday lives. In this way, at least, he was forced to recognise the significance of social relations of power and subordination.

1 THE INSTITUTIONALISATION OF DEPENDENCE

We have already drawn attention to Kant saying that, in giving to the poor, the rich 'must carefully avoid any appearance of intending to put the other under obligation'.[1] He should give as if this 'duty is merely something that he owes'. With this in mind we are likely to be a little surprised at the way Kant opens his discussion of the Duty of Gratitude:

Gratitude consists in *honouring* a person because of a kindness he has done us. The feeling connected with this recognition is respect for the benefactor (who puts one under obligation). But the benefactor is viewed as only in a relation of love to the one who receives his favour. (*The Doctrine of Virtue*, 454)[2]

Is this supposed to be true of a relationship in which people are assumed to be more or less equal, or does this also refer to the help which the rich give to the poor? Is the poor person supposed to acknowledge that a 'kindness' has been done, while at the same time feeling that he or she is only receiving their due? Do we not often assume in our moral culture that respect is due to a 'benefactor' in precisely these situations in which the rich help those 'less fortunate than themselves', because we tacitly assume that inequalities of wealth somehow reflect differences in achievement or ability? But is this not the very assumption Kant questions in his discussion of the sources of wealth, and is this not partly what makes us feel that the 'poor' are only receiving what is due to them? At the same time our thinking about the justice of the distribution of wealth very much depends upon our conception of the validity of particular forms of private property.

Kant does assume within his moral theory that we live in a society in which people are independent of each other, and in which people are generally in a situation to repay whatever kindnesses and help they receive from others. In this way his moral theory is tied to particular social assumptions which make sense within a society of small self-sufficient agriculture and crafts, but becomes undermined with the development of the relations of class power and dependency within capitalist society. I want to argue that specific kinds of social relations tend to create but also conceal situations of dependency and subordination. This means we have to investigate their relationship to particular forms of moral theory not only uncovering their social assumptions but also developing our understanding of the moral nature of social relations of inequality. De Tocqueville recognised the different nature of the dependency that was being created with the introduction of manufacturing in the north-eastern United States. He saw the development of a new aristocracy, but one which was different from the traditional forms of aristocracy he knew:

But this kind of aristocracy by no means resembles those kinds which preceded it. It will be observed at once that, as it applies exclusively to manufacturers ... It is a monstrous exception in the general aspects of society ... Not only are the rich not compactly united among themselves, but there is no real bond between them and the poor. Their relative position is not a permanent one; they are constantly drawn together or separated by their interests. The workman is generally dependent on the master, but not on any particular master; these two men meet in the factory, but do not know each other elsewhere; and while they come into contact on one point, they stand very far apart on all others. The manufacturer asks nothing of the workman but his labour; the workman expects nothing from him but his wages. The one contracts no obligation to protect nor the other to defend, and they are not permanently connected either by habit or by duty. The aristocracy created by business rarely settles in the midst of manufacturing population which it directs; the object is not to govern the population but to use it ... the manufacturing aristocracy of our age first impoverishes and debases the men who serve it and then abandons them to be supported by the charity of the people ... the friends of democracy should keep their eyes anxiously fixed in this direction; for if ever a permanent inequality of conditions and aristocracy again penetrates into the world, it may be predicted that this is the gate by which it will enter. (*Democracy in America*, pp. 170–1)

Kant could not be expected to foresee these developments. When de Tocqueville says that 'the object is not to govern the population but to use it', he is not talking about the intentional behaviour of capitalists. He is not judging the kind of people they are, or assessing the moral worth of their actions. But this is to challenge the very assumptions of a moral consciousness that defines morality in terms of the moral worth of individual actions. It calls for a moral theory which is able to illuminate relations of power and dependency which go beyond individual interactions and are not dependent upon the qualities of individuals. It is very possible for the capitalists de Tocqueville is talking about to be pleasant, even generous people. With the best will in the world they might declare that they want to treat people as ends in themselves. They might

97

behave with kindness and understanding in their personal relations with people, being careful not to talk down to them. Capitalists will treat their workers in different ways and workers will often appreciate these differences, but the relations of dependency and subordination remain within the system of capitalist class relations. As de Tocqueville says, 'The workman is generally dependent on the master, but not on any particular master.' It is the nature of this kind of structured dependency which Kant cannot come to terms with.

It has been the very development of the class relations of capitalist society that has also questioned the presuppositions of a Kantian moral tradition. To the extent that the moral culture of a capitalist society remains deeply influenced by a Kantian moral tradition, it encourages us to assume that morality has to do with our individual actions and with the quality of our personal relations. It encourages us to assume that, if only people would relate to others with respect, then the social world would be fundamentally transformed. But, as we have said, however kind and responsive Kafka is to Frau Svatek, she is still in a situation of dependency and subordination which makes her dependent upon the kindness of others who have the power to treat her 'like an old chair'. She is left in a situation in which she almost has to feel grateful for not being treated 'like an old chair', since it is an aspect of the power others have over her that they can so easily abuse her. This is not simply the power to get her to lose her job, though this is important. Rather the power is written into the very bone and marrow of the relationship. It has as much to do with the tone in which people talk, as it has with the ways they carry their bodies as they accept the cup of tea she is offering them.

What is more, liberal moral theory encourages people to think they have made a contract which they have made 'freely', so they have 'chosen' a situation of dependency for themselves. This can have the effect of making people feel they are individually responsible for the situation they are in, even if it is a situation of subordination and indignity. People are left feeling that they only have themselves to blame and, possibly, if they had been brighter or worked harder at school, they could have found themselves in a different kind of job. Responsibility is placed firmly upon the shoulders of the individual. If they find themselves in a situation of misery and subordination, they only have themselves to blame.

This gives a particular meaning to the sense that we are responsible for the lives we live and the choices we make.

If at some level we constantly avoid this particular sense of responsibility, wanting to blame others and the powers that be, at another level we often assume responsibility for situations we have not created but have been forced to come to terms with. Kant has prepared some of the ground for these contradictions. A moral culture which focuses upon the moral worth of individual actions will find it difficult to reveal the moral realities of class relations. It will constantly dissolve social relations which are structured around relations of power and dependency, implicitly legitimating them in terms of individual qualities, as if people can be thought of as individually responsible for the position they have within society. For instance, an assembly-line worker is encouraged to feel that if only he was cleverer or worked harder at school he would not have to do such soul-destroying work. Within liberal moral theory he only has himself to blame. As responsibility is internalised the social relations of the larger society are moved beyond moral criticism. We gain little sense of our moral theory as an integral aspect of the workings of ideology. At the same time, when we learn to talk about the moral relations of a capitalist society, we are not talking about the sufficiency of a moral critique, or implying that it is through coming to share this critique that social relations of power will be transformed. Nor are we denying the importance of individual responsibility and effort when we situate it dialectically within our understanding of social relations of power and dependency. Marx warns us against this, as much as against an abstract moralism which would pose an abstract ideal of relations, with little sense of how these could develop out of the present realities of people's lives.[3] But at the same time we have to learn about the limits of a moral culture which continually works to privatise our sense of morality, making us feel that it is solely about the moral worth of individual actions.

When we try to show the inadequacy of assuming what Max Weber calls 'a conscious acceptance of these ethical maxims on the part of individuals', we do not want to separate our sense of the social relations of power people are involved in as class relations from our sense of capitalism as a system of social relations. If capitalist institutions are reified in this way, this is something we want to understand. It involves grasping the nature of the dependency that is created between individuals, mediated through their class relations. If Weber tended to think of capitalism as a 'system of market relationships', giving less significance than Marx to the relations of production, he does help to focus this critical issue. Marx was sometimes too dismissive about these issues. After Weber identifies 'one's duty in a calling' as 'what is most characteristic of the social ethic of capitalist culture', he warns us:

> Still less, naturally, do we maintain that a conscious acceptance of these ethical maxims on the part of individuals, entrepreneurs or labourers, in modern capitalistic enterprises, is a condition of the further existence of present-day capitalism. The capitalistic economy of the present day is an immense cosmos into which the individual is born, and which presents itself to him, at least as an individual, as an unalterable order of things in which he must live. It forces the individual, in so far as he is involved in the system of market relationships, to conform to capitalist rules of action. The manufacturer who in the long run acts counter to these norms will just as inevitably be eliminated from the economic scene as the worker who cannot or will not adapt himself to them will be thrown into the streets without a job. (*The Protestant Ethic and the Spirit of Capitalism*, pp. 54–5)

The individualistic moral culture that the Kantian tradition has helped foster makes it difficult to grasp the nature of dependencies created and maintained within capitalist society. It promotes a form of moral understanding which works to mystify the nature of power and dependency not only in class relations, but also in sexual and racial relations of power and dependency. It fosters an assumption that individuals are free and independent until they call upon the help and support of others. It is as if individuals themselves can be assumed to be self-sufficient, able to provide a living for themselves through their own labours. What is more, this is assumed to give people 'dignity' and 'respect' for themselves. We find this reasserted in the theories of conservative libertarianism of such people as Milton Friedman.[4] So it is argued that accepting the support of the state in a period of advanced capitalism, say with unemployment benefits, undermines a person's sense of dignity and pride. This draws upon a Kantian tradition which blindly accepts that individuals can be assumed to be 'free' and 'independent' until

100

they ask for the support of the state. It implicitly assumes that meaningful work is available for people on the assembly lines of monopoly capitalism, as long as people show the initiative and drive to look. It is the very dependencies created through the benefits they receive from the state that supposedly undermine this very sense of independence and pride. This has deep sources in the way Kant talks about gratitude and the creation of dependency. Kant helps us focus upon critical issues of dependency, though his assumptions of independence and self-sufficiency become increasingly mystifying with the development of modern capitalism.

Kant tends to assume an economy of independent producers in which people have control over their means of livelihood. This helps foster an individualistic moral tradition that becomes rhetorical, if not speechless, in the face of the realities of class power and dependency. Kant assumes that all forms of dependency are created through the interactions of individuals, and have to take the form of one individual becoming dependent upon another. This is why it is important for people to return the help others give them, since otherwise an assumed 'independence' will be threatened and some kind of dependency created. The balance of generosity, help and kindnesses has to be maintained. This has to be a situation of reciprocity. It is very much taken for granted that it is the help or kindness given that has somehow upset an otherwise balanced relationship. This can illuminate a relationship between people who are more or less socially equal:

> But the *intention* of gratitude – that is, the degree of obligation
> to this virtue – is to be judged by how beneficial the favour
> was to the obligated subject and how unselfishly it was
> bestowed on him. The minimal degree is to do an *equal* service
> for the benefactor, if he can receive it (if he is still living) or if
> he is dead, to render it to others. (*The Doctrine of Virtue*, 445)

The situation between rich and poor is so threatening for Kant, since the poor person will not be in a situation to return the help he or she has been given. It is one thing for Kant to assume a kind of moral equality of people before the moral law, but it is quite another to assume this equality can be maintained in the everyday realities of social life. Kant did not want simply to abstract from the structures of power and dominance to recover a sense of 'equality' and 'independence' guaranteed in the eyes of God, independently of the everyday relations of dependency and power within social life. This is not to say that some notion of 'independence' is not crucial in our sense of what it means to have 'our own individual lives'. But this is also deeply historically influenced. With the early development of capitalist society it was given a particular form in the notion that individuals had to be 'free' to pursue the ends they had set themselves. It was assumed that these 'ends' reflected a person's unique inner qualities. In its own way this separated people from a recognition of the need for certain kinds of equal, caring and loving relationships with others. It prepared people to subordinate their relationships with others and to identify their 'happiness' with their individual achievements.

This helps show that we need to develop a much deeper understanding of the historical context within which these notions of 'independence', 'individual dignity' and 'individuality' were being expressed. This can help reveal their emancipatory significance in individualism and the dangers of contrasting individualistic traditions too quickly with more collective traditions. It is still significant to stress Kant's awareness of how easy it is for people to accept a situation of dependency as 'second nature', so that people are barely aware that they do not have control over their lives. He has a continuing sense of how our understanding can be crippled, and how dependency can threaten our sense of self-respect and our equality with others. His sense of individualism is grounded in the need for us to make certain choices and to take certain steps in our lives:

> Thus it is difficult for each separate individual to work his way
> out of the immaturity which has become almost second nature
> to him. He has even grown fond of it and is really incapable
> for the time being of using his own understanding, because he
> was never allowed to make the attempt. Dogmas and formulas,
> those mechanical instruments for rational use (or rather
> misuse) of his natural endowments, are the ball and chain of
> his permanent immaturity. But if anyone did throw them off,
> he would still be uncertain about jumping over even the
> narrowest of trenches, for he would be unaccustomed to free
> movement of this kind ... (*Kant's Political Writings*, ed. Hans
> Reiss, p. 55)

A conception of 'second nature' could be useful if it helps to understand the ways that people 'even grow fond' of their dependency.

If we have to appreciate the particular nature of the challenge these ideas presented to regimes of aristocratic privilege and the authority of Church, we also have to be ready to grasp the different force and meaning they come to have within a different historical period and social relations. A recognition of the dignity of human reason challenged the authority of faith and allowed people to reclaim this aspect of themselves, even if it was at the high cost of subordinating and inevitably distorting the significance of our bodily experience, emotionality and sensibility. The assertion of 'independence' and the connection with 'respect' and 'dignity' was a profound challenge to the forms of feudal dominance and dependency. Because people come from a period of being humiliated through being dependent upon others for their very means of livelihood, people treasured their 'independence'. But this notion of 'freedom' or 'independence' also preserved the position of a relatively small number of men who gained power and control with the emergence of the bourgeoisie as a class, and legitimated the subordination and domination of a far greater number of men and women who had been deprived of their means of independent existence with the emergence of the factories. Very briefly, it was with the transition from feudalism to capitalism and the democratic revolution in the eighteenth and nineteenth centuries that new relations of dependency and power were brought into existence.

The moral consciousness with which we attempt to grasp the realities of class power and dependency is deeply influenced by a Kantian moral tradition formulated within an earlier period. The limitation of our moral consciousness to a concern with individual action, and its privatisation as a form of 'personal opinion', makes it harder to realise how it can both challenge one kind of dependency and legitimate another kind. This is not to argue that moral theory simply has to illuminate the moral realities of a particular period. It is important to recognise how Kant's notions of individual autonomy and independence can retain a critical relevance within a very different historical period, even if this means transforming their significance. It is the strength and importance of our moral consciousness that it can often help us challenge this kind of sociological relativism. We can be struck by the ways we share moral concerns with others if we also learn to identify moral traditions we take for granted in our everyday thinking and living.

103

But we barely have an adequate framework within which we can identify critical issues about the social and historical character of our moral consciousness. At one level we can be warned about an ahistorical form of conceptual analysis which can so easily make us insensitive to the ways, say, notions of 'dependence' and 'independence' come to live within a particular organisation of social relations. Of course it can help us to an awareness of the complexity of some of these notions if we investigate the different ways they enter our ordinary language and consciousness. But we also have to be aware of how deeply these are influenced by the history and social relations in different societies. This does not mean we simply have to appreciate that some societies value 'independence' while others have tended to value 'dependence'. This just reveals the poverty of our discussion of 'values and beliefs' within orthodox traditions of sociology. [5]

So, for instance, notions of 'independence' and 'self-sufficiency' refer illuminatingly to a particular period of independent producers. It is bound to carry a more ambiguous meaning, given the forms of class, sexual and racial dependency which exist within a capitalist society. It does not mean simply that people do not value 'independence' but the material conditions of people's lives have so changed as to give this a new meaning and significance. Within a capitalist society this can confront people with different tasks and difficulties, depending upon their position within the class relations of power. It is one thing, for instance, for John to feel bad because he has had to seek a loan to keep his business going, but quite another for Jack to be working in his firm. Within a capitalist society Jack is forced to work to support himself and his family. He knows that he is dependent upon John for a job. He knows that he has the 'freedom' to get another job, but he also knows this involves accepting very similar conditions of subordination. He has a sense of pride because he works for his living, though he feels that the routine assembly-line work does not call upon his skill or ability. If anything he finds it degrading to be virtually a slave to a machine. Even though part of him thinks he works for a living so he is not dependent upon the state, he knows that he is so dependent upon his boss that he hardly dares say what he really thinks about the routine work he is forced to do, because he knows he will be out of a job. This is not simply a question of one individual being dependent upon the help of another. It is a question of the nature of dependency created between individuals because of the class relations of power that exist between capital and labour within a capitalist society.

John is in a different situation as the owner of the firm, even if he still feels he has to prove himself. When John asks for his loan he feels ashamed. This compromises the picture he has of himself as an independent business man. He knows that this has little to do with how hard he has been working. It is just that the competition from abroad makes it difficult for him to compete. John might feel that he 'stands a step lower than his benefactor' when he asks his uncle for a loan. He feels he needs to apologise for himself, since this means he cannot survive in business without the help of others. But at another level which John might be barely aware of, partly because he knows he pays his workers well and could always get others to work for him, it is only because of the hard work of Jack and other workers in the factory that John has made the profits he has. But when we say that 'John is dependent upon their hard work', we illuminate a different kind of dependency involved and show something of the inequality of the relationship.

It is difficult to understand these forms of dependency unless we situate them within the relations of power and dependency reproduced within capitalist society. It is partly because the notion of exchange between equal individuals seems to legitimate the wage contract that relations of power and dependency are concealed. So Kant's ideas of individual independence which were so threatening to traditional relations of authority could easily work to legitimate relationships of power and dependency within capitalist society. Again we need to be sensitive to the ways in which particular ideas can come to life in a renewed critical role.

But Kant is also uncovering connections between 'dignity', 'independence' and what we could think of as 'sense of self' or 'sense of identity', which have a more pervasive influence upon our moral traditions. Even if we have to recover the particular connection between these notions within particular cultures and particular moments of history, we want to acknowledge the critical importance they assume, especially within a broadly conceived Western bourgeois culture. Within this tradition we meet an identification between 'independence' and 'individuality' that often assumes, in C. B. McPherson's language, a form of 'possessive individualism'.[6] We identify our sense of self in competition with others, so we become suspicious of the help and support others give us, thinking this is bound to threaten our independence or allow others to feel superior to us. We cannot help feeling within this moral tradition that others are almost inevitably trying to compromise us. So we find ourselves assuming that the kindness of others is some kind of burden we would do better without. People will easily think that others have stolen some kind of advantage through the help they have given us:

> But one cannot, by any requital of a kindness received, rid oneself of the obligation for this kindness, since one can never win away from the benefactor his *priority* of merit: the merit of having been the first in benevolence. (*The Doctrine of Virtue*, 454)

Kant invokes a metaphor of 'winning' since, as we have mentioned, it is easy to construe the moral life as some kind of race in which we are continually trying to prove ourselves individually. There is an implicit competition in which we are proving ourselves to be 'morally worthy'. So that even though we are encouraged to think of ourselves as each working out our individual relationship to the moral law, there is an unavoidable reference to others. We find it hard not to compare ourselves continually with others, because this is the way we establish our 'sense of self'. It is hardly surprising that within this implicit moral framework being kind to others, or helping them, is often mistrusted, or seen as a way others want to prove themselves morally worthy at our expense.

Kant is so aware of the ways the kindness of others can be experienced as 'burden' that he warns us explicitly against this. He wants us to welcome this situation, while at the same time recognising this is going against the stream of social relations. This is hardly surprising, since Kant also acknowledges that 'the person favoured stands a step lower than his benefactor':

> [The minimum of gratitude requires one] not to regard a kindness received as a burden one would gladly be rid of (since the person so favoured stands a step lower than his benefactor, and this wounds his pride), but to accept the occasion for gratitude as a moral kindness – that is, an opportunity given one to couple gratitude with love of man ... (*The Doctrine of Virtue*, 455)

Kant prepares us to accept that at some level this must be experienced as a moral setback by telling us we can use this situation
ourselves to prove ourselves. This presupposes it is already some
kind of defeat to need the help and kindness of others. This can in
no way be acknowledged as an integral aspect of our relations with
others. So, for instance, a person living down the road might help
me fix my car knowing that on another occasion he would be able
to draw upon my help. I might not feel I should have been able to
fix this on my own. I do not think this has to be a sign of weakness
or inadequacy. I might just accept this as part of what it means to
be 'neighbourly'. On the other hand, I might think twice before
borrowing some paint from Pete, knowing that he is bound to
think I am disorganised for not having got things ready myself.
This all assumes a society in which people take it for granted that
they should live their own individual lives. It would be very different within a more socialist society, in which people took it for
granted that they would help each other out if they were decorating
their houses. It would not simply be that people would expect this
kind of help in return. This does not have to be a simple situation
of reciprocity. The challenge is deeper. People might assume that
it is much easier and more pleasant if people learn to do things
with each other. This would challenge the basic idea that people
always have to be proving themselves individually, which is often
taken for granted within a more possessive individualism.

Even within capitalist societies there has often been a fuller sense
of community and sharing within working-class communities.
There was more open recognition of the ways people needed each
other, especially in periods of difficulty. There is often also a deeply
held suspicion of a middle-class ethic in which people are continually trying to prove themselves one better. People have recognised
that they need each other without feeling that this compromises
them – or means a person 'stands a step lower'. The notions of
'dignity' are given a different meaning, sometimes related to the
dignity of labour, when they are not so closely connected with
notions of 'self-sufficiency' and 'independence' as they are within a
more middle-class situation. There is a more socialist and com-
munitarian ethic which challenges the assumed individualism of the
hegemonic moral culture. This reminds us of the reality of different
class moralities, traditions and cultures which often remain sub-
merged until they are invoked within new movements, and of the

complex ways they relate to each other, especially because of the power of the middle class in the organisation of social relations within the larger society. Richard Hoggart's *The Uses of Literacy* can give us some sense of the human complexities involved:

> Towards 'Them' generally, as towards the police, the primary attitude is not so much fear as mistrust: mistrust accompanied by a lack of illusions about what 'They' will do for one, and the complicated way – the apparently unnecessarily complicated way – in which 'They' order one's life when it touches them. Working-class people have had years of experience of waiting at labour exchanges, at the panel doctor's, and at hospital. They get something of their own back by always blaming the experts, with or without justification, if something goes wrong – 'Ah never ought to 'ave lost that child if that doctor 'ad know what'e was doing'. They suspect that public attention is not so readily and effectively given to them as to the people who can telephone or send a stiff letter. (*The Uses of Literacy*, p. 74)[7]

Kant recognises the ways in which our 'independence' can be threatened as we become dependent upon others. He tends to identify 'independence' with 'self-sufficiency' which makes it difficult to grasp how this legitimates a particular form of social relations. It makes it difficult to identify traditions in which independence is not threatened within a community in which people are ready to give help and support to each other, recognising the value and importance of bringing into reality more equal human relationships as a guarantee of human dignity and self-respect.

2 LIBERALISM, CITIZENSHIP AND SOCIAL DEPENDENCE

If the notion of equal respect for individual ends involves a partial abstraction from the relations of class power and dependency, it is at least supported within liberal moral consciousness in the notion of equal citizenship, civil rights and equality before the law. In these areas of public life people are to be treated as equal so that, for instance, it is not supposed to matter whether we are talking about a cabinet minister or a bus driver, say, if it is an offence of drunken driving. What matters is simply whether people are guilty of having driven with a certain level of alcohol in their blood. The law presents itself as impartially existing in a realm of its own above the conflicts of social life and does its best to establish criteria which it can apply equally to all. This helps establish a sense of equality, which encourages people to think that inequalities of power and wealth in society are somehow 'incidental' to equality before the law and an equality of citizenship acknowledged publicly.

Sometimes this notion of equality in citizenship is established through the demarcation between the public and private realms of life. This is deeply institutionalised within liberal society. This tends to make even a person's job and income a matter of 'private concern' that they do not have to reveal to others. This can even encourage the concealment of an area of work life in which someone is constantly bossed about by the foreman in a factory. It can make it difficult to identify and articulate the ways in which people are constantly being undermined through these everyday conditions of subordination and control, since people are supposed to rest secure in their knowledge of equal citizenship. Our moral language is often powerless to illuminate these contradictions between liberal rights and the everyday experience of subordination.

Kant acknowledges the ways in which forms of dependency threaten the 'independence' of people. This does not only threaten his sense of moral equality of people, but also his sense of citizenship which also 'presupposes the independence of people in society'. To some extent he sees the inadequacy of the dichotomy between equality in citizenship and inequality in wealth and power. As far as Kant is concerned 'only the ability to vote provides the qualification of the citizen', but

> this ability, however, presupposes the independence of such
> people in society, since they wish to be not only a part of the
> community but also members of it, that is, a part which acts in
> accordance with its own will in communication with the
> others. (*Metaphysical Elements of the Theory of Right*,
> Introduction)[8]

This encourages Kant to draw a distinction 'between active and passive citizen', though he also acknowledges that 'the concept of passive citizen seems to be in contradiction with the definition of

the concept of a citizen in general'. But, even though he acknowledges this 'contradiction', he does not allow it to threaten his basic
conceptions. Rather, he tends to admit that some people 'must be
given orders or protected by other people' so that 'they possess no
civil independence'. We have already indicated this in referring to
his discussion of women. It is almost as if we should not worry
about this 'contradiction' with 'the definition of the concept of a
citizen in general', since we would not expect to claim equality with
those who are so obviously in a position of subordination, rather
than simply made unequal because of the help or kindness we offer
to them:

> The following examples can help to remove this difficulty. The
> apprentice employed by a manufacturer; the servant (not the
> servant in the service of the state); the pupil ... all women ...;
> the woodcutter I employ in my yard ...; the private tutor ...;
> the peasant who works on a daily basis for the farmer, and
> people of this kind – are simple dependents of the state, since
> they must be given orders or protected by other people, and in
> consequence they possess no civil independence, i.e. they lack
> civil personality (*Metaphysical Elements of the Theory of Right*,
> 2nd Sec.)

Galvano della Volpe in his book *Rousseau and Marx* is right to
point out that at this moment 'the "*difficulty*" is not really "re-
moved" but only exposed' (*Rousseau and Marx*, p. 81),[9] when he
goes on to quote Kant saying that:

> his dependence on the will of others and this (civil) inequality
> are not, however, at all contrary to the freedom and equality
> of these same individuals as men, who all together make up a
> people; also it is only on the basis of their conditions that this
> people can become a state and enter into a civil constitution.
> In this constitution, however, not all can claim the right to
> vote by that same title, that is, the right to be citizens and not
> merely associated. For the fact that they can demand to be
> treated as passive parts of the state by all the others, according
> to the laws of natural freedom and equality, does not allow
> them to derive therefrom the right of acting as active members
> of the state itself, nor that of organising the state or
> cooperating in introducing laws, but only that right, whatever

the character of the positive laws voted in by those who have the right to vote, that these laws must not be contrary to the natural laws of liberty and the subsequent equality of all members of the people in the capacity to raise themselves from their passive state to an active one. (*Metaphysical Elements of the Theory of Right*, Part 2)[10]

So Kant does not want this 'dependence on the will of others' to compromise 'the freedom and equality of these same individuals as men', though he does acknowledge that this makes a difference to whether they should only assume positions of 'passive' citizenship. It is as if a person *as* an 'apprentice', 'servant', 'pupil', or 'peasant' has only a 'price', since he or she is dependent on the will of others and 'must be given orders or protected by other people'. To the extent that we see people as workers or labourers, it is as if they are to be seen as a 'commodity' which has no intrinsic value. This is partly because *as* a worker, servant, pupil, peasant 'they possess no civil independence', but must 'be given orders or protected by other people'. Kant recognises that the relationships of dependency and subordination that people are in denies 'the independence of such people', and so denies them the right of active citizenship. This opens up a contradiction that Galvano della Volpe was aware of, between considering the manual or external activity of people and considering people as moral beings. This essentially fragments our understanding of people, and involves abstracting from the everyday activities of work and community to consider people having the 'dignity of mankind':

> And yet, insofar as he is a *man*, the individual labourer cannot help having intrinsic '*dignity*' and '*value*', etc., for the Christian, natural law theorist, Kant. It is unnecessary to dwell on this – at least in the sense that nothing prevents the worker as a man, in the spirit of the system, being himself the '*subject of practical reason*' and hence 'virtuous', on occasion, and a 'person' with all that entails. But that does *not* concern him as a *worker*. This is also true not only in the abstract but in the concrete as well, i.e. for a worker who lives in a human community, as worker-citizen ... (*Rousseau and Marx*, p. 80)

Kant maintains the logic of his concerns when he denies the rights of active citizenship to those who are 'dependent on the will of others'.[11] At least he recognises the nature and character of this dependency. In this sense he does not take the option of abstracting from the social relations of power and dependency, which he tends to do when he thinks about us as moral beings. But the very considerations of the relations between rich and poor potentially threatened this notion of the autonomy of morals. But this is the deeper questioning which he wishes to avoid when he says that his 'dependence on the will of others and this (civil) inequality are not, however, at all contrary to the freedom and equality of these same individuals as men'. It is as if this 'freedom and equality' is to be guaranteed within this moral realm in which we are working out our individual relationships to the moral law. It is as if we can exclusively conclude that it is within this realm that we consider 'these same individuals as men'. This is automatically to subordinate our understanding of people as, say, workers, craftsmen, tutors, mothers, peasants, fathers. Since the relations with nature which work involves create their own forms of dependency, it is only within the moral realm that people can be assumed to have true freedom.

Kant is forced to acknowledge relationships of power and dependency. It is deeply held by Kant that 'Innate equality is the same as independence ... and yet it is the quality man has to be his own master' (*Theory of Right*, Introduction). This is why in the passage we quote Kant becomes a little uneasy in saying that 'dependence on the will of others' is not 'at all contrary to the freedom and equality of these same individuals as men', so that he ends by talking of 'the subsequent equality of all members of the people in the capacity to raise themselves from their passive state to an active one'. But this is to beg the very questions Kant raises in his discussion of the relations of rich and poor. It is difficult for him to have it both ways. It is difficult for him to assume that people can 'raise themselves' through their own will and determination. At the same time even if he acknowledges that 'dependence on the will of others' means people do not have the independence which entitles them to active citizenship, he still wants to preserve his assumption of the autonomy of morality. I have tried to show the difficulty in maintaining this assumption, while acknowledging difficulties in the moral relations between rich and poor that call for more than sensitivity to the ways these relations are 'handled'. It begs the question of challenging the material basis for these relations of power and dependency, so that people are in a situation to use the capacity Kant acknowledges we all share 'to raise themselves from their passive state to an active one'.

Kant does follow through his arguments to deny people active citizenship if they are dependent upon the will of others. Sometimes in his discussion of women it seems clear that he thinks they have to be 'protected by other people'. He does not want to recognise the consequences of this subordination and dependency, but tends to take it for granted. He does not really develop a full sense of the ways people are hurt, denied, compromised, oppressed within these relations of subordination and dependency. It seems as if Kant barely acknowledges the capacity of women 'to raise themselves from their passive state'. It is partly because Kant can believe in a notion of moral equality guaranteed in our relation to the moral law, that he does not give weight to the sufferings and indignities people are forced to endure within a class and patriarchal society. This is something we need more understanding of.

It turns out that the people who have this 'independence' are a small class of men who are not 'dependent on the will of others', but who are their own masters. As della Volpe says, the citizen-labourer has 'the independence and dignity and being-an-end-in-oneself and possession *also* of *civil* personality – but only *potentially*, through his chance of *"promotion"* from labourer to bourgeois ... Alternatively, the labourer has no choice but to remain a chrysalis of man, or, if one prefers, a pupil or minor, with all that implies' (*Rousseau and Marx*, p. 82). This is part of his argument to show that it is only the bourgeois individual who can work for himself, and is not thereby dependent upon the will of others, who can be regarded as a 'person' in all senses, not only as a moral being but also as a citizen. This is what allows della Volpe to recall Marx's reminder to his opponents in the *Manifesto*: 'You must, therefore, confess that by "individual" you mean no other person than the bourgeois, than the middle-class owner of property.'

Once Kant recognised the moral relevance of relations of dependency, he was forced to deny certain rights of citizenship to many people in society. At least he does not pretend that people have an independence and autonomy which they do not enjoy in their everyday lives. In this sense he exposes one of the raw nerves of liberal conceptions of freedom and equality. He recognises the ways in which relations of power and dependency undermine autonomy and independence in people's lives, and so denies people effective control over their own lives. He tends to describe this in the patriarchal language of being 'one's own master'. Since there is no way of making people 'independent' without challenging these relations of power and dependency through questioning the moral legitimacy of property relations within society, Kant had to deny these political rights to people. Kant drew back from questioning these property relations, since these threatened to challenge fundamentally his assumption of the autonomy of morals. It is a mark of the greatness of Kant's thinking that he does not avoid these contradictions but faces the choices they present him with, though at the same time he wants to maintain his deep assumption of the autonomy of morals which allows him to preserve 'the freedom and equality of these same individuals as men'.

Within liberal political and moral theory there is a desire to grant these rights of citizenship to all and to think that these rights somehow preserve a sense in which people can be thought of as being 'independent'. This involves avoiding some of the implications of Kant's moral theory, particularly his discussion of the relations between rich and poor, and invoking different tendencies of moral theory which will allow people to more easily abstract from the social relations of power and dependency, be they relations between classes, sexes or races.

So in thinking about issues of citizenship Kant had to acknowledge the social relations of power and dependency. He had to acknowledge that if some people are dependent upon others for their very means of livelihood then we have to recognise that they cannot live autonomous and independent lives. They no longer enjoy the material conditions which would give them effective control over their lives. If a relationship of dependency was sufficient to deny people full political rights, Kant was reassured that people could always *become* free and independent and so eventually assume equal rights with others. But Kant was less clear how this was to be achieved or what kind of moral issues were raised by these social relations of power and subordination. For most of the time he had been able to construe the sources of inequality in a way which protected his assumption of the autonomy of morality, of people's equality before the moral law. Sometimes Kant was ready to secure his assumptions of independence and self-sufficiency as transcendental qualities guaranteed through abstracting

114

from the structures of power and inequality. But sometimes Kant wanted to go further to assume this independence as a feature of people's everyday lives. He was forced to recognise how this independence could be threatened by social relations of power and subordination.

But Kant never really wanted to think about the nature and character of moral relations once the notion of the autonomy of morality had been challenged. Kant had all along wanted to challenge those empiricist philosophers who were content to study man 'only in the varying forms in which his accidental circumstances have moulded him, in the distorted forms in which even philosophers have almost always misconstrued him'. Kant's notions of autonomy and independence enable us to be critical of forms of life and social relations of power and subordination for the hurt and misery they can bring into people's lives. We are not simply left to accept these relations, as if the fact that they exist means they have always existed or cannot be changed. Against this Kant was concerned to restore to us a sense of 'what is enduring in human nature, and the proper place of man in creation'. But this remained to the end a deeply patriarchal and Christian vision. This made it easier for Kant to feel that dignity and respect could always be restored to people in their relationship to the moral law. It made it relatively easy for him to escape from the revelation of the moral significance of social relations of power and subordination.

It also meant that Kant could continually trust his individualistic vision, safe in his knowledge of the primacy of an individual's relationship to the moral law. If this could work to sharpen our sense of individual autonomy giving us terms in which we could morally criticise relations in which people were being used for the ends of others, it could never develop into an understanding of how dependence had been institutionalised. To do so would be to bring our moral theory into a closer relationship with social theory. It would involve developing a moral language in which we could identify and criticise these relations. This would involve recognising the hurt and indignity that people do to each other, even while thinking they are treating others with respect. The very individualism of Kant's moral theory which provides its critical edge could also be used to legitimate social relations of power and subordination. He did this himself in his discussion of relations between the sexes.

Kant could never fully appreciate the ways in which people can be undermined and their individualities disorganised through a systematic denial of their emotions and sensibilities as well as through class and sexual relations of power and dependency. His individualism tended to protect his moral theory from the full force of these realisations. Not only would this require a challenge to the autonomy of morality but it would also involve a critique of prevailing social relations of power and subordination. It would involve not simply a change of attitudes towards others but a transformation of social relations so that the autonomy and independence which Kant valued could be more widely realised.

I have tried to show how both the rationalism and individualism within Kant's moral theory make it difficult for us to realise the kind of control over our lives which his moral theory would seem to promise. In reserving the notion of respect for our rational moral selves, he encourages us to subordinate important aspects of our experience, activities and relations which could otherwise help us define and strengthen our individualities. This is something his rationalism never allowed him to recognise. In reserving the notion of dignity to our inner relationship to the moral law and guaranteeing us equality in an independent moral realm, he makes it difficult for us to understand how people can be undermined, hurt and humiliated through the indignity and oppression they suffer in their everyday lives. In making morality into an individual quest, his individualism makes us less able to understand our need for more equal relations with others – not only to give meaning to our lives but also to validate and confirm our experience.

It is partly through recognising both the strengths and limitations of Kant's influence within the moral and political consciousness of liberalism that we can begin to articulate and clarify a moral language that is less threatened by and estranged from the social and material conditions of independence and autonomy. This challenge to the autonomy of morality would not dispense with the powerful insight it has given us into the reality of our moral experience, nor would it seek to reduce morality to other aspects of our social and political experience. But it would have to challenge the tendency for us to abstract from the inequalities and injustices of social life. These would recover their central position within our moral theory. What is more our moral theory would have to be open to discovering sources of dignity and respect in our needs, desires, feelings and emotions as well as in our personal and social relations. Notions of dignity, respect, autonomy, independence and individuality, far from being dispensed with, would have a central role within the renewal of our moral language and experience.

VIII

LIBERALISM AND THE AUTONOMY OF MORALITY

Liberal moral and political theory has turned towards Kant for philosophical foundations for a liberalism in which notions of justice, fairness and individual rights play a central role. This is part of a major change in moral, political and legal philosophy which H. L. A. Hart has described as a 'transition from a once widely accepted old faith that some form of utilitarianism, if only we could discover the right form, *must* capture the essence of political morality', to a 'doctrine of basic human rights, protecting specific basic liberties and interests of individuals, if only we could find some sufficiently firm foundations for such rights'.[1] But this shift has assumed the very autonomy of morality and the fragmented conception of the person upon which Kant's moral theory is built. It is a liberalism that has been built upon shaky foundations because it has ignored the tensions and contradictions in Kant's less formalistic later writings.

Even though Kant's moral theory seems to provide a firm basis for the integrity and separateness of individuals against a utilitarianism which seems to sacrifice the happiness or pleasure of individuals for its goal of maximising aggregate or average general welfare, we have to be careful in assessing this claim. Though the accusation of ignoring the separateness of persons is often seen as a version of Kant's principle that human beings are ends in themselves, it is rarely connected to the difficulties Kant had in elucidating the moral significance of this principle. Liberal moral theory has inherited the weaknesses as well as the strengths of its Kantian inheritance.

While Bernard Williams's article 'Persons, Character and Morality' opens with the recognition that 'Much of the most interesting recent work in moral philosophy has been of a basically Kantian inspiration' he also recognises its difficulty of relating a moral point of view 'specially characterized by its impartiality and its indifference to any particular relations to particular persons' (*Moral Luck*, p. 2) to other points of view. He recognises that though the motivation of a moral agent 'involves a rational application of impartial principles' this is not supposed to preclude more intimate and personal relations. But, as Williams shifts away from thinking of this in the liberal terms of 'the relations between those points of view' he focuses the issue in more illuminating terms, saying that

> the deeply disparate character of the moral and non-moral
> motivation, together with the special dignity or supremacy
> attached to the moral, make it very difficult to assign to those
> other relations and motivations the significance or structural
> importance in life which some of them are capable of
> possessing. (*Moral Luck* p. 2)[2]

I do not think this can be done without challenging the fundamental assumptions upon which the autonomy of morals is built.

In this conclusion I argue that we need to find other ways of relating morality to other areas of our lives. Notions of respect, autonomy and independence can no longer be secured and guaranteed within a rationalistically conceived moral realm. Without succumbing to a moral relativism that Kant deplored, we need to grasp the moral significance of relations of power and subordination that can undermine our existence as independent human beings. If this can only be done through restoring dignity to our emotional lives, activities, needs and desires, it can help us establish a firmer grasp than Kant was able to do of why we should not treat others merely as means, but always as ends in themselves. But this is to bring issues of power, dependency and oppression into the heart of moral theory.

1 AUTONOMY AND DEPENDENCE

Kant was prepared to deny civic rights to those in relationships of subordination and dependency. He denies people active citizenship if they are dependent upon the will of others. So, as far as Kant is concerned, workers, servants, pupils, peasants and all women 'must be given orders or protected by other people, and in consequence they possess no civil independence'. Few liberal theorists, however indebted to Kant, would want to admit this conclusion. Nor do they often explore the tensions in Kant's discussion of the relations between rich and poor. Rather they draw strength from Kant's general observation that these forms of independence and inequality 'are not, however, at all contrary to the freedom and equality of these same individuals as men'. In this sense, Kant's reassertion of the autonomy of morality has been crucially used to sustain, against Kant, the idea that people are equally entitled to full political and legal rights, or as Dworkin has it, to 'equal concern and respect'.[3] So we find the idea that individuals are equally capable of living moral lives serving as a justification for equal treatment within the legal and political realm.

But possibly Kant should not be surprised, since he seems to have prepared the ground for this in his separation of our individual relations to the moral law from our empirical social lives. We exist in different spheres. As I have shown, this has its basis in Kant's conception of the person as fragmented between the sensible world and the intelligible world. It is our rationality which gives us access to the moral realm which is also the realm of freedom. It is here that our moral autonomy and independence is guaranteed. This is the way we are made invulnerable to relationships of power and subordination within the social world. Our individuality is given prior to our participation and involvement in social relations. This also reflects a hierarchy within ourselves in which we learn to identify the 'self' with our existence as free and equal moral agents. We are to identify with our intelligible, noumenal selves. Our autonomy and freedom have to do with our inner relationship to the moral law. This is at the core of a rationalist vision in which we are always struggling to make our experience conform to the ideals and images we have of ourselves. This has to do with the sovereignty of reason that gives us access to a moral law that exists independently, even if we have constantly to discover it anew for ourselves.

Kant wants to say that when we act morally out of a sense of duty we are expressing our humanity, our freedom and autonomy. We have to raise ourselves above the empirical world, the world of nature which is essentially a realm of unfreedom and determination. There is no way we can express our individualities in our activities and relationships, since these take place in a realm in which our behaviour is constantly being externally influenced. This is the world in which we naturally pursue our happiness, as we strive to pursue ends we set for ourselves. But this can hardly be an expression of our individuality, since Kant essentially sees this as a matter of pursuing our own self-interest. This gives our lives no dignity nor moral worth. There is little of value that can be learnt from our experience. It is not a source of knowledge or insight. Rather it is a realm we are constantly trying to escape as we draw ourselves up to identify with our noumenal aspects. This helps explain our ability to abstract ourselves from ongoing social relations of power and subordination. It also explains why the indignities and humiliations of social life should not really matter to us.

Our freedom and autonomy are guaranteed to us in the intelligible world. Here we can experience ourselves as equal with others and as equally deserving of respect. This is part of what draws us to accept both the autonomy and the priority of the moral since it seems to promise us our freedom and equality. But this is to deny moral significance to relationships of power and subordination and to the ways individuals can experience themselves as undermined and invalidated. If our autonomy and independence is to be guaranteed in our individual relationship to the moral law, what is it that is being undermined and invalidated? This can easily make people feel they have nothing legitimate to protest against and that it is only envy or personal gain that can be motivating them. If the social world is simply a space in which we can prove ourselves morally, through acting out of a sense of duty, then our inherited moral traditions threaten to become powerless in illuminating the moral significance of social relations of power and subordination. If we grow up within a Kantian moral tradition to accept the implicit identification of the moral with the rational and the universal, then we are bound to minimise the moral significance of the hurt and indignities of social life since they become powerless to affect our equality and freedom as moral agents. The split between autonomy and dependence reflects the division between the moral realm and the world of social relations. Since the social world is inevitably a world of determination and unfreedom our energies are being misplaced if we expect our individuality and freedom to find expression there.

This leaves us with a fundamentally fragmented conception of the person. This has been inherited into modern, liberal, moral and political theory as an ethic that asserts the priority of the right over the good. The independence of the moral law has been used to secure the primacy of justice among moral and political ideals and the sanctity of individual rights. As Sandel has pointed out 'the right is prior to the good not only that its claims take precedence, but also in that its principles are independently derived' (*Liberalism and the Limits of Justice*, p. 2). This means that 'principles of justice are justified in a way that does not depend on any particular vision of the good' (p. 2). Within this view justice is identified with the moral law so that it can be argued against utilitarianism that 'the virtue of the moral law does not consist in the fact that it promotes some goal or end presumed to be good. It is instead an end in itself, given prior to all other ends, and regulative with respect to them' (p. 2). Even though Sandel's stimulating argument recognises that 'the problem is not simply that justice remains always to be achieved, but that the vision is flawed, the aspiration incomplete' (p. 1), he tends to accept the fundamental fragmentation of the person that is so much part of the rationalist vision.[4]

Kant's moral theory rests upon the crucial distinction between duty and inclinations. This establishes a hierarchy within our inherited conception of the person which, as I have shown, leaves us fundamentally divided against ourselves. Our very humanity is to be identified with our reason and morality. Our moral theory has to go beyond finding space for acts of care, generosity and concern that Kant grants no moral worth, to a more basic challenge to this rationalist conception of ethics. This is not to argue against the place of reason in our moral lives, but against a particular form of rationality which conceives our self-control as a matter of the *domination* of our emotional lives and desires. Hopefully I have helped weaken the hold of this picture over our moral conceptions. It is also important to grasp how it is written into the distinction we draw between the concept of right as a moral category given prior and independent of the good.

Liberal theory has developed itself on the idea that individuals should be free to advance their own conceptions of happiness. We partly show our respect of others by recognising they have their own ends, interest and desires which they should be free to pursue. This means that any regulative principles of justice should not themselves presuppose any particular conception of the good but should guarantee an equal freedom to individuals. This is the only way we can supposedly make sure that we do not impose on some the values of others and so deny them the freedom to pursue their own conceptions. For Kant this meant that the moral law could not have its basis in happiness and could not be implicated in any contingent interests and ends. It is duty which gives the moral law a basis prior to all purposes and ends. So the basis of the moral law is to be found not in the object of practical reason, since people inevitably disagree, but in a subject capable of rationality and so to the independent demands of duty. This connects the priority of right to freedom, since as moral beings, we are equally subject to an autonomous will, But again this depends upon a fundamental split between the moral realm of freedom and the empirical world in which we pursue our individual conceptions of happiness.

Since the sensible world is conceived of as a world of determination our choices can never be free, but will always be conditioned by the desire for some object. 'When we think of ourselves as free, we transfer ourselves into the intelligible world as members and recognize the autonomy of the will' (*Groundwork of the Metaphysic of Morals*, 461). In this way the issue of autonomy is reserved for the intelligible world as an issue of moral autonomy. This makes it difficult even to raise issues about how individuals can be undermined and their existence as independent moral beings threatened because of the workings of social relations of power and subordination. The issues of autonomy and dependence have been divided into separate and distinct realms. In this way we are fundamentally detached as moral beings from everyday empirical relationships. This is because, in this vision, we only ever freely choose for ourselves when we are completely unconditioned by the contingencies of circumstances. It is this notion of freedom that has to be challenged along with the conception of the person upon which it depends.

Sandel helps clarify these issues when he says that 'On the deontological view, what matters above all is not the ends we choose but our capacity to choose them. And this capacity, being prior to any particular end it may affirm, resides in the subject' (*Liberalism and the Limits of Justice*, p. 6). It is this notion of 'a subject prior to an independent of experience' which Sandel sees as an inherited flaw in liberal theories of justice. It is an essential part of their claim for the primacy of justice:

> It is grounded in the concept of a subject given prior to its ends, a concept held indispensable to our understanding of ourselves as freely choosing, autonomous beings. Society is best arranged when it is governed by principles that do not presuppose any particular conception of the good, for any other arrangement would fail to respect persons as beings capable of choice; it would treat them as object rather than subjects, as means rather than ends in themselves. (*Liberalism and the Limits of Justice*, p. 9).

This ties our understanding of ourselves as freely choosing and autonomous beings to our existence as rational moral agents. This can blind us to the difficulties we face in identifying our individual needs, wants and desires, let alone the connection this can have to defining our autonomy and independence. Fried puts this clearly when he says that by comparison with the good, the concepts of right and wrong 'have an independent and overriding status because they establish our basic position as freely choosing entities' (*Right and Wrong*, p. 8). This is what makes the idea of respect for persons central to liberal moral and political theory. But this is to focus our sense of respect on our capacity to make free choices within an independent moral realm. It also limits our notions of the good to the quest for individual conceptions of happiness. At some level, it seems to be the basic distinction, however useful in drawing a contrast with utilitarian consequentialism, that seems to disorganise our moral consciousness. Not only does it make our sense of respect more formal and abstract than it needs to be, but it hides the fragmented conception of the person upon which it is built.

The idea, as Sandel expresses it, that 'As the right is prior to the good, so the subject is prior to its ends' (*Liberalism and the Limits of Justice*, p. 7) shows how the terms of our moral discussion are formed in opposition to utilitarianism. When we talk about 'the good' we are already talking in utilitarian terms about the ends and goals individuals choose for themselves. This notion is essentially self-interested, though it accords well with the generally hedonistic assumption that Kant makes about individuals left to

themselves without the guidance of the moral law. This is to deprive the notion of 'the good' of a broader meaning that could
itself challenge utilitarian conceptions of morality.[5] Liberal theory
has tended to accept an essentially utilitarian conception of the
good, even if its theory of right is set in fundamental opposition to
utilitarianism. This shows itself in the distinction between 'individual' and 'society' that has provided a fundamental antinomy for
liberal theory. Rawls, for instance, in his *A Theory of Justice* has
no complaints with utilitarianism as an account of individual or
private morality. Its mistake is to think we can conceive of society
in similar terms and so adopt 'for society as a whole the principle
of rational choice for one man' (p. 26).

As far as Rawls is concerned, utilitarianism does not go wrong
in conceiving the good as the satisfaction of my immediate wants
and desires. Rawls is quite clear that 'A person quite properly acts,
at least when others are not affected, to achieve his own greatest
good, to advance his rational ends as far as possible.' (*A Theory of
Justice*, p. 23.) He is concerned that we do not fall into explaining
the justice of society by imagining that we can conflate the desires
of all individuals into one coherent system of desires which we seek
to maximise. This is to reduce social choice to a question of efficient administration. The appeal of a contract theory of justice is
that, in opposition to utilitarianism, it can take seriously the distinction between persons. But if justice as fairness seeks to restore
the separateness of individuals in the way they enter into a theory
of justice, it makes itself powerless to explain how individuals are
vulnerable to social relations of power and subordination. It inherits
the weaknesses, as well as the insights, of a contract theory. There
is no way of situating individual moral experience within larger
social and historical relationships of power and subordination.

Rawls does not worry about inheriting utilitarianism's impoverished conception of the good since he tends to think that morality
exists at a social level along with justice. Like Kant he thinks that
no person's values or conceptions of the good can escape the determination of our desires and feelings. Morality has to discover an
independent source and inspiration. This reflects the basic duality
between nature and reason. So we should not be surprised when
Rawls says 'That we have one conception of the good rather than
another is not relevant from a moral standpoint. In acquiring it we
are influenced by the same sort of contingencies that lead us to rule

out a knowledge of our sex and class.' (Rawls, 1975: 'Fairness to Goodness' *Philosophical Review*, 84, p. 537.) Not only should this encourage us to rethink our inherited conceptions of morality, but, as I have tried to show, issues of sex and class could well become integral aspects of our sense of moral identity. We are not only challenging a rationalist conception of morality that defines itself in terms of impersonal and universal reasons, but the attenuated conception of the person upon which this relies.

Sandel is ready to challenge Rawls for his failure to realise that the fact the utilitarianism cannot take seriously the distinction between persons is 'a mere symptom of its larger failure to take seriously the qualitative distinctions of worth between different orders of desires' (*Liberalism and the Limits of Justice*, p. 167). Sandel wants us to conceive a 'system of desires' as ordered in a certain way, arranged in some kind of hierarchy of relative worth and essentially connected with the identity of the agent. This is part of his challenge to the Kantian concept of the person which sees it as a subject existing prior to its ends. But this is to bring reason into a sphere in which it does not belong, into the realm of our inclinations. This is to acknowledge, as I have argued, that our feelings, emotions and desires can have their own rationality. Sometimes our anger is a legitimate and appropriate response to the way we are being treated, though this does not always mean we are free to express it. This is also to admit that our emotions and desires can give us insight and understanding of ourselves. But for Kant they are inherently sources of unfreedom that can only be controlled through being dominated and silenced. Our sense of ourselves as moral beings has to come from a completely different source. It is this fundamentally dualistic conception that needs to be challenged if we are not to be trapped, as Sandel is, into giving relative weight to the good and the right. But at least it does help him to the insight that

> the morally diminished status of the good must inevitably call
> into question the status of justice as well. For once it is
> conceded that our conceptions of the good are morally
> arbitrary, it becomes difficult to see why the highest of all
> (social) virtues should be the one that enables us to pursue
> these arbitrary conceptions 'as fully as circumstances permit'.
> (*Liberalism and the Limits of Justice*, p. 168)

There is something flawed in organising our moral consciousness around the distinction between the right and the good. This seems to reflect too closely Kant's distinction between the intelligible world and the sensible world. If happiness can only be ours through wrongful means, say stealing or lying, then as Fried says 'We would have to wave it away because right and wrong are the foundations of our moral personality. ... Right and wrong are the expressions of respect for persons – respect for others and self-respect.' (*Right and Wrong*, pp. 8–9.) As for Kant, our capacity to abstract ourselves from the empirical world into the intelligible world is the source of dignity and moral worth. The very concept of right is used 'to refer to the whole domain of the obligatory, the domain of duty, the domain of deontology as opposed to the domain of the good' (*Right and Wrong*, p. 9 fn.). Fried makes it clear that for the deontologist the two realms are not only distinct, but the right is prior to the good. This is because we can only be said to exist as freely choosing subjects within the moral realm of right and wrong. Implicitly this accepts that when it comes to our desires, needs, emotions and feelings our behaviour is being externally determined. As we have shown this is to define respect, dignity and moral worth exclusively in relationship to our 'moral personality'. Our very humanity exists in our capacity as sovereign moral subjects able to legislate for ourselves.

Liberal moral and political theory rests upon Kant's dualistic conception of the person. The idea of 'moral personality' is tied to the idea of ourselves as free and equal rational beings. The autonomy and independence of the self is antecedently established, given prior to the choices it makes in the course of experience. As in Kant's earlier, more formalistic, ethics, the unity of the self is guaranteed and rendered invulnerable to the exigencies of social life. Again we tend to find this in Rawls's *A Theory of Justice* as established in contrast to utilitarianism. He is concerned, against teleological accounts, that the rights should not be instrumental to the advancement of some end held to be prior, since this makes insecure the equal liberty of individuals. Rawls wants to guarantee that the denial of liberty for some cannot be justified in the name of an overriding good for others. Though Kant seemed to lose faith in the idea that these rights could be guaranteed irrespective of the social relations of power and subordination which, say, separated rich and poor, Rawls is still concerned to make the attempt. Rawls thinks that if we realise that what is most essential to personhood is not the ends we choose but our capacity to choose them, we will avoid the error of teleology which has been to misconceive the relation of the right to the good. This is, as Rawls says, because:

> It is not our aims that primarily reveal our nature but rather
> the principles that we would acknowledge to govern the
> background conditions under which these aims are to be
> formed and the manner in which they are to be pursued. For
> the self is prior to the ends which are affirmed by it. (*A Theory
> of Justice*, p. 560)

This is part of Rawls's argument that in choosing the principles of justice we are 'revealing our nature'. In itself this transforms the dichotomy that Kant drew between our 'natures' which are part of the empirical world of unfreedom and determination and our 'reason' which gives us access to the intelligible realm, to morality. Rawls seems prepared to trade upon Kant's dualism while thinking that he has avoided the necessity of positing a noumenal or intelligible realm. He wants to say that we are only expressing our 'true nature' when we act out of a sense of justice. Kant was only prepared to say that our lives only have dignity and moral worth when we act out of a sense of duty. This allowed Kant to think about duties to ourselves as well as to others, while Rawls seems trapped into thinking that 'morality' has only to do with collective decisions of justice. This is part of the way Rawls explains the primacy of justice, since, as Sandel points out, 'the self owes its constitution, its antecedent status, to the concept of right' (*Liberalism and the Limits of Justice*, p. 22):

> The desire to express our nature as free and equal rational
> beings can be fulfilled only by acting on the principles of right
> and justice as having first priority. ... It is acting from this
> precedence that expresses our freedom from contingency and
> happenstance. Therefore in order to realise our nature we have
> no alternative but to plan to preserve our sense of justice as
> governing other aims. (*A Theory of Justice*, p. 574)

For Rawls it is important for us 'to express our nature as free and equal rational beings' since at one and the same time it seems able to guarantee our autonomy and independence, while also allowing Rawls to include features he takes to be shared and common to all human beings as such. Unlike Kant, Rawls is prepared to rely on certain generalised human preferences and desires, such as that each is a person who chooses his or her ends and values certain primary goods, such as respect and self-respect, as instrumental to their realisation. Since Rawls's concern is to develop a theory of justice that is fair between persons, only those contingencies that differentiate people from each other need to be ruled out. As Sandel points out, 'Contingent attributes common to human beings as such are not only not a problem for Rawls, but are essential ingredients in his moral theory.' (*Liberalism and the Limits of Justice*, p. 39.) This is the way Rawls thinks that the principles of justice derived from the original position apply to human beings in the real world, rather than simply to beings in a transcendental world. Rawls is quite happy that moral philosophy uses contingent assumptions and general facts about human nature. But if Rawls is prepared to accept a less stringent conception of contingency than Kant, who would think that any reference to desires, however widespread across human beings, would be an appeal to heteronomy, he also transforms Kant's conception of rationality. This is clear when he says that 'given human nature, wanting them [primary goods] is part of being rational. ...' (*A Theory of Justice*, p. 253). Where Kant was concerned to separate our rationality from our nature, Rawls wants to situate it in 'the elementary facts about persons and their place in nature' (*A Theory of Justice*, p. 257). As far as Rawls is concerned, human freedom is to be regulated by principles chosen in the light of natural restrictions of moderate scarcity and competing claims.

As long as the original position works with the assumption of the veil of ignorance, Rawls can be sure that it abstracts from personal differences between rational beings and from the content of their private ends. This allows him to think that 'The original position may be viewed, then, as a procedural interpretation of Kant's conception of autonomy and the categorical imperative.' (*A Theory of Justice*, p. 256.) When we act from these principles we are supposedly expressing our nature 'as free and equal rational persons'. Rawls takes one of the strengths of his account to be that these notions are no longer purely transcendent or dependent upon a reference to a noumenal realm. He thinks we can always avail ourselves of this 'way of thinking', regardless of the social relations we find ourselves in. Rawls is able to sustain what he takes to be the central Kantian insight, namely, 'the idea that moral principles are the object of rational choice' (*A Theory of Justice*, p. 251) while making clear that the principles of right are not legislated a priori by pure reason, but 'may be conceived as principles that would be chosen by rational persons' (*A Theory of Justice*, p. 16). This is one of the merits of a social contract conception. If this strengthens Rawls's sense of people as 'free and equal rational beings', it tempts him into thinking that we are always free to treat others with equal respect, since it is always possible for us to appreciate that others have ends they wish to be free to pursue. Paradoxically it is the very compromise Rawls makes with the empirical characteristics of social life that limits his insight. People always have a freedom to choose the point of view from which noumenal selves see the world. Since we are assumed to have a desire to express our nature 'as rational and equal members of the intelligible realm with precisely this liberty to choose, that is, as beings who can look at the world in this way and express this perspective in their life as members of society' (*A Theory of Justice*, p. 255) Rawls has turned into an effortless aspect of our nature what Kant took to be an endless struggle against our inclinations.

The idea of justice as fairness is that the principles of justice are agreed in an initial situation that is fair. But Rawls also realises that society cannot be a voluntary scheme of co-operation and that, in reality, 'each person finds himself placed at birth in some particular position in some particular society, and the nature of this position materially affects his life prospects' (*A Theory of Justice*, p. 13). How are people to think about justice in the unequal situations they find themselves in? Are they to compare themselves with the principles of justice as fairness knowing that these are the principles which free and rational persons would accept in an initial position of equality? Does this help to strengthen people or are there ways it serves to disempower them, making it harder to think clearly about the unequal situations they find themselves in? One of the features assumed, by Rawls, to be common to all human beings and thereby non-contingent, is his sense that we all desire to choose our own ends. This is partly what defines us as free and equal rational beings and is embodied in Rawls's principle of equal liberty. But it is this very ability to choose our own ends which is threatened in the relationship of power and subordination between rich and poor. For Kant it was crucial to realise that if someone was dependent for their very means of livelihood, it would be difficult for them to conceive their individual ends. Kant could only save his assumption of the autonomy of morality by assuming that this was a situation that was freely chosen. Effectively, this was to blame the victim for his or her subordination, though Kant had earlier recognised how this had grown out of an unequal distribution of property which gave the rich more than they needed while the poor had less than they needed. This helped produce a relationship of dependency and subordination. But Rawls seems more willing to guarantee our existence as free and equal rational beings by making it an aspect of our nature which we can choose to display. As Rawls says 'men exhibit their freedom, their independence from the contingencies of nature and society, by acting in ways they would acknowledge in the original position' (*A Theory of Justice*, p. 256).

Rawls wishes to guarantee a situation in which people are equally free to pursue their own ends. This is the way we show our respect to others. The essence of Kant's moral writings, for Rawls, is not 'a morality of austere command' but 'an ethic of mutual respect and self-esteem' (*A Theory of Justice*, p. 256). As far as Rawls is concerned,

> by arranging inequalities for reciprocal advantage and by abstaining from the exploitation of the contingencies of nature and social circumstances within a framework of equal liberty, persons express their respect for one another in the very constitution of their society. (*A Theory of Justice*, p. 178)

But the issue still emerges about how people are to think about justice when society does not follow these principles. Briefly, how are we to behave justly in an unjust society? Are we simply to behave towards others as if the society was just, knowing that in this way we at least 'express most fully what we are or can be, namely free and equal rational beings with a liberty to choose' (*A Theory of Justice*, p. 256)? I have challenged the idea that as long as we behave towards others with equal respect, we have done all that can be morally expected of us. The idea that we are equally able to live independent and self-sufficient lives was shown to be an implicit assumption of the autonomy of morality. It also remains implicit within Rawls's theory of justice as fairness.

When Rawls thinks that the 'essential unity of the self is already provided by the concept of right' (*A Theory of Justice*, p. 563) he is also confirming the independence of people from each other. We are free to choose our ends and follow our own conception of happiness. It is the autonomy and independence of the person which is guaranteed. But as Sandel has realised, the priority of the right over the good mirrors the priority of the self over its ends and that:

> To assert the priority of the self whose sovereign agency is assured, it was necessary to identify an 'essentially unencumbered' self, conceived as a pure subject of possession, distinct from its contingent aims and attributes, standing always behind them. (*Liberalism and the Limits of Justice*, p. 121)

This helps identify an important weakness in liberal theory, though Sandel's wish to recognise how certain ends are 'constitutive' of our sense of self, rather than voluntaristically chosen as an act of will, still poses the issue in terms of an individual's relationship to his or her own ends. But at least it does help him recognise that both Rawls and Dworkin's right-based theories which seek to defend certain individual claims against the utilitarian calculus of social interests 'both rely on a theory of the subject that has the paradoxical effect of confirming the ultimate frailty, perhaps even incoherence, of the individual whose rights they seek above all to secure' (*Liberalism and the Limits of Justice*, p. 138). Even though Sandel repeatedly refers to the irony that a 'person so morally disempowered should be the product of a liberal ethic designed to establish the rights of the individual as inviolable', it is much harder to explain this, let alone provide an alternative conception. One reason is that we are repeatedly trapped within a framework within which deontological liberal theories are set against utilitarianism. Hart is probably right when he thinks that 'a satisfactory foundation for a theory of rights will [not] be found as long as the search is conducted in the shadow of utilitarianism' (*The Idea of Freedom*, p. 98). Possibly we go astray as long as we separate the right from the good, as long as we accept the distinction between a morality defined in terms of reason and our emotions, desires and needs. Kant left us with a clue in the difficulties he himself faced in giving a more substantial account of respect as not treating others merely as means, but as ends in themselves. At the very least we need an account of the ways we as human beings hurt and mistreat each other which is not set in utilitarian terms.

Sandel also helps when he draws our attention to the grounds Rawls has to depend on to reject the idea that one race may be inherently more worthy than another. The fallacy for Rawls is not that it 'denies the intrinsic worth of blacks but that it falsely attributes an intrinsic worth to whites, and so attributes to them an unfounded claim of desert' (*Liberalism and the Limits of Justice*, p. 128). Though Kant thinks it is only our moral actions that make us morally worthy, the confusion we discern in Rawls between morality and justice makes it impossible for him to recognise even this. As far as Rawls is concerned the concept of moral worth, like the concept of the good, is 'secondary to those of right and justice, and it plays no role in the substantive definition of distributive shares' (*A Theory of Justice*, p. 313). Persons can no more have intrinsic worth than intrinsic merit or desert, that is, as Sandel makes clear, 'a worth or merit or desert that is theirs prior to and independent of what just institutions may attribute to them' (*Liberalism and the Limits of Justice*, p. 138). In denying that justice has to do with giving people what they deserve or recognising their intrinsic worth, justice as fairness departs decisively from traditional theories. In truth no substantive theory of the person antecedent to social institutions, and the legitimate expectations created by them, exists. So a person's moral worth depends upon fulfilling the expectations created by just institutions. Once a person does what established institutions encourage him or her to do, certain rights are acquired, but not before. What people are entitled to is not proportional to or dependent upon their intrinsic worth. In Rawls's view people have no intrinsic worth, in the sense that it is prior to what just institutions attribute to them. As Rawls says, the concept of moral worth is secondary to that of right and justice. But it is exactly this which makes it difficult to understand the ways people hurt each other when they act unjustly towards them.

Kant has prepared the ground for some of these difficulties. He talks in terms of the respect for persons only to prepare us for the recognition that it is only the moral law which is due our respect. But Kant, unlike Rawls, gives less weight to the importance of people having equal liberty to pursue their own ends, which is a basic principle of justice for Rawls. Kant thinks that people will naturally pursue their own happiness, but this is of no moral worth.

133

But if people learn to act out of a sense of duty, their actions can accumulate moral worth. The focus is upon the moral worth of our individual actions, not as in Aristotle, on the cultivation of qualities such as compassion and honesty which are accepted as intrinsically worthwhile in themselves. It is part of the attenuated conception of the person we inherit within a Kantian tradition that we can only attribute moral significance to particular qualities and capacities to the extent that they result in our acting out of a sense of duty. But this makes it difficult to investigate the different ways we mistreat and hurt others. Rawls has inherited this difficulty in the priority he gives to the right over the good and the way he conceives of the right as the product of a collective choice in the original position, while conceptions of the good are the products of individual choices in the real world. The fragmentation of the moral universe which this creates leaves no space for consideration of intrinsic moral worth, or really for making any distinction between needs and wants. Rather we are dazzled by the idea that different things are good for different people and that it is quite wrong for us to make any judgements about the relative value of the ends which individuals are supposedly free to choose for themselves.

We find it difficult to articulate the moral significance of social relationships of power and subordination, especially the impact they have on the quality of individual lives, since we find ourselves with no way of connecting considerations of right and justice with individual moral lives. As far as Rawls is concerned the principles of justice have to be antecedently derived if we are to be able to guarantee 'the freedom of choice that justice as fairness assures to individuals and groups within the framework of justice' (*A Theory of Justice*, p. 447). But this depends upon the very ideas of independence and self-sufficiency which Kant was brought to question in his reflection upon the relations between rich and poor. Kant was forced to recognise that individuals cannot stand in the same relation to the moral law where the rich have more than they need when the poor have less than they need, so creating a relation of subordination and dependency between them. This situation is rendered morally invisible if we learn to think of the moral world in Rawls's terms. Since individuals are assumed to be free to choose their own ends, it is difficult to recognise the moral significance of relationships of subordination and dependency. Or, if this is conceived of as a situation ruled out because of the principles of

justice, then justice as fairness would supposedly demand a transformation of capitalist relations. But these considerations are connected because if we cannot assume that people in the original
position can be conceived of as independent and self-sufficient and
so free to choose their own ends and visions of happiness, then the
whole process has great difficulty in getting going.

Rawls has a strong sense of the need for a conception of justice
to 'publicly express man's respect for one another' and the need for
people to 'insure a sense of their own value'. The two principles of
justice are designed to meet this end:

> For when society follows these principles, everyone's good is
> included in a sense of mutual benefit and this public
> affirmation in institutions of each man's endeavour supports
> men's self-esteem. The establishment of equal liberty and the
> operation of the difference principle are bound to have this
> effect. (*A Theory of Justice*, p. 178)

As far as Rawls is concerned this is how people can 'express their
respect for one another in the very constitution of their society'
(p. 178). In this acknowledgment of the importance of a *public
recognition* of the equal value of the ends people choose for themselves. Rawls is enriching the territorial conception of respect. He
recognises the importance of self-respect and he takes this to be
one of the primary goods people will value whatever their individual
ends happen to be. He thinks of self-respect as having two aspects:

> First of all ... it includes a person's sense of his own values,
> his secure conviction that his conception of his good, his plan
> of life, is worth carrying out. And second, self-respect implies a
> confidence in one's ability, so far as it is within one's power, to
> fulfill one's intentions. When we feel that our plans are of little
> value, we cannot pursue them with pleasure or take delight in
> their execution.' (*A Theory of Justice*, p. 440)

This is a generous conception but it assumes that individuals can
meaningfully abstract themselves from relations of dependency and
subordination. It blinds us to the nature of the difficulties people
face in establishing themselves as autonomous human beings. The
autonomy and independence that people supposedly enjoy in the
moral realm is somehow taken to guarantee the independence
people have to work out their own conceptions of the good. Unlike

Kant, Rawls wants to value this as an exercise of people's freedom and autonomy. But he is left without a moral language in which to explore how people can be *undermined* and their autonomy threatened through the workings of relationships of power and dependency. This is essentially a masculine vision since it is easier as men to assume we have the freedom to make our own lives. In contrast women are often brought up to find their fulfilment and vision of the good in living in relation to men. This brings the issue of autonomy into a much sharper focus, since if you take for granted that your own happiness will only come in caring for others, it can be frightening to even formulate a notion of individual ends.

Rawls enriches liberal theory in bringing in the need for public institutions of society to express the equal value of its citizens. But his idea of the way this is expressed, in a recognition that people should have an equal liberty to pursue their own conceptions of the good, embodies an important limitation of liberal theory. We are left powerless to theorise a distinction between human needs and wants and so to investigate different ways people can be hurt, denied, negated, invalidated. Even though individuals will differ over how to define a conception of shared human needs, we should not thereby think this is the same as defining our individual ends. This could be no less contingent than the other features which Rawls takes to be common to all human beings as such. Rawls wanted to restrict the description of the parties in the original position to those characteristics which all human beings share as free and equal rational beings. If Rawls does not want to rely, even implicitly, on the idea of a noumenal realm, then he has to wonder, as Kant did, about the assumptions of independence and self-sufficiency which underpin our conception of ourselves as 'free and equal rational beings'.

We should be able to concede easily that things that are good for one person may not be good for another, without thereby thinking we have dissolved the possibility of an investigation into human needs. Rawls acknowledged that in different situations different kinds of agreements are called for:

> individuals find their good in different ways, and many things
> may be good for one person that would not be good for
> another. Moreover, there is no urgency to reach a publicly

136

accepted judgment as to what is the good of particular individuals. The reasons that make such an agreement necessary in questions to justice do not obtain for judgments of value. (*A Theory of Justice*, p. 448)

Recognising the moral importance of an investigation of human needs is not connected to drawing up a list which people can agree to. This quest has often been misplaced since it has classically conceived needs as given prior to people's relationships in society. In traditional contract theory it is conceived that we enter society to fulfil pre-given needs.[6] Against this it has been taken as a strength of deontological liberalism that it does not depend upon any particular conception of human nature. Thus Rawls can claim that the key assumptions of justice as fairness involve 'no particular theory of human motivation' (*A Theory of Justice*, p. 129). Likewise, Dworkin can say that 'liberalism does not rest on any specific theory of personality' (*Taking Rights Seriously*, p. 142). But as Dworkin makes clear, the force of this is in the idea that liberals can be 'indifferent to the ways of life individuals choose to pursue' (p. 143). Contemporary versions of liberalism take pride in the fact that they do not depend upon any particular theory of the person, at least in the traditional sense that they do not attribute a determinate nature to all human beings. Rather than being a strength this turns out to be a fatal flaw.

Rawls is concerned to develop a viable Kantian conception of justice. This means denying that a prior and independent self which is distinct from its values and ends can only be a transcendental or noumenal subject, lacking all empirical foundation. For Rawls this means detaching the content of Kant's doctrine from its background in transcendental idealism and recasting it within the 'canons of a reasonable empiricism' ('The Basic Structure as Subject', *American Philosophical Quarterly*, 14, p. 165). It is an essential part of Sandel's argument in *Liberalism and the Limits of Justice* that for justice to be primary we must be independent and distinct from the ends and values we hold. As subjects we must be constituted independently of our ends and desires. He seeks the limits of justice in the partiality of this self-image and argues that 'Rawls' attempt does not succeed, and that deontological liberalism cannot be rescued from the difficulties associated with the Kantian subject' (*Liberalism and the Limits of Justice*, p. 14).

I have argued that to understand this fully we have to challenge the very character of Kantian rationalism. The deep antagonism between morality as a creation of reason and our emotions, feelings, desires and needs still organises our liberal moral consciousness. It is embodied in Rawls's conception of us as 'free and equal rational persons'. Even though Rawls wants to connect our principles of justice to the empirical conditions of human conduct, he still assumes that the contingent social and natural conditions are morally irrelevant. Since he takes himself to be developing a theory of justice that is fair between persons, only those contingencies that differentiate people from each other need be ruled out. This helps him develop a 'thin theory of the good' in which he can think of respect and self-respect, say, as primary goods that people will want whatever their individual ends and goals happen to be. Their inclusion does not threaten the basic idea of ourselves as beings who are free to choose our own ends. But of course this is not enough to develop a substantive theory of the person antecedent to social institutions. For Rawls the worth of persons has to await the creation of social institutions with the power to create legitimate expectations.

Rawls's *Theory of Justice* is basically concerned to guarantee our equal freedom to follow whatever ends we have chosen for ourselves. It is essentially a liberal vision in its critical assumptions that people are independent and self-sufficient enough not only to formulate their own conceptions of happiness, but to realise them. It is suspicious of any conception of needs, since this seems to threaten people with an external judgement of what they should value. But if we can respect the insight of the liberal vision and the crucial importance of the freedom for people to develop their own understanding of themselves, this is equally true of our individual and collective needs, wants and desires as it is of the ends we set for ourselves. We can quote Mill that 'If a person possesses any tolerable amount of common sense and experience, his own mode of laying out his existence is the best, not because it is the best in itself, but because it is his own mode' (*On Liberty*, p. 197). But the issue also concerns the material conditions of autonomy and independence. If people do not have their basic needs met and do not have control over their means of livelihood, then it is hard for them even to visualise their own individual ends. This is what Kant faced in his discussion of the relationship between rich and poor.

As I have argued, autonomy and independence is something that cannot be assumed, but in class, sexual, racial and ethnic relations of power and subordination it has to be struggled for. It is a feature of the workings of relationships of power and subordination that the oppressed accept the dominant definitions of their reality, without often realising the ways they can be helping to invalidate their own experience, history and culture. But this is something people have to discover for themselves. The first step is often to learn to value and respect aspects of identity that people have been brought up to despise and feel ashamed of.

Rawls would need to strengthen his sense of the material conditions for our existing as 'free and equal rational persons', if he could no longer assume the sharp distinction between the self, taken as a pure subject of possession and its aims and values. As Sandel describes the situation, 'Given the distancing aspect of possession, the self *itself* is dispossessed. On Rawls' theory of the person, the self strictly speaking, *has nothing*, nothing at least in the strong constitutive sense necessary to desert.' (*Liberalism and the Limits of Justice*, p. 85.) There is nothing essential or constitutive of my person in the ends or values I have chosen, since otherwise my status as a sovereign moral agent could not be epistemologically guaranteed but would supposedly then depend upon the contingent conditions of my existence and so be vulnerable to transformation by experience. This has always been basic to a rationalist project which sees the individual as a bearer of these contingent qualities, but as having no substantial identity itself.

Within a rationalist tradition our autonomy is vested in our reason and our dependency is seen as a feature of our emotions and desires. This dualistic conception still disorganises our moral consciousness. In truth our ideas are no less our own than are our emotions and desires. Oppressed groups have continually had to liberate themselves from mental slavery. Liberal political theory would seem to guarantee our freedom to pursue our ends without thinking that unless we develop what Gramsci calls a 'critical consciousness' we are likely to accept tacitly the values, ends and aspirations we have inherited from our families. We seem to be left with a limited grasp of moral psychology. We inherit a limited sense of how to develop as individuals as we come into a fuller relationship with different parts of ourselves. This means challenging a Kantian inheritance which assumes that it is through reason alone that we will discern the true significance of our lives. But for Kant this rested in a recognition of an identity between reason and morality. But in Rawls we seem to be offered the idea that reason will also give us our ends and values. In both accounts it becomes impossible to recognise a distinction between our wants and our needs and the significance of their denial for our developing sense of identity.

A consequence of identifying our 'selves' with our reason and the ends we set for ourselves is that we learn to discount our emotions, feelings and desires automatically. Accepting this as a realm of unfreedom, we learn to despise this part of ourselves as showing weakness and irrationality. This is especially threatening for men, as I have argued. We rarely learn as men that our autonomy can rest as much in learning to have our own feelings, desires and needs, as it rests upon our having our own ideas and thoughts. Rather than seeing them as necessarily opposed we could see them as offering different ways of building a deeper contact with ourselves. Our moral vision is limited as we commit ourselves to too narrow a conception of rationality as we identify it exclusively with our mental or intellectual qualities. This automatically encourages us to think there can be no rationality in our emotions and feelings so that they can be no source of knowledge and understanding of ourselves. Sometimes it is our intellectual selves that can block a deeper contact with ourselves. We only have to remember the difficulties that Roger had in trusting his feelings to be a dancer, even though he recognised it might be more 'rational' to go to university as his father had advised. He has to sort out whether this is what he really wanted to do for himself, or whether he was simply reacting against his father. In recognising that dancing is a need for him, he is acknowledging its centrality to his being able to realise himself as a person. He had to discover the seriousness of his decision because he did not want to go against his father's advice easily. This did not mean he was making a decision that would hold true for his whole life, but that it felt important at some core level for him to train as a dancer now. It has been important for him to take this moral stand against his father, though he could not begin to say what others might do in his situation. He knew that he could not have made this decision unless he had learnt to trust his feelings about himself. He felt that he was exercising his autonomy, possibly for the first time in his life.

140

A Kantian tradition which stresses the impersonal character of morality and which stresses that reasons have to be universally appropriate if they are to be moral, often fails to illuminate the individuality of our moral experience, even though this is supposedly one of its strengths. We find it harder to value the particularity of our experience as we do the cultural and historical experience we share with others. We learn to discount too much that is valuable in our experience when our needs, desires, emotions and feelings find no place in the respect we feel for ourselves and others. As we learn to accept the integrity of our feelings and emotions we recognise that as they can bind us unwillingly to a past dependency, they can also express our autonomy and independence. We can feel hurt because others do not accept the validity of our feelings, always thinking they know better how we should feel. We can feel we have not been respected. The truth is that our emotions and feelings, our needs and desires are an integral part of our individuality. As we learn to listen and accept them, learning to appreciate what they say about ourselves, however hard it might be, we are often developing a fuller relationship to ourselves. We are not so concerned to judge our emotions and desires as 'right' or 'wrong', but we are concerned to give them their own voice and form. Since Kant could never recognise the moral significance of developing this kind of inner relationship to ourselves, he could never really substantiate the individualism he wanted to foster. In his desire to make morality impartial, impersonal and disinterested he had to simplify the nature of our moral experience. As long as we lived in his image we would work to construe our moral experience in his terms, thinking that in the domination of our inclinations we were living out a higher vision of ourselves. Our moral traditions seemed incapable of illuminating the hurt and pain which the self-denial implicit in the Kantian vision cost us, since in so many crucial respects they shared his assumptions.

A Kantian tradition encourages us to think of ourselves as independent and self-sufficient, free to work out our individual relationship to the moral law. It finds strong echoes in traditional conceptions of masculinity in which our autonomy seems to be threatened if we acknowledge as men that we have needs for others. Too often we automatically interpret this as a sign of weakness which threatens to question our very masculinity. This can produce its own form of insensitivity as the very identification of masculine

141

identity with reason can make us seem invulnerable to the hurt we cause and are caused in our relationships. Often we are slow to recognise our needs ourselves, especially if we strongly identify ourselves with our achievements in the public realm. I have shown how Kantian moral theory can work to *impersonalise* our experience as we become used to identifying ourselves with the external goals and ends we set ourselves. This can make it difficult, especially for men, to explore the tension between what we need for ourselves individually and the ways we can nourish our selves and what is expected of us in the public world of work. Our experience becomes *externalised* as we find it difficult, if not impossible, to say what we are individually feeling in an emotional situation. We have learnt how to control ourselves, only to discover that this has limited our access to our emotional lives and desires. We find it easier to assess a situation externally, as if we are not part of it ourselves. We can feel speechless when we are asked to give an emotional response ourselves.

When liberal theory talks in quite general terms about the freedom it guarantees to people to pursue their own ends, it rarely thinks that this helps articulate the experience of men rather than women. Since a rationalist conception of morality promises that the independent workings of reason will alone clarify what we should morally do, it discourages us from recognisimg any need to develop more contact with our emotions and feelings. This can only be a distraction from the main task. This leaves no space within which to illuminate the tension between what we want and need for ourselves and the demands institutions make upon us. Rawls also makes this impossible as he tears into two separate worlds considerations of justice which concern the basic organisation of society and the moral worth of individual lives. But often it is the interrelationship between these different spheres that is so crucial. If we think for a moment about men's relationships to children we are immediately struck by how this is mediated by the organisation of work. There is a definite tension between the kind of person I have to be to relate to children in a close and loving way and the person I have to be to compete in the impersonal world of work. This tension cannot be dissolved through making an intellectual decision, nor can we simply switch our identities in the different spheres of our lives. If I want to develop a fuller relationship with my child then I have to be ready to give time and space to this relationship. How I learn to cope with this situation will partly depend upon how much I need this fuller relationship and how much I am prepared to give up for it. I am likely to feel deeply torn as I realise there is no way of resolving this situation, especially as long as I am forced to work full-time. I might feel that both my life and probably the life of my child would be enriched if we could develop our relationship while feeling hopelessly torn between the different things I want for myself.[7]

A distinction between needs and wants could be crucial in making me aware that this is not something I just want for myself. Too often we think of wants as if they are matters of taste without realising the difficulties involved in clarifying our wants. I have argued against Kant that rather than being a necessary sign of our dependency, this can be an important moment in clarifying our autonomy. We can be so used to identifying ourselves with what we ought to want, think or feel that there can be considerable risk and fear involved in asserting even simple wants and desires. At the very least this is a form of self-expression in which we are making ourselves vulnerable to being rejected or refused by others. So again we have to be morally prepared to make qualitative distinctions in the full awareness of the reality of individual lives. Certainly people can be trapped by their emotions, feelings and desires, but they can also learn to use them to express their autonomy and independence. In learning to accept the reality of our emotions and feelings we are learning to accept part of ourselves. We are extending the respect we feel for ourselves as well as opening ourselves to a greater sensitivity to the difficulties others face in discovering their autonomy and independence. At the very least this makes us aware that we can seem to be autonomous when we are not, since we have learnt to silence our emotional lives and desires rather than live in an ongoing relationship with them. Often Kant has limited our moral vision through offering us a false notion of autonomy as the domination of our emotions and desires. As we extend our notions of rationality so we develop different senses of self-control.

As far as Kant is concerned it is only when we act out of a sense of duty that we exercise our autonomy. Since this is supposedly the only way our lives have dignity and moral worth, we are strongly encouraged to identify our sense of self with our reason which gives us access to what is morally required of us. Similarly, within deontological liberalism our rights are supposedly guaranteed through the independent workings of reason. But, as I have argued, this trades upon Kant's idea that it is only in the exercise of our reason that we can express our choice and so our freedom. Rawls wants to think of our conception of our happiness, goals and ends as a similar exercise of our freedom. Though at other times only when we use our reason to articulate our rights and sense of justice are we expressing our nature as free and equal rational beings. But our experience remains essentially fragmented as long as our emotions, feelings and desires are to be discounted as genuine sources of knowledge.

There is an uneasy line where morality can turn into moralism. The strength which Kant gives to stand up for our principles, say to a liberal in South Africa who refuses to treat blacks and whites differently, or to a civil servant in England who refuses to lie to Parliament about the sinking of the Belgrano in the Falklands War, remains essential to liberal moral and political theory. If we have the moral strength we learn to stand up for our principles regardless of the consequences we will suffer. We know that we are doing what we believe to be right. This gives strength and integrity to liberal theory and speaks to a sense of autonomy and independence that needs to be valued and nurtured. But we also have to be aware of where the language of principles can limit our moral vision and sensitivity. It can encourage us into thinking that people share an equal control over their lives. We can think it is only an issue of strength of will if people are to do what is morally required of them. But, as Kant's discussion between rich and poor shows, we cannot assume that people stand in the same relation to the moral law. Kant realised that people show their moral worth in their inner struggle against their inclinations. Simone Weil works to extend our sense of the difficulties people face to include the external relations of power and subordination. She had learnt for herself that most working people are not in a position to 'abstract' themselves from social relationships. In a letter Weil wrote to a pupil in Spring 1935, she describes her first experience of factory work saying that:

> Goodness especially, when it exists in a factory, is something real; because the least act of kindness, from a mere smile to some little service, calls for a victory over fatigue and the

144

obsession with pay and all the overwhelming influences which drive a man in upon himself. And thought, too, calls for an almost miraculous effort of rising above the conditions of one's life. (*Seventy Letters*, pp. 11-12)[8]

Our moral theory should illuminate the nature of the difficulties people face in living autonomous and independent lives. The very universalism of Kantian ethics can make us think that we only have ourselves to blame if we cannot live up to the moral vision we have of ourselves. The very fragmentation between our principles and our experience can encourage us to mould our experience so that it conforms to the moral conceptions we have of ourselves. Often we fool ourselves because we do not want to acknowledge the reality of our feelings and emotions. We do our best to feel and desire in the way we think we are supposed to feel or desire. So, for instance, a woman might feel the greatest difficulty in allowing herself to feel angry at her husband for his alcoholism that had broken up their marriage. She cannot help feeling that somehow it must have been her fault because she had always thought that it was up to women to keep a marriage going. She cannot help blaming herself, though others have told her that her husband has to take his own responsibility for what has happened to the relationship. Even if she felt angry she did not want to acknowledge it because she did not want to think of herself as an angry kind of person. In this way she can deny the reality of her experience because it does not fit with the image she has of herself. She could be blocking the possibility of change for herself since it can make it harder for herself to regain a sense of her independent life. If she had felt as a matter of principle that it is wrong for people to get divorced this could make it even more difficult for her to build a new kind of relationship with herself.

For Kant our autonomy and independence is guaranteed in our relationship to the moral law. Deontological liberalism has inherited this conception in the idea that our individuality is guaranteed in the rights we possess. Kant was prepared to deny equal rights to people unless they were also socially independent of each other, but liberal theory has tended to silence his concerns with its idea that we show our respect by being prepared to abstract ourselves from social relations of power and subordination. In this way the idea that we are equally capable of living moral lives supposedly serves as a guarantee that we can enjoy equal political and legal rights. Kant himself never thought through the challenge to the autonomy of morality, preferring in the end to blame those who are powerless for their subordination and dependency. This sustains the idea that people only have themselves to blame for their unhappiness and lack of success, especially in a liberal society which guarantees to them an equality of opportunity. The moral significance of the structures of power and subordination are mystified as people learn to blame themselves for not taking fuller advantages of their education, which supposedly could have turned them into a factory manager rather than an assembly-line worker.

Once it is acknowledged that we are not equally able to live moral lives, issues of moral autonomy can no longer be separated from social relations of power and subordination. This issue is clearly focused in Simone Weil's discussions with a factory owner in Bourges, when she was trying to initiate a factory newspaper. She challenges the very universalism that is implicit in the autonomy of morality when she challenges our right to judge others because of the ways we think we might ourselves act in the same situation. We blind ourselves to the moral realities unless we are prepared to acknowledge the realities of power and dependency in our expectations of others. As Weil writes:

> The fact that you yourself in the past were bolder with your superiors gives you no right to judge. Not only was your economic position totally different, but also your moral position – if, at least, as I think I understood, you were at that time holding more or less responsible jobs. I myself, I think, would run equal or even greater risks in resisting my university superiors if necessary (suppose we had some authoritarian type of government) and with far more determination than I should show in a factory against the overseer or manager. And why? ... In the university I have rights and dignity and a responsibility to defend. What have I to defend as a factory worker, when I have to renounce all rights every morning at the moment I clock in? All I have left is my life. It would be too much to be expected to endure the subordination of a slave and at the same time to face dangers like a free man.
> (*Seventy Letters*, pp. 33-4)

As long as we think of morality in terms of providing reasons for action which are supposedly universal, we think we are asking of others no less than we ask of ourselves. Often we end up blaming people for not using opportunities available to them. This seems to add legitimacy to our own positions of power. This partly explains the touch of contempt the manager felt when the workers remained silent at a meeting of the Co-operative. But as Weil was concerned to stress, against the force of a Kantian tradition:

> These people are defenceless at the mercy of a force completely
> disproportionate to their own, against which they can do
> nothing, and by which they are continually in danger of being
> crushed – and when, with bitter hearts, they have resigned
> themselves to submission and obedience, they are despised for
> lack of courage by the very men who control that force.
> (*Seventy Letters*, p. 34)

Kant acknowledged the importance of people not being dependent upon others for their very means of livelihood. This makes it difficult for people to speak their own minds, let alone formulate ends for themselves. The only way he could preserve his assumption of the autonomy of morality was to assume that people are independent and self-sufficient unless an inequality is created because some people have voluntarily accepted the help of others. This helps him sustain the notion that it is inner difficulties, such as a weakness of the will, that can explain why people fail to act out of a sense of duty. So we might hear a liberal idea that a worker is always free to tell his boss what he thinks. If he believes in what he has to say he should be prepared to risk his job. Such a sentiment illuminates the difficulties which a liberal moral consciousness has in grasping the reality of class, sex or racial relations of power and subordination. Even the idea that we are always free to have our own ideas and feelings, even if we do not feel free to express them, betrays difficulties in revealing moral relations of autonomy and dependence. As long as we think of this in terms of an act of will and determination we fail to appreciate, for instance, the depth and complexity of the issues of emotional dependence faced by the woman who is struggling to free herself from the marriage she has just ended. Freud helps us to realise that it is not simply an issue of pulling herself together and putting her past behind her. Sometimes we can only free ourselves from our histories by acknowledging them and painfully working through the sources of dependency in our early family relationships. This is one of the ways psychoanalysis can enrich our sense of ourselves as historical beings who have to work through the pain and difficulties of a past we have often chosen to repress or ignore, if we are to discover a more genuine autonomy and independence. This is partly to develop the very sense of inner struggle with ourselves that is an integral part of Kant's inheritance, even if it is, at least in Freud's case, to extend and enrich the rationalist framework within which this is placed.

But we have to place these efforts in a broader social and historical context. Issues of autonomy and independence have to be recognised in their outer and inner relations, if we are to grasp the nature of the social transformations necessary if people are to live free and independent lives. If Kant was right to stress a link between our existence as moral beings and our sense of dignity and moral worth, he limited himself in his identification of morality with reason. If we discover a broader sense of dignity and moral worth, recognising ways our feelings and desires can have their own dignity, we extend our conception of morality. Kant's sense that our dignity lies in our not being determined by external conditions could never be given a clear enough focus, since he brought our emotions and desires as well as our social and historical conditions under the same category of 'externality'. He assumed that emotions and feelings were determining our behaviour, getting us to do things we would not rationally choose to do. But if our feelings, say of anger, seem to be overwhelming us in just this sense, there can be times when our anger is an appropriate and rational response, say to someone who is bullying us. If we adopt Kant's general conception of our emotional lives and assume that we can only control our feelings if we dominate them through some kind of externalised relationship, we could be creating the very situation in which they do seem to be continually threatening us. If we are continually struggling to eradicate and silence their influence on our lives, we can never learn to build a form of control through developing an inner relationship to our emotional lives. This seems to be the form of control the young Freud was interested in creating.

Sometimes relationships of power work to make it difficult for us to have our own feelings. This can help us appreciate our feelings as an integral part of our autonomy. Again Simone Weil makes us aware of how factory work can even deny us our fits of irritation and bad humour as workers struggle to 'make the grade':

In front of the machine, the worker has to annihilate his soul,
his thought, his feelings, and everything for eight hours a day.
If he is irritated, or sad, or disgusted, he must swallow and
completely suppress his irritation, sadness, or disgust; they
would slow down his output. And the same with joy. ... As
for one's own fits of irritation or bad humour, one must
swallow them; they can have no outlet either in word or
gesture. All one's movements are determined all the time by
the work. (*Seventy Letters*, p. 22)

Learning to control our feelings can help still the pain and keep us
out of trouble. This is clear in a factory when it must seem prefer-
able not to feel anything, if you never have a chance to express
your feelings. But just as Kant stressed the critical importance to
our autonomy and independence to express our own ideas, rather
than simply to accept the ideas of others, it could be as significant
for us to have our own feelings and emotions. Both can be externally imposed and both can be sources of our individual dignity.
As we have to *work* to separate our own thoughts from those we
have automatically inherited, so we can *work* to make our emotions, feelings and desires our own. These can equally bring us into
conflict with dominant institutions. But in neither case is this something we can simply decide to do as an act of will, though we can
decide to *begin* such a process of exploration. As we gain a deeper
contact with ourselves our words and feelings come to have a
different weight and integrity. As an expression of our developing
autonomy they have an intrinsic worth, though Rawls is left without a way of fully acknowledging this. In relation to our ideas this
is something Kant is aware of and connects to his understanding
of moral autonomy. We have to learn to legislate for ourselves
rather than passively accept the dictates of the moral law. Like
other Enlightenment rationalists Kant learnt to privilege our mental faculties, since this is what makes us superior to animals and
also helps us challenge traditional authorities.

Feminist theory has helped illuminate a connection between a
rationalist moral tradition and the experience of men. Kant's ethics
illuminates the experience of men rather than women. This is
equally true of its universalism since, as men, we have often appro-
priated to ourselves the right to speak for others. Partly because
women have traditionally been more closely identified with emo-

tions and feelings, they have tended to conceive issues of autonomy and independence in different terms. Often brought up to find meaning and fulfilment in caring for others, it has often been more difficult for women to exist in their own right. Kantian ethics has made it harder for women to recognise the validity and integrity of their experience as it has held up ideals of independence and self-sufficiency. As Jean Baker Miller has pointed out in *Towards a New Psychology of Women*, women are more likely to define themselves in the context of human relationships and judge themselves in terms of their ability to care. But within a moral tradition which stresses individual autonomy and self-sufficiency, concern with relationships appears as a weakness of women rather than as a human strength. This insight is put to good use by Carol Gilligan when she realises that 'Women's deference is rooted not only in their social subordination but also in the substance of their moral concern. Sensitivity to the needs of others and the assumption of responsibility for taking care lead women to attend to voices other than their own...' (*In a Different Voice*, p. 16). So an apparent diffusion of relevant considerations and a reluctance to judge others according to categorical principles, which is often interpreted as a sign of women's moral weakness, is in fact inseparable from women's moral strength, an overriding concern with relationships and responsibilities.[9]

In liberal moral and political theory we are centrally concerned with acknowledging that people will have different values and ends. But it is harder to grasp that men and women might have different values, let alone different ways of conceiving morality. It is simply a matter of chance if individuals come to share the same values or ends. But for Virginia Woolf it was not only 'obvious that the values of women differ very often from the values which have been made by the other sex', but also that 'it is the masculine values which prevail' (*A Room of One's Own*, p. 76). It is because men often have the power to define values in a patriarchal society that women are left to question the normality of their feelings and responses. Often they will feel that their experience of themselves and their relations with others will not be acknowledged or validated. Often this will lead them to alter their judgements in deference to others. It will be harder for women to trust their own experience and find a voice which expresses themselves truthfully. You could say that because men and women stand in a relationship of power and subordination within the larger society, they do not stand equally before the moral law. But probably this does not go far enough. Our moral traditions themselves need to be reformulated if women are to feel recognised and validated in their experience. Again this calls for a sense of respect that can give due weight to the moral significance of our emotional lives and relationships.

It is hard to realise that when we think of morality in terms of rules and universal principles we are unwittingly universalising from the experience of a particular sex or class. It is a continuing strength of both a Marxist and a feminist tradition to remind us of the ease with which are able to universalise a particular social and historical experience. We develop a standard we use to judge an experience that can no longer be grasped in its own terms. Gilligan has argued that women's moral development has somehow to be understood in its own terms. If we begin with a recognition of the *validity* of women's own experience we discover the outline of a different moral conception than described by Freud, Piaget or Kohlberg who have all insistently judged and found wanting the experience of women, having judged them by the standards of men. She discerns a crucial difference between a morality of rights and a morality of responsibility which comes closer to expressing the ways women often seem to conceive moral issues. A morality of rights differs in its emphasis on separation rather than connection and in its consideration of the individual rather than the relationship as primary. In a morality of responsibility 'the moral problem arises from conflicting responsibilities rather than from competing rights and requires for its resolution a mode of thinking that is contextual and narrative rather than formal and abstract' (*In a Different Voice*, p. 19). This is illuminating even if it makes the distinction too generally without really connecting it to the historical relationship of power between the sexes. It reveals an important contrast between a conception of morality as fairness which is geared to arriving at an objectively fair resolution to moral dilemmas upon which all rational persons could agree, and a conception which is more concerned with the understanding of responsibility and relationships.

Since men are often brought up to identify their masculinity with independence and self-sufficiency, we are more likely to feel threatened by dependency and intimacy. As long as we think of autonomy in terms of reason, it is unlikely to be an issue for us.

But for women who learn to identify themselves in relation to others there is the task of modulating what can so easily become an excessive sense of responsibility. Often women learn a sense of autonomy through recognising that other people have to take their own responsibility for their lives. But as Gilligan appreciates this can help make clear 'why a morality of rights and non-interference may appear frightening to women in its potential justification of indifference and unconcern' and also why 'from a male perspective, a morality of responsibility appears inconclusive and diffuse, given its insistent contextual relativism' (*In a Different Voice*, p. 22).

If, for instance, someone cannot accept any longer that abortion is wrong as a matter of principle, they may still think along with Kant that their personal emotions and feelings are irrelevant in the situation and can only cloud what should be a rational decision. This can become a repressive assumption which imposes a particular moral conception of what can be considered relevant in the situation. Reasons have to be impersonal and generally applicable. This could well make it harder for a woman to share her feelings about the situation. Even if this is allowed it is only as an emotional release which may show how deeply people feel about the situation, but can be no part of a moral clarification of what is involved in the situation. This can produce a form of emotional and moral control in which people are encouraged to distance themselves from the situation, thinking this is the only way to become clear and objective in our moral thinking. But this can serve as an instance of men's control in relation to women, especially if both parties take for granted that only reason can give us genuine knowledge. Often women are silenced as men appropriate the right to work out what the 'right thing to do is'.

Not only can this help men to separate themselves from their own feelings about the situation but it can give us a way of sustaining and legitimating control of the situation. This makes it difficult to realise that taking responsibility for the situation might involve both men and women sharing their feelings about the situation. The fact that our feelings are ambiguous, contradictory and difficult to contact does not make it any the less important to share them. It has been a misleading assumption of Kant's to think that because our feelings change they are essentially unreliable. We can learn from these changes as they can help us recognise how complicated a situation we are often facing. Kant does not realise that

152

clarity is a process and that often we have to share our confusions, resentments and hopes before we can think clearly about the situation. Often it is only if we can feel clearly and honestly without judging or shaping our experience so that it fits in with what we think we ought to feel, that we seem to gain clarity in the situation. But we are not helped in this process if we are continually trying to be disinterested and objective. This can make it more difficult for us to take responsibility in the situation. We can be left intellectualising our experience without realising difficulties we have individually in sharing our individual feelings about what is going on.

Paradoxically the idea of a woman's right to choose in relation to abortion has often reinforced a traditional male attitude that abortion does not have anything to do with us. This itself is a denial of our responsibility and involvement in the situation, even if it remains crucial to realise a woman's right to choose because of the overwhelming impact that having a child has on a woman's life. This can sharply focus the issues of autonomy and dependence as a woman, say, realises that she has always assumed that she will be looked after and has never really learnt to take responsibility for herself. At the same time this can mean learning to have her own feelings about the situation. Kantian morality can make us think that if we have made the right decision then we have no 'reason' to feel sad or upset. Often, as men, it is difficult to appreciate the depth of feelings women can feel in relation to an abortion. Often we do not want to acknowledge our own feelings, especially if we know we can do nothing to change the situation. We find it hard to accept that a woman might feel the need to mourn the loss of a child, even if she has clearly made the decision herself and knows there was not an alternative for her. This can accompany feelings of relief. Unfortunately our moral traditions rarely recognise the moral significance of working through our feelings in this way. Even though we think we are helping others to recover, often we are simply making things easier for ourselves.

Within a Kantian tradition it is rationality which becomes a moral quest. We learn to control our feelings through dominating them and work for a time when our emotions and feelings have less and less influence over our lives. This is a process of reformulating our experience and accepting a certain vision of our lives. I have shown the different ways it disorganises crucial features in our moral experience. It limits the respect we can learn to have for ourselves and our sense of the moral experience of others. In a crucial sense we are left divided against ourselves, as we learn to devalue and disdain our natures so that we can elevate our sense of ourselves as rational moral beings. We are constantly trying to mould our experience and our lives to live up to these moral ideals which our moral traditions set for us. Not only do we often fail to live up to these ideals of ourselves, so that we often blame and punish ourselves, but we rarely imagine that these ideals could themselves be flawed.

I have argued that Kant leaves us with an attenuated conception of the individual, even though this is traditionally taken as a strength of his moral theory. Likewise he is unable to substantiate, for similar reasons, his idea of respect that we should not treat people merely as means but always as ends in themselves. This idea continues to echo and promises crucial insights into the realities of subordination and oppression. But it is an idea that Kant cannot develop without challenging his basic conception of the autonomy of morality.

2 MEANS AND ENDS

Kant's injunction that we should not treat people merely as means but always as ends in themselves was at the heart of his conception of respect. It was an insight he constantly returned to, but was never able to elaborate or explain. I have attempted to show that this was a failure which goes to the core of the rationalism and individualism of his more formalistic ethics. It is only later when he comes to the edge of challenging the very assumptions upon which the autonomy of morality was based, in his discussion of the relations between rich and poor, that he glimpses what this would involve. The notion of respect as an attitude we can freely take up towards others or the idea of respect as non-interference both sustain our freedom in our moral relations. The autonomy of morality is guaranteed in the idea that we are equally able to live moral lives as we are free to relate to others in any way we choose.

The idea that people should not be treated merely as means towards the ends of others is situated in Kant's opposition to a market which would reduce all objects to commodities which have a price. Kant's sense that human life has an intrinsic value means showing that people are not objects who can be exchanged on the market. But as long as Kant assumed that the sensible world as a world of determination becomes a world of equivalence and price, there was no way in which our everyday material lives could be a source of dignity and moral worth. Kant was led to assume that all our activities were done for individual advantage and that it was only morality which could redeem us. But this was to fragment our experience of ourselves and leave us with a fundamentally divided conception of the person.

It is only to the extent that we are moral beings that we are owed equal respect with all other rational beings and are to be recognised as ends in ourselves. This gives a particular character and form to our sense of dignity and self-esteem since our 'dignity as a moral man' is heightened in a comparison with our 'insignificance as a natural man'. This is the sense in which our Kantian inheritance leaves us divided against ourselves. We learn to disinherit and disown our emotions, feelings and desires, willing that they be no part of our identities. As we learn to dominate external nature so we also learn to dominate and control nature within ourselves. Often we unknowingly project this rejected part of ourselves. We barely realise the ways we disempower ourselves as we reject these aspects of our experience. We weaken our connection with our somatic experience as we identify with our ideas and thoughts. We learn to despise our emotions and feelings when they do not accord with the images we have created for ourselves. We judge ourselves harshly, finding no way to accept these emotions and desires as an integral part of ourselves. Unwittingly we live out Kant's familiar distinction between 'man regarded as a person' and 'man in the system of nature'.

Our abilities and talents have a market value which can make us more useful to others but they leave us in the system of nature. They have no place in expressing our individualities nor can we distinguish when they are being abused or exploited. There is no way of giving *moral weight* to the importance of people being able to express their abilities and talents in their everyday activities and relationships. As Hegel realised there is no way to acknowledge the moral significance of human labour, of people discovering ways of expressing themselves through exercising their abilities and talents. We simply have to reconcile ourselves to being part of the world of equivalence and price as long as we remain within the system of nature.

For Kant it is only morality which 'is exalted above all price and so admits of no equivalence' that can give our lives dignity and moral worth. But this is to separate dignity and moral worth from the expression of our individualities in our activities and relationships. Kant assumes that things have either a price or a dignity but they cannot have both. It is only to the extent that we can raise ourselves above the world of equivalence and price in the sensible world that our lives can find dignity or moral worth at all. To the extent that we have duties laid upon us by our own reason, we can transfer ourselves to the intelligible realm. This helps explain why Kant thinks that we can treat people as means if we relate to them in the system of nature, as long as we realise we cannot treat people 'merely' as means without denying that they also exist as moral beings within the intelligible realm. It is this fragmentation of our experience as lived between different realms that has been crucial to a liberalism that has wanted to insist that working people can exist as equal citizens, despite the relations of subordination they are forced to endure at work. This is to draw distinctions between different parts of the social world which Kant regarded as part of the determinations of the system of nature.

This has helped liberal political theory acknowledge the importance of the different realms within which people live their lives. Social democratic politics has given working people a sense that they exist as equal citizens sharing definite legal and political rights, whatever the indignities and humiliations they are forced to endure at work. An awareness of the historical struggles which have been fought to establish these rights makes these more precious to working people than we can grasp, if we think of them as simply mystifying, underlying relations of class power. Where the conditions of work, say in factories or offices, tend to be similar, working people often appreciate an employer who treats them with respect in their personal relations. Working people often become sensitive to the ways they are treated in different jobs, often assuming that the basic conditions of hierarchy and subordination are unchangeable. An ethical theory, which limits moral relations to personal relations on the assumption that we are free to relate to others with respect, at least acknowledges how sensitive people are to being hurt and humiliated in personal relations with others. If people

156

suffer at the hands of machines it does not seem to affect them in the same way. It is as if people accept a necessity in their relations with a machine that is governing and controlling their every movement while they feel that people could relate differently towards them, if only they would make the effort.

Kant assumes that we have the power not to treat others merely as a means but as ends in themselves. Sometimes this means little more than recognising that others are also moral beings who have duties laid upon themselves by their own reason. But even this declares certain forms of human relationships as morally inadmissible, for instance slavery. Kant also learnt to worry about the relations between rich and poor. He became less convinced that people could abstract themselves from the social relations of power and subordination. If the rich could learn to relate to the poor as if there was equality between them, the poor had to learn gratitude for the help given them. Kant could only sustain his conviction in the autonomy of morality through assuming that these inequalities were voluntarily incurred, as the poor accepted help they did not really need. But this assumed an independence and self-sufficiency that Kant had himself been forced to challenge, when he discusses the sources of wealth in the unequal distribution of property. But this threatened to turn it into an issue of justice as some had more than they needed while others had less. The idea of the autonomy of morality could not then be sustained.

Kant was concerned to show that people shared a human dignity that needed to be affirmed in the face of an indifferent universe. Within an emerging capitalist market economy all value was being reduced to the single measure of exchange value. Qualitative distinctions were being subverted as different commodities were brought into relation with each other through the medium of money. Everything had its price and this seemed no different when it came to the skills and talents of people. Kant perceived this as a threat to human dignity, but felt unable to challenge the reign of the commodity within the system of nature which was essentially a realm of determination. Our dignity and moral worth could not be affirmed within the organisation of the social world, but only if we elevate ourselves above this world into an intelligible world of moral values. It was in this sense that we can recognise ourselves as ends in ourselves. We were to be continually drawn back to an awareness of our duties as moral beings. But this is to fragment our experience as we seem left without moral terms to challenge the prevailing relations of power and subordination. It can seem as if the poor and oppressed have to learn to bear the indignities and humiliations of social life secure in the knowledge that salvation is only to be sought in a spiritual realm.

But Kant's injunction that we should not treat people merely as means but always as ends in themselves seems also to contain a stronger critique of prevailing relationships of power. Certainly, to the extent that this is a reminder of how we are to relate to others in our personal relations, it can limit our moral awareness to a sensitivity to how we have been treated, especially if we assume that people are always free to relate with equal respect. So, for instance, we can find ourselves blaming an insensitive teacher for our miserable experience within the educational system. We think that if the teacher had been prepared to make more of an effort we would have experienced school quite differently. So we are encouraged to personalise institutional relationships of power. Within a Kantian tradition we find it harder to develop a larger framework of analysis in which the issues concern not only the teacher but the inadequacies of an educational system which trains and employs them. Within the common sense of a liberal moral culture inequalities become *individualised* as people learn either to blame their teachers or else blame themselves for not having worked harder at school. The educational system has assumed a critical position in legitimating social inequalities, especially if people are ready to accept that they have enjoyed an equality of opportunity. This means that if a man ends up as an assembly-line worker he only has himself to blame. If he had tried harder or been cleverer, he could have been the managing director. It becomes difficult to think of inequalities in different terms. People turn in on themselves as their anger no longer seems to have a legitimate external focus. People learn to take out their frustrations on themselves or those close to them.

Social theory often gets locked into an arid framework where we think it is either the individual teacher to blame or else it is the social relations of education we have to transform. We are presented with the stark alternative of either individualistic or social explanations. This is echoed in the debate between liberalism and orthodox Marxism as it is between positivism and phenomenology. We feel forced to choose between notions of individual and social responsibility, thinking that either the individual has to be held responsible for the life he or she makes, or else it is society which is to be blamed. But these are false choices which themselves frustrate our ability to grasp our individual experience within a social and historical network of relationships. If we begin to grasp the significance of our class background, our ethnicity or our gender for the kind of individual experience we have had or the ways we have been treated, our individuality does not have to be threatened. I have argued that it can be deepened as we learn to define ourselves more clearly. If this kind of dialectical grasp is associated with Hegel and Marx, it is also part of the continuing appeal of Kant's idea that we should not be treated merely as a means. This is something Simone Weil realised when in her *Lectures on Philosophy* she defines oppression as 'the negation of Kant's principle. Man is treated as a means' (p. 136). She also goes on to say that from a moral point of view 'Oppression is an insult to the dignity of human nature' (p. 138).

The uncertainties in Kant's later writings show a concern with the inequalities of social life, especially where some have more than they need while others have less than they need. This produces a form of dependency that threatens the idea that people can exist as ends in themselves. Kant seems to admit that he had attempted to establish the dignity and intrinsic worth of human beings, against the idea of their being treated as replaceable commodities, on too narrow a foundation. He had assumed that we could simply abstract from everyday social relations of power and subordination and guarantee our existence as beings who exist in our own right in an independently defined moral realm. But this was to appropriate a limited conception of morality and so make it impossible to explore the *moral* issues involved in social relations of power and subordination. Paradoxically, it would also leave him unable to explain what it meant to treat others as means. These were issues Kant did not have to face in his earlier writings since he tacitly assumed that people were independent and self-sufficient, at least as moral agents. Liberal theory has tended to sustain this earlier view.

Structured relations of dependency threaten the ability of a person to live an independent life. Kant seems to promise an enriched conception of autonomy when he seems aware of how much he had assumed material conditions of independence and self-sufficiency. If we cannot any longer assume that our autonomy and independence is guaranteed in our relations to the moral law, then we have to be more concerned with the material conditions of autonomy and independence. Not only do we have to be prepared to consider the moral issues of inequality and dependency, but we can no longer assume that we can abstract ourselves from prevailing relations of power and subordination. Kant could free himself from a concern with the inequalities of the social world because he did not think they produced structured relations of dependency that threatened our equality before the moral law. When it became clear how issues of dependency threatened his sense of moral autonomy, he could no longer stand aloof from the moral issues of inequality and dependency. This also meant considering how people can be treated as means, especially if this threatened their autonomy and independence. This has been an insight that has become central to the development of a feminist theory concerned to articulate the nature of women's autonomy in a man's world.

For instance, women have been concerned to challenge the ways they have been treated as sexual objects. Women have not been seen as people in their own right, but as means to satisfy the pleasures of men. I have alluded to this in different examples, but the point here is to illuminate Kant's discussion of being treated as an end in oneself. This connects to Kant's discussion of dependency, since women have talked about the difficulties of seeing themselves in their own terms, rather than solely in relation to men. So the idea, for instance, of being 'attractive' is automatically in relation to men, rather than in relation to themselves. Women have sought to define themselves in their own terms but have recognised that this has to be done collectively as well as in individual relationships. But this has also involved recognising the limits of a rationalism which has assumed that people could simply decide to relate differently. As men have learnt how difficult it is to relate to women not as sexual objects we have had to admit this is not solely under our rational control, as Kant would have us think. It also means coming to terms with our inherited traditions of masculinity.[10] For instance, we might become aware of how we rarely listen to what women have to say. Taking women intellectually seriously might be our way of learning to see them as individuals in their own right. But it also involves recognising the larger social relations of power and dependency which organise the context in which men and women relate. Kant realised the crucial importance of people defining their own terms and articulating their own ends, rather than tacitly accepting those with authority and power over them. Even though he denies this right to women, he leaves a language of autonomy and dependency which helps identify critical issues.

Put in different terms, Kant can make us suspicious when we speak for others, rather than let people discover their own voice. He seems to recognise that structured relations of dependency work to deny those who are powerless or oppressed their own voice. But if Kant helps sustain the idea that people need to learn to exist in their own right, not simply in relation to others, his moral rationalism only dimly perceived the nature of the *difficulties* people face in this quest. He constantly feels drawn back to acknowledge the inner difficulties of will. But if it is one of the strengths of his ethical theory to guarantee our dignity as 'an absolute inner worth' it is also a source of its weakness. It makes us insensitive to the different ways our dignity can be *undermined* by social relations and people can *fail* to treat us as people in our own right. This makes it difficult to recognise the need we have to be confirmed and acknowledged in our relations with others if we are to believe in ourselves. This is hardly surprising since Kant is concerned to confirm the sovereignty of the individual against feudal and aristocratic relations of dependency. The idea of the individual as choosing his or her own ends and finding fulfilment in achieving these individual ends has to be placed historically. We have to be wary of generalising to different historical contexts where relations of power and dependency assume a very different form.

In a society in which people can live independent and self-sufficient lives we can also imagine that people can be free to choose their own ends. But in a capitalist society where the relations between rich and poor have been structured according to the ownership of the means of production the issue of dependency becomes central. It also becomes more pressing to consider the various ways people are treated as means, rather than as ends in themselves. The assumption that we are free to relate to others with equal respect becomes suspect. We can no longer define our moral concerns as about how we are individually to relate to others. The Kantian definition of morality as centrally concerned with the issue of 'what ought I to do?' is itself, as I have argued, built upon a material assumption of independence and self-sufficiency. But Kant makes us crucially aware that it is when relations of dependency threaten

161

our autonomy that we are likely to be treated as means to the ends of others who have power over us, especially if it is power over our means of livelihood. This can potentially extend the language of autonomy beyond a critique of class relations of power to include issues of gender and ethnicity. Wherever we tacitly accept the definitions of those with power, as definitions of our own reality, issues of autonomy are raised.

At the same time as our moral traditions can help articulate and identify crucial aspects in our moral experience, they can also disempower us and weaken our vision. Though Kant can help us value our independence and autonomy he also makes it difficult to identify the process through which we can become ends in ourselves. As a duty-based conception of morality Kant focuses our attention on doing what we ought to do. He implicitly sets this in opposition to what we might want to do, assuming that our desires are inherently selfish and self-seeking. But this can make it difficult to define our own ends, especially if we do not live in a society of independent farmers but within relations of class, sexual and ethnic power and dependency. If we are anxious to do the right thing, this can extend beyond morality to different spheres of our lives. Rather than help us develop a strong and independent sense of self, we can become weakened and undermined if we are always doing what is expected of us without a sense of what we want to do for ourselves. We feel scared of getting it wrong, first with our parents and then with our teachers. Kant has undermined the very trust and confidence we might otherwise have developed in our feelings, desires, needs and intuitions. Rather we have often learnt to despise this part of our nature, having learnt that at some basic level our natures are not to be trusted. This has been an integral part of a Protestant inheritance that has unwittingly weakened the very individuality that it is supposedly championing. We weaken ourselves as we become suspicious of our own natures. We can become fearful of discovering our own desires, lest they leave us in too much conflict with what is expected of us.

Mill was aware of this deeper conflict in the liberal inheritance, though he tended to think it was an issue of excessive calvinism. Mill shows the influence of a Kantian moral education and the weaknesses of a rationalist tradition that insists upon weakening our connection with our inclinations. He shows how we come to define ourselves externally:

I do not mean that they choose what is customary in
preference to what suits their own inclination. It does not
occur to them to have any inclination, except what is
customary. Thus the mind itself is bowed to the yoke: even in
what people do for pleasure, conformity is the first thing
thought of; they like in crowds; they exercise choice only
among things commonly done: peculiarity of taste, eccentricity
of conduct, are shunned equally with crimes: until by dint of
not following their own nature they have no nature to follow:
their human capacities are withered and starved ... (*On
Liberty*, Chapter 3, p. 190)

People become incapable of any strong wishes or pleasures and
generally cease to have 'either opinions or feelings of home growth'
(p. 190). Mill asks us rhetorically whether we think this is a desirable condition of human nature, while at the same time expecting
us partly to recognise ourselves in this picture. Even though we
may not like to recognise ourselves in this mirror, Mill thinks it is
a condition that has become quite common. But it presents a challenge that liberal theory has rarely faced being ready to guarantee
a situation in which people are supposedly equally free to choose
their own ends.

Within a moral culture in which people assume themselves to be
free because they are guaranteed the freedom to choose their own
ends it becomes difficult to discover a reality of unfreedom. We
discover, contrary to Kant, that as we have weakened our inclinations, we have *also* weakened our capacities for independent
thought and judgement. Our reason does not have the kind of
independent existence that a rationalist moral tradition has assumed. Where we expect to praise a public discourse of individuality and self-expression we are forced to recognise a reality in which
'our human capacities are withered and starved'. We can no longer
take a liberal political theory at face value but need a language in
which to investigate the moral realities it helps produce.

The enlightenment tradition had established its claim to human
equality on the basis of an independent faculty of reason. It is
because we are rational beings that we can be moral beings and so
deserving of equal respect. But this tradition carried a central weakness in that it could only affirm our humanity through denigrating
our natures. We had to learn to dominate a nature that was con-

stantly threatening our claim to exist as equal rational beings. Since women were deemed closer to nature, the relationship between the sexes had to be established as a relationship of domination, as an identification of masculinity with rationality was established. Kant was important in giving a secular expression of the idea that we are equal in the eyes of God, in the notion that we are equal before the moral law. But, as I have argued, this leaves us with an impoverished conception of the person, as we realise that respect for the person is respect for the moral law. Our sense that we are equal human beings 'who are as good as other people' could only be given a limited expression within this tradition. This shows itself most clearly in the difficulties Kant has in exploring what it means to be treated as a means and what it means to exist as an end in ourselves.

Kant was concerned to strengthen a person standing up for what he or she knows to be right regardless of what this costs them in the favour of others. He wanted us to learn that this would often mean doing things we did not want to do, or things that were not in our interest. It is in this sense that morality makes independent demands upon us. This is partly what led Kant to stress the impersonal, disinterested and universal character of morality. If this helps illuminate central aspects in our moral experience, it also disorganises our grasp of both the individuality and the collective character of other aspects of our moral experience. It can make us think that when we face a moral decision, such as the decision about an abortion, we have to begin by putting our feelings aside, or that reasons have to be universal if they are to count as morally relevant. This can make it harder to appreciate that we are facing what is also a crucial personal decision in our lives. We can find ourselves *displaced* as if the situation it not really happening to us at all. Very soon this can become a form of pathology as we discover ourselves disconnected from our experience, as if we are trapped into being some kind of impersonal observer of our own lives. The fact that this is sometimes recommended as an appropriate moral standpoint, rather than simply helpful in particular situations, is disturbing about the condition of our moral theory.

Within a Kantian moral tradition we learn to discount our desires, feelings and needs to do what is right. This can so easily build fear and tension into our character formation as we can become continually anxious to do what is right. We learn not to risk ourselves because we fear being made to feel small in front of others. This is clear in a school situation in which pupils can be scared of the wrath of their teachers if they get the answers wrong. I heard from a young girl how her teacher had ripped up a story she had written about herself because it had spelling mistakes. She felt humiliated, even though the teacher may well have thought he had to be strict if they were to learn. He was interested in results. John Lennon expressed some of this painful experience in his song 'Working Class Hero':

As soon as you're born they make you feel small
By giving you no time instead of it all
Till the pain is so big you feel nothing at all
A working class hero is something to be
A working class hero is something to be

They hurt you at home and they hit you at school
They hate you if you're clever and they despise a fool
Till you're so fucking crazy you can't follow their rules.

In a moral culture where the focus is often on 'doing what is right' we do not sensitise ourselves to responding to the needs of others. This is hardly surprising if we have learnt to deny our own needs. We automatically assume that if we give people what they need, even at a very early age, then we are indulging them. Even newly born babies can be thought of as manipulating their mothers with their cries, so the babies have to learn 'who is in charge' before they leave the maternity hospitals. Since babies are assumed not capable of reason, there is no basis for our respect. But this itself is a challenge to our moral conceptions since parents can learn to respect a baby's needs and wants as they learn to differentiate the different cries. The baby can feel validated in its own needs, rather than made to feel it is not entitled to have needs at all, which is the way 'they make you feel small, by giving you no time instead of it all'. It can become difficult for parents to learn to trust their judge-ment even about the needs of their children, if they have learnt that there is an externally established set of rules they have to conform to. People feel disempowered and weakened as they become anxious about doing things wrong, rather than learning to trust themselves. We learn not to listen to the cries, as we have learnt not to listen to ourselves.

165

This is also critical of a permissiveness which would ignore the needs of parents. Children have also to learn boundaries as they learn to respect their parents, partly through learning that their parents have needs of their own, so they cannot be expected to be constantly available, nor would this be a desirable ideal in itself. But a Kantian tradition does not begin to help us acknowledge our own individual needs, nor does it help us think of respect as an acknowledgment and balance of different needs and desires. Children do not only learn through what their parents say, but through what they do. This recognition fosters a different vision of moral education and equal respect. If parents want a child to respect their needs for their own space and time, they can expect children will also learn to look on their room as their own space. Children will expect to be equally listened to when they limit access. This is a vision of mutual respect which fosters a recognition that individuals have needs they are entitled to fulfil. We mistreat people when we do not acknowledge their needs, or when we assume that we know better. According to psychoanalytic theory this core sense of entitlement is often established in our early family relationships. This is something we might never have learnt if we were made to feel we had constantly to fit into the requirements of others if we are not to be immoral or disobedient.

How are we to learn to respect our abilities, needs and capacities? What transformation in our moral traditions does this call for? Unless we can do this we have no basis for choosing our ends, even if we have the chance to. Only if we have developed our powers and capacities and discovered means of expressing them in our everyday lives can we exercise more effective control of our lives. John Lennon goes on to express the harsh reality which turns a capacity for choice into a fiction that is used against those who are subordinate and powerless:

> When they've tortured and scared you for 20 odd years
> Then they expect you to pick a career
> When you can't really function you're so full of fear
> A working class hero is something to be
> A working class hero is something to be.
> ('Working Class Hero', John Lennon/Plastic Ono Band, 1970)

Lennon talks of fear and pain as integral parts of relationships of power. This makes it difficult to explore our desires and feelings, lest we discover yet a further ground for people to put us down. As we learn to shape our experience so it fits images of right behaviour, we unconsciously use ourselves as means. We learn to take up an instrumental attitude towards ourselves. We do everything for the approval of others. Even though this was directly against the intention of Kant, the moral culture he has helped produce encourages this form of instrumentality. It is partly because we learn to treat ourselves in this way that we are less sensitive to the ways we hurt and abuse others.

This is partly fostered in Kant's sense that it is only when we are acting out of a sense of duty for the moral law that our lives have any dignity and moral worth. This is the only way we build a true sense of self. Rawls says as much when he has us acting out of a sense of justice. But, unlike Rawls, Kant gives little weight to the fact that we will naturally pursue our individual conceptions of happiness. This is why it is also hard for him to recognise the *moral significance* of treating someone merely as a means unless this can also be shown to compromise a person's ability to live a moral life. What matters to Kant is that we are denying due recognition to a person's moral and spiritual nature when we deny people as ends in themselves. This is because when we follow our individual ends we are following a false sense of self which is not only self-interested but denies us a fulfilment of our higher self. A categorical distinction is drawn between a true and false self which mirrors the distinction between reason and inclinations. This leaves us with no way of *differentiating* between our different wants and desires as we come into closer contact with ourselves. This can be no part of defining and clarifying a sense of self nor can it help transform an instrumental attitude as we learn to clarify what we want and need for ourselves as opposed to what others – like our families and teachers – want from us. Nor is this part of learning to respect our own process and development.

When Kant reminds us that we have an intrinsic value, he is inculcating a certain vision of ourselves. But his reliance upon our individual relationships to the moral law to sustain our human dignity does not help us create a strong enough sense of our individuality. It leaves Kant without a way of explaining why people should not be exchanged on the market like other commodities. If he can argue that our dignity as moral beings means we should not be treated 'merely' as means, he has great difficulty substantiating our existence as ends in ourselves. He wants to acknowledge the individuality of our moral experience so that we do not simply value ourselves according to the price of our labour on the market. If we begin to experience ourselves as beings whose value is fixed through the market, we deny the humanity in our moral being. But it is harder for Kant to say what forms of human labour and treatment are morally unjustifiable because they are an offence to our human dignity. Nevertheless this seems to be what he is reaching for in parts of *The Doctrine of Virtue*.

This is why it is important to show that issues of autonomy and independence cannot simply be guaranteed in our relationship to the moral law. We cannot assume a self that exists prior to its ends as if our independence remains invulnerable to social relations of power and subordination. As Kant was to discover for himself, issues of autonomy and independence have to be related to the empirical world. We cannot assume, as Sandel makes clear, 'that the values and relations we have are the products of choice, the possessions of a self given prior to its ends' (*Liberalism and the Limits of Justice*, p. 176). But Sandel settles for the point that for our deliberation about ends not to be an exercise in arbitrariness, we need to acknowledge constitutive attachments. We cannot regard our identities as never tied to our aims and attachments, our loyalties and convictions. In assuming that we exist as independent selves, deontological liberalism assumes that 'No transformation of my aims and attachments, however deeply held, could possibly engage my identity to begin with' (*Liberalism and the Limits of Justice*, p. 179). But Kant was led to question his assumption of moral autonomy and independence of the self when he considers relations between rich and poor. It is the issue of dependency which enables a challenge to Kant's dualistic vision of a world of determination and a world of freedom. It also helps clarify what it means to treat others as means and shows the weakness of a liberal tradition which has insisted, even against Kant, to assume the integrity and invulnerability of the individual. We cannot simply assume the human subject as a sovereign agent of choice who is free to come to his or her aims and purposes by acts of will. Nor can we assume, as Rawls does, that 'The essential unity of the self is already provided by the conception of right' (*A Theory of Justice*, p. 563).

In a relationship of subordination and dependency it can be

threatening for an individual to discover what he or she wants or needs since this can bring him or her into conflict with authority. Kant seemed to recognise that if the poor are dependent for their very means of livelihood, they have to learn to silence themselves. It will be so much easier if people limit the vision of their own lives and accept the definitions of the powerful. They do not have the material conditions in which they can realistically imagine different individual and collective ends. So, for instance, a peasant in Central America may know that his family was dispossessed from the fertile lands generations ago. He may also know that as far as the land-lord is concerned peasants are simply beasts of burden, a pair of arms and a strong back. These ideas may legitimate struggling against the difficulties of organising a collective resistance. People who want to be recognised as equal human beings can draw strength from Kant's sense of human dignity and moral worth. But they have to challenge the terms of a liberal moral theory which would assume that their dependency was somehow voluntarily in-curred. Otherwise, Kant at least seemed to acknowledge the justice of a struggle against unequal land distribution. It is then the con-ditions of life that need to be transformed, not simply the character of personal relations. In this situation justice cannot simply be detached and impartial but calls upon us to take sides. This acknowledges the prior claim of justice as a precondition for the autonomy of morality.

It is easy to think that as long as we treat others with respect and acknowledge their rights, we have exhausted our moral re-sponsibilities. We cannot be held responsible for the sins of the world. But we also cannot assume that individuals are free to make their own lives which only blinds us to the workings of social relations of power and dependency. Our moral theory has to illu-minate the contradictions in our social experience. It has to recog-nise that people's sense of self can be undermined as it works to connect our liberal moral language of equality and respect with the lived experience of dependency and subordination. We have to go beyond a Kantian tradition which focuses upon the accumulation of moral worth by a pre-existing self. With Kant we are left con-stantly judging ourselves as to whether we have done what duty has demanded. We tend to conceal our weaknesses which will often include our feelings as well as our needs. This remains an ethic of right actions. I have argued that this is not only an ethic of self-denial but it often unwittingly leaves us treating ourselves instrumentally, even as means. It does not help us understand the process through which we can learn to exist as people in our own right, either in our inner struggles or externally in defining ourselves against relationships of power and subordination.

Liberal moral and political theory inherits from Kant a weak and attenuated conception of the person. Since respect for a person is in effect respect for a moral law which is established through the independent workings of reason, we never learn what it means to respect our emotions, feelings, needs and desires. We learn to reject and silence these parts of our experience, not to respect them. A fuller conception of respect would involve an acceptance of our emotional lives and needs. At least we would have to know them and develop some kind of relationship with these different parts of ourselves as we learn to develop control in relation to them. But this would not be self-control *as domination* of our inclinations. Rather it would develop out of a sense that respect for our feelings and desires has to be an integral part of a fuller conception of my respect for myself as a person. For instance, if I acknowledge that I am scared of a teacher I can go on to decide what to do with this fear. If I learn to deny and ignore this fear, thinking that it is a sign of weakness, I am not learning to respect my feelings. Rather I am helping to produce a false sense of self. I am limiting the contact I have with myself as I am left feeling ashamed of a fear I do not want to know myself. It will give me yet a further reason to feel inadequate and put myself down. But as I learn to conceal my vulnerability I do not give myself a chance to accept these feelings and learn from them. I cannot learn what it could mean to be true to myself or learn to respect my feelings and desires, even if I decide not to act upon them. Rather I limit and constrict myself as I get trapped into living out images of myself that bear little relation to my lived experience. As Freud makes central to psychoanalysis, the rejection of this fear does not mean it disappears or becomes powerless to influence our behaviour. But this is a knowledge we often refuse.

For Kant learning to be true to ourselves means learning to value our rational moral selves in comparison with a nature we have to denigrate and deny. I have shown how this establishes a hierarchical split within ourselves in which we often unwittingly project feelings we cannot accept in ourselves. This shows the importance of our moral conceptions in the formation of our characters and sense of self, though it has rarely been explored. Crudely this has meant that our rationalist tradition has founded its sense of humanity too narrowly in its identification of morality with reason. Historically we have inherited the contradictory nature of the enlightenment tradition which the Frankfurt school did so much to explore. Somehow our moral theory has to face the sight of chamber music being played in the midst of Auschwitz. It is as if we can only sustain a rationalist sense of respect inherently threatened by the revelations of our natures, by projecting this nature on to others, who we reduce to the status of animals or beasts. This fate of being seen as less than human because of somehow being closer to nature has at different times been the lot of women, blacks, Jews and colonial peoples.[11] We should never forget that Kant was not simply a creature of his times in his denials of equal citizenship.

Liberal theory has tended to rely upon Kant for its sense of the integrity and separateness of persons, which seemed to be denied in a utilitarian theory that does not limit the permissible trade-offs between the satisfaction of different persons. In its recent forms liberal theory has been anxious not to offend Kant's principle that human beings are ends in themselves. But at the same time it has failed to challenge Kant's fragmented conception of the person which would be necessary to give a full enough account of being treated as a means. We are left with the idea that respecting others can only mean respecting their ideas, thoughts or opinions, or else being ready to see the world from their point of view. This is the only way people can make themselves visible and deserving of respect. But this is to view social life as a vast debating chamber in which we all have an equal right to talk. In the early 1970s, feminists insisted that women had to gain their own confidence if they were to set their own terms, rather than simply adapt to existing terms of discussion. This was to awaken new insights into a discussion of autonomy and independence which had always been crucial to liberal theory. Kant had thought of independence as an issue of self-sufficiency, though this could not be sustained when he thought about relations between rich and poor. Mill had also wanted to think of liberty as independence, that is, as Dworkin describes it 'the status of a person as independent and equal rather than subservient' (*Taking Rights Seriously*, p. 262). Dworkin is concerned to distinguish this from liberty as licence, the degree to which a person is free to do whatever he or she wants to do, which is an indiscriminate concept since it does not distinguish between forms of behaviour. But Mill differed from Bentham who thought the idea of liberty as independence would be sufficiently secured by a wide distribution of the right to vote and other political liberties in a democracy. As Dworkin has it, 'Mill saw independence as a further dimension of equality; he argued that an individual's independence is threatened not simply by a political process that denies him equal voice, but by political decisions that deny him equal respect' (*Taking Rights Seriously*, p. 163).

Though Dworkin recognises that 'Mill insists on the political importance of these moral concepts of dignity, personality and insult', wanting to make them 'available for political theory, and to use as the basic vocabulary of liberalism' (*Taking Rights Seriously*, p. 163), he tends to accept that some form of Mill's distinction between self-regarding and other-regarding actions can 'define political independence, because it marked the line between regulation that connoted equal respect and regulation that denied it' (*Taking Rights Seriously*, p. 263). Dworkin fails to explore the significant tensions in Mill's *On Liberty* where he talks about our capacities and abilities being 'withered and starved' because he agrees to limit subservience to a denial of our competence to decide what is right for ourselves. This places Dworkin's idea of equal respect firmly within a liberal rationalist framework. This makes it impossible to develop the political and moral importance of dignity, personality and insult. This is partly because, as Hart has shown, Dworkin differs from most philosophers in the liberal tradition in insisting along with Rawls, Fried and other deontological liberals that he does not appeal to any theory of human nature. Unlike Mill he is not prepared to 'make any appeal to the important role played in the conduct of individual life by such things as freedom of speech or of worship or of personal relations' (*The Idea of Freedom*, p. 88). Mill wanted to claim that these liberties are among 'the essentials of human well-being' and 'the very groundwork of our existence'. But possibly the crucial tension in Mill, as for Kant, concerned the issue of independence and subordination.

How can the idea of liberty as independence be secured? Liberal theory has tended to assume this could be settled within the political realm in which people could be guaranteed equal legal and political rights. But this has assumed, as Mill sometimes grasped, that people's very sense of identity is secured and cannot be undermined through the workings of social relations of power and subordination. But if people do not exist as persons in their own right, the rights they share in the political realm will not be enough to secure this. This is something Mill himself seemed to learn from feminism. He was aware that economic dependence, even within personal relationships, works to undermine women's autonomy and independence. If women grow up to find their meaning in caring for others, they can so easily cease to exist as persons in their own right. Neither an equality before the moral law or an equal share of political rights can secure this independence. Nor is it enough for people to conceive of marriage, say, as an equal partnership in which people learn to respect what each is doing individually. If women are left with exclusive responsibility for the domestic sphere and childcare, experience shows how easily they can be undermined and lose an independent sense of self. A man's work as the source of family income comes to assume an importance in the family which can make it hard for a woman to give equal value to her own time and activities. The crucial issue is that relationships of subordination come into existence even when people insist on showing an attitude of equal respect. If women are brought up to feel that they should be grateful for their situation, they will not feel they have any grounds for legitimate protest. The point is that within our inherited moral culture it will be seen as a 'psychological' problem which will be the only way of acknowledging the hurt and damage to a person's sense of self, rather than a crucial moral and political issue. This is because within our liberal moral traditions we assume that the self is invulnerable and exists prior to the social relations it freely enters.

Dworkin acknowledges that we lack a psychological theory which could help explain that the loss of particular liberties involves likely psychological damage. Given his challenge to the idea of a right to liberty as a 'misconceived concept that does a disservice to political thought' and because he resists the idea that a restraint on free speech or the exercise of religion is especially unjust because they have a special impact on liberty as such, he is forced to think out these issues. Since we want to defend these rights, even if they would not be in the general interest, we need to discover something beyond utility that argues for these rights. This

173

is when he acknowledges that 'We might be able to make out a case that individuals suffer some special damage when the traditional rights are invaded' (*Taking Rights Seriously*, p. 271). But he cannot take this quest seriously since he assumes a clear distinction between the 'psychological' and the 'moral' and shares a Kantian assumption that the moral point of view is basically different from the non-moral. This is clear when Dworkin asserts that 'We must argue on grounds of political morality that it is wrong to deprive individuals of these liberties, for some reason, apart from direct psychological damage ...' (*Taking Rights Seriously*, p. 272). He then goes on to

> presume that we all accept the following postulate of political morality. Government must treat those whom it governs with concern, that is, as human beings who are capable of suffering and frustration, and with respect, that is, as human beings who are capable of forming and acting on intelligent conceptions of how their lives should be lived. (p. 272)

The idea that governments must treat citizens with equal concern and respect defines Dworkin's notion of the liberal conception of equality.

This avoids the critical issue that a relation of subordination can undermine a person's sense of self. If a person is treated as a means to the ends of others, even if this is a situation they originally accepted, they can lose an independent sense of identity. They can come to exist in the shadows of others and become fearful of having to talk for themselves. Kant was certainly aware that 'it is difficult for each separate individual to work his way out of the immaturity which has become almost second nature to him' (*Kant's Political Writings*, p. 55). He recognises that people can even grow fond of their dependency and that

> The guardians who have kindly taken upon themselves the work of supervision will soon see to it that by far the largest part of mankind (including the entire fair sex) should consider the step forward to maturity not only as difficult but also as highly dangerous. (*Kant's Political Writings*, p. 54)

He knew that people will be intimidated and frightened from claiming their autonomy.

Kant at least acknowledges the moral character of the damage that is being done to people. He recognises the efforts people will have to make, though it was mainly against inner difficulties, since people were generally assumed to be independent and self-sufficient, or at least men were. But it is the relation between a person's sense of autonomy and their coming to have ideas of their own, rather than ideas they have inherited from others, that makes freedom of speech a crucial liberty for Kant. He knew that people had to learn to think for themselves if they were to gain more control over their lives. He knew that people had to free themselves from mental slavery. It was only later he had to acknowledge that this could also mean disentangling themselves from the workings of social relations of power when he could no longer assume people were generally independent. This does not make freedom of speech any less important, but it does mean that he could no longer assume it is sufficient on its own to guarantee people equal respect. But it was always clear that Kant was less concerned with how government should treat its citizens, than with the ways individuals could live free and equal moral lives. It was in these terms that postulates of political morality needed to be justified.

The liberal conception of equality seems to commit us to seeing others as 'capable of forming and acting on intelligent conceptions of how their lives should be lived'. But what kind of control does this assume people have over their lives? Does this depend upon people having control over their means of livelihood? Does this mean that respecting a person involves respecting the plans they have made for themselves, even if we know that the class, sexual or racial relations of power make it an impossible dream? The headmistress who, with the best intentions, tells the school assembly that if they only work hard enough they can get to university, as did Sally Brown, the first person to go to university from an inner city school, is surely deceiving the children about the reality of their situation. Is she lying if she knows that it would be an exceptional year if more than a couple made it, especially in a period when university places are being cut back? If we are simply being asked to acknowledge a 'capacity' people share to make plans, rather than the plans themselves, we need to be aware, if we are assuming people have the material conditions to realise their plans. We also need to realise that our capacities can themselves be hurt and undermined because of the social relations in which we have to make our everyday lives. If we are not simply to assent to a moral principle that assumes the material independence Kant was led to challenge, we have to face the moral and political issues that enable people to live as persons in their own right.

For Kant, morality remains an essentially rational quest. Any tradition of moral thought attempts to reformulate and reorganise our moral experience. A recent focus on the language of morals, as if it could somehow be separated from an engagement with our inherited moral traditions, has made this harder to realise. I have argued that in undermining our contact with our bodies and emotional lives, Kant has unwittingly undermined the autonomy and independence he seems to value. He has also made it difficult to explore what is involved in being treated as a means or to exist as an end in ourselves. It is only if we are sensitive to the tensions in our moral experience that we can acknowledge this, since otherwise it is easy to limit ourselves to the moral arguments and reasoning which sustain a sense of the 'moral' within a rationalist tradition. Williams seems to recognise this issue when he says that 'the special dignity or supremacy attached to the moral, make it very difficult to assign to those other relations and motivations the significance or structural importance in life which some of them are capable of possessing' (*Moral Luck*, p. 2).

As long as we think of morality as the rational application of impartial principles it is hard to think that in respecting others we can be called upon to validate and confirm their experience. But this is the way we can strengthen their sense of identity. This is partly a matter of helping people to trust themselves. Though Kant can help us identify the problem, he often blinds us to the ways we can learn to work with people to restore a sense of self. Kant understands that in the end people have to take the first step themselves. He is more likely to throw people in at the deep end. Since experience is part of the world of determination, he cannot acknowledge that in affirming a person's experience, including their experience of being treated as a means by others, we can be showing our respect for them. Similarly, self-respect has to do with *validating* and *confirming* our own experience, not just with putting value on the plans we have set for ourselves, as in a rationalist tradition. In undermining the trust we might otherwise have in our emotions and desires, Kant is unwittingly giving power to those who have the authority to define correct behaviour. Since what is 'right' is defined impersonally and universally the powerful can claim to have reason on their side. People are being disempowered if they cannot trust their natures but somehow have to contest on the same impersonal grounds.

So, for instance, Ann can feel that her mother never respected her because she never listened to her. She wanted her daughter to be a means to her own self-glorification and she felt that Ann somehow owed this to her because she had worked so hard for her. She would never admit this, but in reality her daughter was a means to her own ends. She often said that she could do whatever she wants but this only seemed to work as a way of making Ann feel guilty. Her mother always seemed to know what was best for her, even the kind of dresses she looked best in. She did not want to disappoint her mother and she often felt her mother did seem to know best. She lacked confidence in herself and in her own judgement. When she was told that she could not trust her feelings, she did not know what else she could trust. It seemed as if her feelings could sometimes help to bring her into closer contact with her individuality. She learnt that she somehow had to separate from her mother and build an independent sense of identity. It was as if she ceased to exist when her mother was around. Even years later she was forced to realise that she seemed to lose all her new-found strength when she visited her mother. She becomes the child she once was. This makes her realise how vulnerable her sense of identity is and how dependent it still seems to be on the affirmation and recognition of others. She knew it had been crucial for her to learn to respect her own feelings and thoughts. She used to be too anxious that others would like her so that she would use herself as a means, doing whatever would find favour with others. She is no longer so concerned to please others. She has found, paradoxically, that the more she learns to listen and accept herself, the more she seems to get on with others. She now feels she has the resources with which to challenge people who think they know what is best for her. She knows that for her autonomy to be firmly grounded, it has had to concern not only her thoughts but also her feelings.

Liberal theory has little sense of the difficulties people have in discovering what they individually need or want. It tends to assume an autonomy and independence that is invulnerable to social relations of power and subordination. Since individuals are assumed to be free to choose their social relations, including their conditions of work, there is little sense of how a sense of self develops and grows within particular relationships of power, initially within the family and school. Kant comes to realise that respect is not simply a matter of how individuals choose to treat each other. But it remains difficult for him to explore what is morally involved in a person being undermined or made to feel worthless. He is limited to thinking that this means people cannot conceive of ends for themselves or else are treated according to the ends of others. Rawls thinks of this in terms of individuals putting more or less value on themselves and their ends. In neither case can we really develop a sense of people being *undermined* or *invalidated* since this involves referring not only to our ends rationally conceived, but also to our emotions, feelings and desires. This is equally true if we are to grasp what it means to be treated as a means and how this can undermine our very sense of self.

We should not allow Kant's guarantee of our dignity as 'an absolute inner worth' to make us insensitive to the ways our dignity and sense of self can be undermined by social relations. This helps us grasp that when people are being oppressed it is not just that their dignity is being offended, but their very sense of self is being undermined. It is because liberal theory has tended to assume a self that exists prior to its ends and prior to social relations, that relations of subordination and dependency cannot threaten the very integrity and autonomy of a person. This is part of what makes it difficult to explore the damage, at once both psychological and moral, that is being done to people when they are treated as means. It is a significant strength of Freud's psychoanalytic theory that while it operates within a Kantian framework, it does not take the integrity of the individual for granted. In this sense he breaks with a central assumption of liberal theory to show that it is the very integrity of the individual that can be damaged when the individual is emotionally dependent or exists in pieces. This is a repression that Kant has crucially helped to prepare in his denigration of nature and identification of the self with our reason. He has prepared the place for 'oughts' and 'shoulds' in our lives so that we are constantly forming and shaping our experience according to how we think things ought to be. We do not really want to contact the reality of our experience and Freud has shown the efforts we make to deny this knowledge of ourselves. He wants us to acknowledge that it is quite natural to have our feelings, even if we choose not to act upon them. Often, for instance, a married man will not want to acknowledge his attraction for another woman because the feeling itself seems tantamount to making a new relationship and, in any case, reveals what a treacherous nature we really have. Freud wanted to create a space between our feelings and our actions which had been closed and limited within a Kantian tradition. For Freud this meant that we should be able to control our emotions more reliably.[12] We are less likely to be overwhelmed by them, as we are when we constantly shun them. It is no surprise that if we are struggling to live in the acceptable images we have of ourselves, people will talk of the 'unreality' of their experience, since we learn to have such a limited relationship to ourselves. This will limit not only our respect for our emotional lives, but also the sensitivity we can have for others. This is particularly clear for a masculinity that has historically been so closely identified with self-control.

Freud recognised that our identity is much more precarious than our moral theory has supposed. The repression of our emotional lives gives us a false sense of control over our inner lives. It makes it difficult to identify the damage people do to themselves in sustaining this form of control. Marx had already realised that we do not have the kind of external control to make our social lives that liberal theory has tended to assume. Within a capitalist society, according to Marx, our experience is fundamentally formed within class relations of power which can help account, if we are prepared to acknowledge them, for the ways we experience ourselves individually. It can leave people scared with a sense that they have constantly got to prove to themselves that they are as good as others. But it can also leave people with a deep sense of the injustice of the prevailing relationships of power and a felt sense that people do not have an equal chance to make their own lives. This is not simply an issue of unequal distribution of resources, as liberal theory would have it, but of the power this gives some people over the lives of others. This is to recognise a moral and political issue of dependency, especially when it threatens the very integrity and autonomy of a person. This also means acknowledging the need for a *morality of relationships*, since this cannot be explained in terms of the individual moral actions of the individuals involved. Nor can we assume, as Rawls wants to, that the essential unity of the self can be provided by the concept of right.

Kant learnt to question his assumption that social relations could be thought of as external, determining our behaviour. He learnt how they could come to threaten a moral autonomy he had assumed invulnerable. Likewise, if he had thought similarly about forms of emotional dependency, without assuming they could be overcome as a matter of will, he would have glimpsed the territory Freud was to investigate. In both areas he would have had to question his assumption of morality as essentially an individual quest. He would have been forced to recognise the moral importance of people learning to *situate* themselves both within the social and historical relations of power in society as well as emotional relationships of dependency within the family. Autonomy and independence could not be achieved solely as an issue of will and determination, but would also call for a transformation of relations of power and dependency. This would not be to see 'inner' and 'outer' as separate and independent realms, but as necessarily interrelated to each other, since otherwise this would simply reproduce Kant's fragmentation.

Liberal theory has tended to assume that the notion of rights can guarantee the independence of people and embody the separateness of people which is taken to be the strength of Kant's inheritance. The fragmentation upon which Kant's rationalist notion of the person depends is rendered *invisible* as individuals are guaranteed a framework in which they are free to pursue their own visions of happiness. This is how our respect for others is to be embodied in the very organisation of society. Though the idea of rights tends to assume the independence of people, notions of independence and the conditions sustaining them are rarely discussed. There is little sense that particular liberties are crucial because they support and nourish an independence which is a precondition of our moral autonomy. Rather, as in Kant's more formalistic ethics, our moral autonomy flows directly from our capacity to reason. This allows Rawls to assume that the unity of the self is antecedently established. In contrast to utilitarianism it is the moral personality so defined, and not the capacity for pleasure and pain, that is the fundamental aspect of the self. As Rawls says, 'it is not our aims that primarily reveal our nature' (*A Theory of Justice*, p. 560) but our capacity to choose our aims that matters most. It is this capacity that supposedly finds expression in the principles of justice. But if we acknowledge that this capacity itself is not beyond the reach of relations of power and dependency but is vulnerable to being hurt or injured, we cannot think of justice simply in distributive terms, even if this includes such social goods as respect and self-respect.

Rawls and Nozick would give different responses, but would probably agree with Dworkin that 'The sovereign question of political theory, within a state supposedly to be governed by the liberal conception of equality, is the question of what inequalities in goods, opportunities and liberties are permitted in such a state and why' (*Taking Rights Seriously*, p. 273). This assumes the independence of a government very much as Kant wanted to assume the independence of the moral law. It is a view of the powerful that does not start with an investigation into the suffering and indignity of people's everyday lives. Rather it assumes an independence and integrity of people that in reality has long been undermined by social relations of power. Questioning whether individuals are related to their ends externally through acts of will and choice, or whether our ends are somehow constitutive of our very sense of self, still assumes that the integrity and independence of people are not violated through social relations of power and subordination. This limits our sense of the depths to which people can be mistreated, humiliated and abused. It is the very separation of the rational moral will which can alone make universal laws from our empirical world of desires, needs and emotions that establishes for liberal theory the distinction between the right and the good. This distinction cannot be sustained if we are to grasp the nature of oppression as an insult to the dignity of human nature. It is not only that our integrity is not acknowledged for what it is, but it is actively undermined and damaged. However, this involves rethinking our inherited conception of human rights and Kant's early assumption that as long as we respect the rights of others we can be doing them no wrong.

Conservative libertarians, such as Nozick in his *Anarchy, State and Utopia*, attempt to build a theory of rights on the moral importance of the distinctness or separateness of human persons which utilitarianism is said to ignore. In contrast, the liberal left of Rawls and Dworkin wants to construct such a theory of rights on the moral title of individuals to equal respect and concern. Both have different conceptions of the place and responsibility of governments, as Hart makes clear, since 'while the first theory is dominated by the duty of government to respect the separateness of persons, the second is dominated by the duty of government to treat their subjects as equals with equal concern and respect' (*The Idea of Freedom*, p. 77). Even though both theories draw on Kant, they had not heeded Kant's doubts and uncertainties in his later writings. They assume that our political philosophy can usefully suppose that individuals are independent and self-sufficient, if only to establish a vision of a just social order which can be compared with existing realities. Though Hart thinks the new theories which seek a doctrine of basic human rights underestimate strengths in the utilitarian tradition, there are more grounds than he supposes to think that 'the new insights which are currently offered us seem to dazzle at least as much as they illuminate' (*The Idea of Freedom*, p. 77).

Simone Weil thought that the notion of rights, which the revolutionaries of 1789 made the keynote of their deliberate challenge to the world, has proved unable to fulfil its role because of its intrinsic inadequacy. She warns us that 'To set up as a standard of public morality a notion which can neither be defined nor conceived is to open the door to every kind of tyranny' (*Selected Essays:* 'Human Personality', p. 10). This can be difficult to hear when the notion of rights is used specifically to protect specific basic liberties against the demands of general welfare. But the point Weil is continually returning to is not that we cannot talk about rights, but we have to be able to discriminate between the different ways people can be harmed. If we assume the independence and integrity of the person in our conception of rights, we can never grasp the nature of people's vulnerability to being treated as a means. This was an insight Weil was developing in her early lectures on politics and social theory, though for her it was only a turn to religious language which eventually gave her the means of expressing the depths to which a person is hurt when they are violated.

Throughout Weil's life she thought it necessary for moral theory not to ignore the existence of social problems. As she says, one can give money to the unemployed, but that does not stop them from being unemployed. Equally we can concern ourselves with the education of working-class children, but that does not mean that they will find work when they leave school. The familiar tendency to treat her life as somehow divided between politics and religion misses her constant recognition of the impossibility of avoiding social problems and the first duty it places on us not to tell lies. In the notes taken by Anne Reynaud-Guerithault of her lectures to students at the Roanne lycée in 1933–4 we find:

> The first form of lie is that of covering up oppression, of flattering the oppressors. This form of lie is very common among honest people, who in other ways are good and sincere, but who do not realise what they are doing. Human beings are so made that the ones who do the crushing feel nothing; it is the person crushed who feels what is happening. Unless one has placed oneself on the side of the oppressed, to feel with them, one cannot understand. (*Lectures on Philosophy*, p. 139)

But the people who feel what is happening do not have the language in which to express their suffering, nor, as Weil says, is it the professionals of speech who can express it for them. This was a task she had accepted for herself.

In her later writings Simone Weil thought in terms of affliction not oppression. She wanted to find words which 'express the truth of their affliction, the words which can give resonance, through the crust of external circumstances, to the cry which is always inaudible: "Why am I being hurt?"' (*Selected Essays 1934–43:* 'Human Personality', p. 24). But she tended to interpret this task too severely, thinking that if we want to be sure of using the right words, we have to confine ourselves to such words as 'truth', 'beauty', 'justice' and 'compassion' which everywhere, in all circumstances, express only the good. If this was the way she wanted to nourish the afflicted whom she saw as starving for good, it led her to diminish the place of rights which she concluded were 'alien to the good' because 'To possess a right implies the possibility of making good or bad use of it' (*Selected Essays*, p. 24). It is one thing to challenge the notion of rights as a general term in which our liberties are to be defended and quite another to reject the place of rights completely. She sometimes thought of rights as a contamination which was essentially alien to the Greek mind she cherished. The Greeks had no conception of rights and no words to express it. The fact they were content to think in terms of justice is important, however, because it reminds us of a tradition in which justice is not thought about in terms of rights. She also thought it monstrous that Rome should be praised for having bequeathed us the notion of rights.

If we examine Roman law in its cradle, to see what species it
belongs to, we discover that property was defined by the jus
utendi et abutendi. And in fact the things which the property
owner had the right to use or abuse at will were for the most
part human beings. (*Selected Essays*, p. 20)

Weil helps us understand that our moral language has to be able
to illuminate the reality of people's suffering and misery. This is
something utilitarianism singularly failed to do, thinking that all
suffering could be equally thought of in terms of pleasure and pain.
Kant's sense that human dignity is offended when we treat someone
as a means promises a different insight, but one which could not
be developed as long as a person's individuality and moral autonomy could be guaranteed in their relation to the moral law. Weil
seeks a religious language of affliction to make distinctions between
different kinds of suffering. This can help us situate the notion of
rights within its proper place while also showing us the necessity of
a conception of people's material and spiritual needs. But it also
challenges the priority which liberal theory has given to the right
over the good. At the very least we learn that we cannot rely
exclusively upon a notion of rights if we want to illuminate the
reality of people's suffering:

Relying almost exclusively on this notion, it becomes
impossible to keep one's eyes on the real problem. If someone
tries to browbeat a farmer to sell his eggs at a moderate price,
the farmer can say: 'I have the right to keep my eggs if I don't
get a good enough price.' But if a young girl is being forced
into a brothel she will not talk about her rights. In such a
situation the word would sound ludicrously inadequate.

Thus it is that the social drama, which corresponds to the
latter situation, is falsely assimilated, by the use of the word
'rights', to the former one.

Thanks to this word, what should have been a cry of protest
from the depth of the heart has been turned into a shrill
nagging of claims and counter-claims, which is both impure
and unpractical. (*Selected Essays:* 'Human Personality', p. 21)

We might recognise that the idea of infringing or not respecting a
woman's rights is 'ludicrously inadequate' to illuminate the horror
and suffering of her violation, without thinking that talking of

184

rights necessarily turns into 'a shrill nagging of claims and counter-claims'.

The force of Weil's distinction, even if it fails to take seriously enough the assertion of rights – which she thinks have always been intrinsically linked with the notion of sharing out, of exchange and of measured quantity – is that it faces us with a suffering and violation we would choose to ignore. She is very aware that the afflicted are not listened to and 'they themselves soon sink into impotence in the use of language, because of the certainty of not being heard' (*Selected Essays*, p. 28). But this makes it important to realise that injury to the personality and its desires is not sufficient to evoke 'a cry of sorrowful surprise from the depth of the soul' (*Selected Essays*, p. 12). As she says, it is not a personal thing. As far as she is concerned there are many cries of personal protest, but they are unimportant since you may provoke them without violating anything sacred. 'Every time there arises from the depths of the human heart the childish cry which Christ himself could not restrain, "Why am I being hurt?", then there is certainly injustice.' (*Selected Essays*, p. 11.) This is the sense of justice which the Greeks cherished, but which we are in danger of forgetting within a liberal culture in which justice has to do with a framework of rights in which individuals are free to pursue their own ends. We need to discern different levels of justice to keep our eyes on the real problems, otherwise we have few ways of illuminating the horrors of rape as well as the degradation of human labour:

> This profound and childlike and unchanging expectation of good in the heart is not what is involved when we agitate for our rights. The motive which prompts a little boy to watch jealously to see if his brother has a slightly larger piece of cake arises from a much more superficial level of the soul. The word justice means two very different things according to whether it refers to the one or the other level. It is only the former one that matters. (*Selected Essays:* 'Human Personality', p. 10)

It is the expectation that is always at the bottom of the heart of every human being, that good and not evil will be done to us, that is sacred in every human being. When this is damaged injustice has been done and we have hurt our souls.

When we degrade or humiliate a person we deny their humanity in a way Kant could never express. I am not sure Weil gets it right, but at least we gain more sense of the depths to which our integrity and independence can be damaged. Liberal theory encloses us into thinking of the choices people can make, as if the freedom workers have to choose to work in different factories or mines, say, is itself enough to guarantee their freedom and independence. Weil recognises that physical labour may be painful, but that it is not degrading as such. But she knew that conditions of factory work can be degrading. If workers really felt that 'the subject of the bargain, which they complain they sell cheap and for less than the just price, is nothing other than their soul' (*Selected Essays*, p. 18), then 'their resistance would have a very different force from what is provided by the consideration of personal right' (*Selected Essays*, p. 18). It would be 'fierce and desperate like that of a young girl who is being forced into a brothel' (*Selected Essays*, p. 18). They would realise that they are not simply making an economic demand. Weil had learnt to use religious language to return Marx's analysis of exploitation as an issue of surplus value to connect again with his core sense of the denial of a person's humanity when their labour is treated as a commodity. It is not an issue of the fair price of labour, but of the institution of wage labour itself. Weil's theology had helped her express the moral edge of a Marxism which had been lost in the orthodoxy of the working-class movement and its trade unions and political parties.

Simone Weil forces us to make moral discriminations concerning the injustice people suffer. When someone is treated merely as a means, an injustice is often being done that goes beyond the infringement of a person's right to pursue their own ends. A person is being violated in a way that goes beyond an injury to the personality and its desires. It can hurt us to realise that our brother is getting a bigger share of the cake, but if this does not mark a deeper rejection of us by our parents, it is something we can live with. As Weil says, 'it comes from a much more superficial level of the soul'. We need to develop our moral psychology to sensitise us to the damage done to people when they suffer different forms of injustice, rather than assume we can dispense equally with all conceptions of human nature and human needs, which has been one of the defining features of deontological liberalism.

If democratic capitalist societies are characterised by class, ethnic and sexual relations of power and subordination, we cannot ignore the place of coercion. As Weil knew: 'Coercion does not go with democracy. It is obviously quite impossible for men to be treated like things in the labour market and in production and to be treated as citizens in public life.' (*Lectures on Philosophy*, p. 151). But she also realised that Russia had proved that it is no use simply driving capitalists out as long as big industry survives, since the capitalists can simply be replaced by bureaucrats. You can be even more helpless when it is the same power which dominates big business and everything else. But if we are to illuminate the moral realities of social oppression, we cannot meaningfully assume the separateness of individuals. We cannot assume, as Nozick's libertarian conservative political theory wants to, that a strictly limited set of near absolute rights can constitute the foundation of morality. For Nozick these rights are so strong and far-reaching that only a 'minimal state limited to the narrow functions of protection against force, theft, fraud, enforcement of contracts, and so on, is justified' (*Anarchy, State and Utopia*, preface). He concludes that 'any more extensive state will violate persons' right not to be forced to do certain things, and is unjustified' (preface).

Nozick thinks that utilitarianism can only give a derivative status to rights and their non-violation. But even if a theory can include in a primary way the non-violation of rights, it can 'include it in the wrong place and the wrong manner' (*Anarchy, State and Utopia*, p. 28). Nozick is concerned to argue that moral views involve what he calls side constraints on action, rather than merely being goal-directed. This central notion is taken to embody Kant's principle as is made clear when he says: 'Side constraints upon action reflect the underlying Kantian principle that individuals are ends and not merely means; they may not be sacrificed or used for the achieving of other ends without their consent. Individuals are inviolable' (*Anarchy, State and Utopia*, p. 31). He acknowledges that more should be said to illuminate this talk of ends and means. He considers the example of a tool where there is no side constraint on how we may use it, other than the moral constraints on how we may use it upon others. There is no limit on what we can do with it to achieve our goals. But when he begins to think of a person being treated as a means, he soon gets lost and withdraws. He is concerned with how we can be used without being aware of it and wonders if someone is obliged to reveal their intended uses of an interaction if they think we are likely to object. This leads him to ask whether we use someone solely as a means when we get pleasure from seeing an attractive person go by. 'Does someone so use an object of sexual fantasies? These and related questions raise very interesting issues for moral philosophy; but not, I think, for political philosophy.' Nozick retreats into a categorical distinction with a declaration that political philosophy is only concerned 'with *certain* ways that persons may not use others; primarily, physically aggressing against them' (*Anarchy, State and Utopia*, p. 32). And then as if to reassure us he says that side constraints express the inviolability of others in the particular ways they specify.

Nozick argues that we may not 'violate' persons for the social good since though we may individually choose to undergo some pain or sacrifice, like going to the dentist or doing some unpleasant work, for a greater benefit or to avoid a greater harm:

> there is no *social entity* with a good that undergoes some
> sacrifice for its own good. There are only individual people,
> different individual people, with their own individual lives.
> Using one of these people for the benefit of others, uses him
> and benefits the others. Nothing more. (*Anarchy, State and
> Utopia*, p. 33)

This assumes the very vision that Kant was forced to consider in the relations between rich and poor. It assumes that, even if there are inequalities, people are free to live independent and self-sufficient lives. There is no relation of dependency, as Kant wanted to think, unless the poor choose to disturb a pre-existing balance by asking for help. Nozick claims that the moral side constraints 'reflect the fact of our separate existence' and 'express the inviolability of other persons'. Any kind of transfer from rich to poor, say through taxation, is talked of as 'using a person', or 'violating persons' since 'there is no moral outweighing of one of our lives by others so as to lead to a greater overall *social* good. There is no justified sacrifice of some of us for others' (*Anarchy, State and Utopia*, p. 33). As far as Nozick is concerned, end-state maximising views are prepared to treat distinct individuals as if they are 'resources' for others.

This language of violation is never explained, possibly because Nozick assumes that moral wrongdoing has only the one form of a violation of rights. This amounts to the violation of a person since our autonomy and independence is assured and we are invulnerable to being undermined by dependency and subordination. Or at least this has been placed beyond the pale of Nozick's conception of political philosophy. As Hart has realised: 'So long as rights are not violated it matters not for morality, short of catastrophe, how a social system works, how individuals fare under it, what needs it fails to meet or what misery or inequality it produces.' ('Between Utility and Rights': *The Idea of Freedom*, p. 81.) The only virtue of social institutions, in Nozick's view, is that they protect the few basic rights, and their only vice is failure to do so. Given that rights are not violated, whether society is grossly inegalitarian or egalitarian, is of no moral significance. Any consequence of the exercise of our rights is morally unobjectionable.

It is as if, as Hart has recognised, the model for Nozick's basic moral rights were a legal one. Just as there can be no legal objection to the exercise of a legal right, so for Nozick there can be no moral objection to the exercise of a moral right. This is something Simone Weil was also aware of when she complained that the notion of rights 'has a commercial flavour, essentially evocative of legal claims and arguments' (*Selected Essays*, p. 18). She thought that rights are always asserted in a tone of contention that must rely upon force in the background, if they are not to be laughed at. She knew that the workers' movement had had to learn to support its claim for rights through learning how to mobilise whatever power it had. But this was to expose a suffering and oppression that insisted that, even if the only moral wrongdoing consists in violating the rights of individuals, these should include not only Bentham's negative services to others, but also a basic right to the relief of great need and suffering, or the provision of basic education and skills. Hart reminds us that, except for a few privileged and lucky persons, the ability to shape life for oneself 'is not something automatically guaranteed by a structure of negative rights' (*The Idea of Freedom*, p. 85).

We can treat misery as a matter of moral concern and require some people to contribute to the assistance of others without having to commit ourselves to a maximising utilitarianism which respects not persons but only the experiences of pleasure or satisfaction. Nozick faces us with a false alternative when he thinks a social philosophy which draws its morality from the single source of individual rights is the only way to acknowledge 'the separateness of individuals'. But, as Hart realises, this involves us in the unexciting chore of 'confronting Nozick's misleading descriptive

terms such as "sacrifice of one individual for another", "treating
one individual as a resource for others" ... with the realities which
these expressions are misused to describe' (*The Idea of Freedom*,
p. 83). But possibly this is not as straightforward a task as Hart
suggests, since, as I have shown, it involves a challenge to the
rationalist character of a Kantian tradition, which itself proved
powerless to illuminate the indignities and suffering involved. But
possibly this is something Hart has sensed for himself when he
declares that:

> once we distinguish between the gravity of the different
> restrictions on different specific liberties and their importance
> for the conduct of a meaningful life or the development of the
> personality, the idea that they all, like unqualified maximising
> utilitarianism, ignore the moral importance of the division of
> humanity into separate individuals and threaten the proper
> inviolability of persons disappears into the mist. ('Between
> Utility and Rights', *The Idea of Freedom*, pp. 84-5)

We can no longer assume that the autonomy of morality can
guarantee our independence and integrity. We can only exist as
persons in our own right through the ways we can express our
individual and collective identities. This means we have to be concerned with the control people have in their everyday lives. Our
'separateness as persons' has to be realised in the control we have
in our everyday lives. In a society characterised by relationships of
power and dependency it can no longer be assumed. Liberal theory
could have learnt this lesson from Kant, if it had not felt this would
automatically result in the reduction of different spheres of life and
the downgrading of morality. Kant had also been forced to challenge the legitimacy of property rights which Nozick insists on
giving an absolute and permanent character. Kant had recognised
that an issue of justice emerged whenever the rich had more than
they needed when the poor had less than they needed. It was an
issue of justice and human needs, not just of rights.

3 RESPECT AND INJUSTICE

For the most part liberal theory has been satisfied to identify and
guarantee our individuality with Kant's rationalist conception of

moral autonomy. This is confirmed in the idea of our dignity as an absolute inner worth that is invulnerable to social relations of power and subordination. This is what supports the idea of the self as existing prior to its ends and the idea that we can respect others, regardless of the relationship within which we meet. Our moral personality is guaranteed in a realm of its own, separated from our activities and relationships in which we seek to express our empirical selves. This can mean that the hurt and indignity we suffer at school or at work can never reach or undermine our dignity as moral selves. Our individuality is rendered invulnerable. It is equally difficult to identify the hurt and damage we can do to ourselves, if, for instance, we grow up feeling we are not entitled to the satisfaction of our needs, since this compromises the image of ourselves as independent and self-sufficient. Our very conception of morality has been limited through its appropriation as exclusively concerned with providing universal reasons for action. If we challenge this idea, we are inevitably taken as attacking morality itself.

The fragmented conception of the person we inherit from Kant finds expression in the difficulties liberal theory has in reconciling two conceptions of equality, namely, as Rawls has it:

> between equality as it is invoked in connection with the
> distribution of certain goods, some of which will almost
> certainly give higher status and prestige to those who are
> favoured, and equality as it applies to the respect which is
> owed to persons irrespective of their social position. (*A Theory
> of Justice*, p. 511)

It is clear for Rawls that equality of the second kind is fundamental. Its deeper significance is explained in its basis in such natural duties as that of mutual respect and the fact that it is owed to human beings as moral persons. Rawls is looking for a theory of justice which, by arranging inequalities for reciprocal advantage and abstracting from 'the contingencies of nature and social circumstances within a framework of equal liberty, persons express their respect for one another in the very constitution of their society' (*A Theory of Justice*, p. 178). This is an attractive vision but in seeing justice in fundamentally distributive terms, even if extended to include such social goods as respect, it is difficult to grasp the interconnection of these two conceptions of equality. It becomes impossible to grasp, as Kant did in his reflections on the relations between rich and poor, that an unequal distribution of property, say, does not simply give its owner higher status and prestige, but gives them power over the lives of others which can threaten the very autonomy of morality.

But Rawls remains trapped in Kant's earlier writings and in the assumption that individuals are free to act justly towards others, just as Kant had assumed we are free to relate to others in any way we choose. So Rawls declares that: 'Properly understood, then, the desire to act justly derives in part from the desire to express most fully what we are or can be, namely free and equal rational beings with a liberty to choose.' (*A Theory of Justice*, p. 256.) This explains, according to Rawls, why failure to act according to the moral law gives rise to shame and not feelings of guilt. This is appropriate because we have failed to do what we could have done and failed to express our nature as free and equal rational beings. As Rawls says, 'Such actions therefore strike at our self-respect, our sense of our own worth, and the experience of this loss is shame. We have acted as though we belonged to a lower order.' (*A Theory of Justice*, p. 256.) This helps explain why Rawls objects to the idea of Kant's ethics as an austere doctrine of law and guilt when according to Rawls, his 'main aim is to deepen and to justify Rousseau's idea that liberty is acting in accordance with a law that we give to ourselves' (*A Theory of Justice*, p. 256). But if this helps provide an ethic of mutual respect and self-esteem, it also helps explain Rawls's attachment to the more voluntaristic aspects of Kant's thought. But this can make it harder to grasp the lack of freedom and control people can have over their lives in social relations of power and subordination. Rawls follows Kant, not in seeing the noumenal realm as transcendental, but as a way of thinking that is supposedly always available to people if they turn towards it. This leaves us thinking that people can always express their nature as free and equal rational beings. It gives us no grasp of ways this could bring them into conflict with prevailing authorities in the factory, at school or at home. Since for Rawls this is an issue of *thinking* differently, we seem safely unaware of the contradictions in our experience. We are made blind to the fact that if we act truthfully and honestly, we can be forced to challenge a structure of power and authority that can often crush us individually. This means we should be constantly aware of the powers we are up against. It should be a central task of our moral theory to illuminate this situation.

If we lived in a society organised according to Rawls's principles of justice, we might enjoy a freedom to act justly towards others. But we have to be careful not to create false expectations in societies which are unequal and unjust. Nor is it clear that we should always act towards others *as if* there is equality between us. It might be better to acknowledge the relationship of power, since to ignore its existence does not mean it will disappear. So, for instance, it might be important for teachers to acknowledge fully the power they have in relation to their students, while doing their best to relate more equally. This is not to pretend that social relations of education would not be quite different if students and teachers shared more control over the educational process. We can work to develop different, more equal relationships, but it is as well to be clear about the larger relationships of power within which this is taking place. Liberal theory can leave us feeling we have more control over our lives than we do. It can make it harder to *identify* the structures of power and subordination within which we live our lives. So, as an example, it can leave a factory worker ashamed that he did not do better at school. He can feel he only has himself to blame and, as I have argued, he will find it harder to assess what he can be individually held responsible for and what demands a recognition, say, of the difficulties even a bright working-class child can have in getting into university.

This is to refuse the simple alternative that it is either the individual who is at fault or else it is society to blame. Liberal theory can encourage us to have unrealistic expectations of ourselves as it makes it difficult to discern relations of power and subordination and as we internalise and individualise unequal relations of power. We have to learn not to feel ashamed for a situation that is not only of our own making. But we also need not feel ashamed if we cannot, by our own individual efforts, always relate justly towards others. We can learn to become more sensitive, but this can also mean, if we are in a position of power and dominance, learning to accept an anger and frustration we have not caused ourselves, but which inequality and injustice have produced. We cannot expect people to be grateful for our fairness without also realising the anger and frustration injustice produces. This is part of learning how to treat people more equally, in an unequal society.

193

Liberal theory persists with the assumption, as Dworkin puts it, 'of a natural right of all men and women to equality of concern and respect, a right they possess not by virtue of birth or characteristic or merit or excellence but simply as human beings with the capacity to make plans and give justice' (*Taking Rights Seriously*, p. 182). Dworkin is convinced that justice as fairness rests on this assumption and feels validated since Rawls does not use the original position to argue for this right, but rather the right to equal respect is a condition of admission to the original position. As Rawls has it, it is 'owed to human beings as moral persons', and follows from the 'moral personality' that distinguishes humans from animals. This is one right, therefore, that does not emerge from the contract. This helps Dworkin to the idea that the deep theory behind the original position must be a right-based theory of some sort. Even though Rawls describes the duties people would impose upon themselves in the original position as 'natural duties', Dworkin is anxious to show this is very different from supposing that the deep theory that informs the original position can be duty-based. But this seems to be part of an attempt to distance Rawls from the Kantian inheritance he himself claims. Dworkin admits it is possible to argue that a person's self-interest lies in doing his duty under the moral law, either because they will be punished or else because fulfilling their role in the natural order is the most satisfying activity. But this means that a person's duties define his or her self-interest, and not the other way round. We would have to set aside any calculation of self-interest except calculations of duty. He thinks a Rawlsian contract only makes sense with a right-based deep theory.

As Dworkin has it: 'The basic idea of a right-based theory is that distinct individuals have interests that they are entitled to protect if they wish.' (*Taking Rights Seriously*, p. 176.) Any right-based theory must presume rights that are not simply the product of legislation, or convention, or explicit social custom, but are independent grounds for judging such legislation and custom. As long as we realise that the assumption of natural rights is not, as Dworkin puts it, 'a metaphysically ambitious one', he feels happy with saying that it must be a 'theory that is based on the concept of rights that are *natural*, in the sense that they are not the products of any legislation, or convention, or hypothetical contract' (*Taking Rights Seriously*, p. 176). It is clear for Rawls that justice has to do

194

with conflicting claims upon the advantages won by social coopera-
tion. The word 'contract' suggests a plurality of persons which
utilitarianism fails to recognise when it conflates diverse systems of
justice into a single system of desire, extending to society as a whole
the principles of rational choice for one person. The fact that the
subjects of co-operation have different interests and ends follows
from Rawls's sense of the nature of a person capable of justice at
all. In contrast, the fact that people have needs and interests which
happen to coincide, so making co-operation mutually advanta-
geous, does not follow from the nature of their subjectivity, but
merely from the happy accident of their circumstances. As Rawls
declares: 'The essential idea is that we want to account for the
social values, for the intrinsic good of institutional, community,
and associative activities, by a conception of justice that in its
theoretical basis is individualistic.' (*A Theory of Justice*, p. 264.)
But this does not at all mean that individuals co-operate out of
selfish motives alone, but rather, as Sandel puts it, that 'our knowledge of the basis of plurality is given prior to experience, while our
knowledge of the basis of unity or co-operation can only come
in the light of experience' (*Liberalism and the Limits of Justice*,
p. 53).

But, as I have argued, it can be difficult to reconcile the different
interests and ends individuals have with the notion of rights which,
according to Dworkin, 'presuppose and protect the value of individual thought and choice' (*Taking Rights Seriously*, p. 172). Right-
based theories supposedly treat codes of conduct as instrumental,
perhaps necessary to protect the rights of others, but having no
essential value in themselves. A person does not live a life of moral
virtue by complying with such a code. Though both right-based
and duty-based theories place the individual at the centre, taking
the decisions of the individual to be of fundamental importance,
they put the individual in a different light. Right-based theories are
concerned with the independence rather than the conformity of
individual action, be it to a code set by society to the individual or
by the individual to himself. Dworkin is concerned to prove that
Rawls's 'original position is well designed to enforce the abstract
right to equal concern and respect, which must be understood to
be the fundamental concept of Rawls's deep theory' (*Taking Rights
Seriously*, p. 181). He thinks Rawls admits as much when he says
that an equality of respect owed to persons, irrespective of their

social position, is more fundamental than an equality concerned with the distribution of goods.

Equal respect seems to mean for Rawls a guarantee of equal liberty to individuals to pursue their own ends and interests. This partly explains why he is ready to subordinate equality in material resources, when this is necessary, to liberty of political activity, by making the demands of the first principle prior to those of the second. But as Dworkin also realises, the original position may also be said to fall short of an egalitarian ideal because 'they do not take account of relative deprivation, because they justify any inequality when those worse off are better off than they would be in absolute terms, without that inequality' (*Taking Rights Seriously*, p. 190). These inequalities are required, not by some competing notion of liberty, but by the more basic conception of equal respect.

But talk of 'relative deprivation' does not touch the critical issue of dependency which challenges the basis of the distinction both Rawls and Dworkin agree to between two conceptions of equality. This also challenges the assumption of equal liberty, since in a relationship of subordination we cannot assume that individuals are equally free to pursue their own interests and ends. Possibly Kant can help us draw a distinction between individual property which gives people power, not over others, but over themselves, and the ownership of capital which gives some people an undemocratic power over other people. This was the substance of Kant's objection to the concentration of wealth. This means accepting a theoretical distinction between the ownership of capital and the ownership of individual property. A socialist tradition which has focused upon the issue of private property, rather than the issue of autonomy and dependence, has assumed that an attack of private property would automatically give people greater control over their lives. This has important implications for our approach to public ownership and to the value and practices of an egalitarian society. Marx himself described capitalist private property as 'the first negation of individual private property as founded on the labour of the proprietor' (*Capital*, Vol. 1, p. 763).

A deontological liberalism fundamentally assumes that what separates us as individuals is in some important sense prior to what connects us. This is an epistemological as well as a moral priority. As Sandel usefully describes it,

We are distinct individuals first, and *then* we form relationships
and engage in co-operative arrangements with others. We are
barren subjects of possession first, and *then* we choose the ends
we would possess; hence the priority of the self over its ends.
(*Liberalism and the Limits of Justice*, p. 133)

This partly explains how Dworkin can say that the idea of rights
that are natural, meaning that they are not products of any legislation or convention, requires 'no more than the hypothesis that
the best political program ... is one that takes the protection of
certain individual choices as fundamental, and not properly subordinated to any goal or duty' (*Taking Rights Seriously*, p. 176). Both
Rawls and Dworkin, notwithstanding their individualistic aspirations, inherit Kant's attenuated conception of the person. The only
way to secure the sovereignty of the self given prior to its ends is
to relegate not only our characters but also our deepest values and
convictions to the contingent, 'as features of my condition rather
than as constituents of my person' (*Liberalism and the Limits of
Justice*, p. 94). If we are to go along with Rawls, even the character
that determines a person's motivation cannot properly be regarded
as an essential constituent of his identity. Hopefully we have been
able to explain how a person so essentially dispossessed has become
the product of a liberal moral theory designed to establish the
rights of the individual as inviolable. This has remained an irony
for Sandel since he has underestimated its strengths in essentially
displacing the moral significance of issues of power and dependency.

Though both Dworkin and Rawls want to take the protection
of certain individual choices as fundamental, they can only do this
at the cost of making our existence as autonomous individuals
invulnerable to social relations of power. They fall back on versions
of the traditional assumption that an individual exists prior to his
or her involvement in social relations. Even if they want to resist
a traditional dependence upon assumptions of human nature, they
share the view that at least some of our qualities are given prior to
our social lives. As I have shown, this limits the sense in which
people can be hurt or damaged in their autonomy as individuals.
It tempts us into thinking that whatever indignities and sufferings
the powerless and oppressed are forced to endure they can only be
of a more or less superficial character. This can only mean an

injury to the personality and its desires, as people are forced to settle for less than they would want. If our egos are hurt, somehow our individuality remains intact. We do not seem to endure damage in our moral capacities to relate to others of the kind Freud helps identify, since our relationships flow from the individual choices we are assumed free to make. Often the assumption of a self that exists prior to his or her ends assumes a self that is invulnerable to being undermined. But as Sandel has realised, a self 'shorn of all contingently-given attributes, assumes a kind of supra-empirical status' (*Liberalism and the Limits of Justice*, p. 94). This is clear when Rawls rejects the principle of fair opportunity which seeks to reward individual skill and effort. The self is still overascribed since these abilities and qualities have to be regarded as arbitrary from a moral standpoint since

> the effort a person is willing to make is influenced by his
> natural abilities and skills and the alternatives open to him.
> The better endowed are more likely, other things being equal,
> to strive conscientiously, and there seems to be no way to
> discount for their greater good fortune. (*A Theory of Justice*,
> p. 94)

For Rawls it is part of a process of liberal enlightenment for us to realise gradually that characteristics we had once accepted as essential to a person's identity are features which are arbitrarily given. They can no longer serve to legitimate the existence of social inequalities. But more and more this means that to speak of the self from a moral point of view is to speak of an antecedently individuated self shorn or dispossessed, as Sadel has it, of most qualities and characteristics.

Rawls challenges the system of natural liberty which is akin to Nozick's entitlement theory, since the distribution it sanctions tends simply to reproduce the initial distribution of talents and assets. It is not enough to define justice as whatever distribution emerges from an efficient market economy in which there is a formal equality of opportunity. This can only be called just on the additional assumption that initial endowments were justly distributed. But since the initial distribution is bound to be influenced by nature and social contingencies, the outcome is neither just nor unjust but simply arbitrary. As Rawls has it, 'Intuitively, the most obvious injustice of the system of natural liberty is that it permits distributive shares to be improperly influenced by these factors so arbitrary from a moral point of view.' (*A Theory of Justice*, p. 72.) But even a principle of liberal equality which seeks to give an 'equal start', regardless of the class, sex or race into which people are born, is too weak a challenge on the arbitrariness of fortune since whatever its success in providing more equal prospects for similar ability and effort, 'There is no more reason to permit the distribution of income and wealth to be settled by the distribution of natural assets than by historical and social fortune.' (*A Theory of Justice*, p. 74.) As Rawls insists, 'From a moral standpoint, the two seem equally arbitrary.' (p. 75.)

The democratic conception which Rawls favours cannot be a simple extension of the principle of fair opportunity since the contingencies of natural fortune have to be acknowledged as intractable. What we need is a different starting-point which works to nullify the effect of these differences. Rather than eliminate these distinctions, we have to arrange the scheme of benefits and burdens so that the least skilled and advantaged may share in the resources of the fortunate. The difference principle defines as just only those inequalities that work to benefit the least advantaged members of society. This is tantamount to an agreement to regard the distribution of natural talents as a common asset and to share the benefits of this distribution whatever it turns out to be.

If people agree to share their fate in this way, it matters less what their individual talents have turned out to be. At least this 'does not require society to even out handicaps as if all were expected to compete on a fair basis in the same race' (*A Theory of Justice*, p. 101). My talents and abilities are no longer to be regarded as my individual possession. The difference principle fundamentally transforms the moral basis on which I claim the benefits that flow from them. Rawls is convinced that the traditional conception of individual desert is based upon a mistake since: 'It seems one of the fixed points of our considered judgment that no one deserves his place in the distribution of native endowments, any more than one deserves one's initial starting place in society' (*A Theory of Justice*, p. 104.)

But it is important to remember that Rawls's theory of the person implies that no characteristics, whether social or natural, can be essential to the self. Since a person's character 'depends in large part upon fortunate family and social circumstances for which he

can claim no credit' (*A Theory of Justice*, p. 104), even those attributes, such as a person's character and values that intuitively seem
closer to defining an essential self, are relegated to a contingent
status. But we can accept Rawls's argument from arbitrariness as
a challenge to liberal equality without accepting the implications
that seem to follow for his conception of the person. We are forced
to rethink the difference principle if we want to make space to
consider it as an issue not simply of a just distribution of resources
but also of relationships of power and subordination. It is not
simply an issue of whether the least well-off can be seen to benefit,
but also of the relationship of subordination and powerlessness this
leaves people in. This connects to the issue that if individual talents
and skills are to be regarded as 'common assets' why are property
and material resources also not being so regarded, especially if this
leaves the poor dependent for their very means of livelihood. It
was because Kant realised that relations of dependency threatened
the independent existence of people that he made this an issue of
justice.

A meritocratic conception, for all its weaknesses, does not disempower individuals to the same extent as Rawls seems to do, since
it leaves individuals with an independent test of the justice of institutions. People have a right to complain if they feel their talents
have not been duly rewarded. Rawls's rejection of pre-institutional
notions of moral worth and virtue means that the intrinsic worth
of the attributes a society elicits and rewards cannot provide a
measure for assessing its justice. It is up to institutions to define
their own conception of moral worth, according to the particular
talents and abilities they have chosen to recognise and foster. As
Sandel makes clear, the priority of just institutions with respect to
virtue and Rawls's rejection of pre-institutional notions of virtue
'reflects the priority of the right over the good and the refusal to
choose in advance between competing conceptions of the good'
(*Liberalism and the Limits of Justice*, p. 76). This is yet another
reason why I cannot be said to *deserve* the benefits flowing from my
natural attributes. If Rawls helps us challenge the meritocratic idea
that I somehow have a right, in a strong pre-institutional sense,
that society, say, values intelligence rather than something else, he
does not help us realise that society has to recognise the hunger
and misery of the oppressed or the suffering of the powerless.

Though Rawls encourages us to think of our individual talents and abilities as 'common assets' we should learn to cherish not just for ourselves, but for the community at large, their worth or value is somehow to be left for institutions to decide upon. We seem powerless, for instance, to demand that the organisation of production calls upon the skills and talents we have rather than degrade them. We seem to slip into thinking that if, for instance, an assembly-line can be shown to maximise production so that working people can be shown to be better off in absolute terms, then it has to be welcomed. There is no space within which to recognise a possible conflict between science and technology organised so as to maximise production and organised with the well-being of the workers at heart. Few people ever imagine that an engineer occupied in technical research could ever have anything other than the objective of producing more at a cheaper rate which seems to be an identical interest of both consumer and producer. As Simone Weil realised, nobody considers the moral well-being of the workers. Nobody thinks twice about the workpeople who will be spending their energies on the machines. What is more, 'Nobody even thinks it possible to think about them. The most that ever happens is that from time to time some vague security apparatus is provided.' (*The Need for Roots*, p. 54.) What is the point of workers struggling for an increase in wages and a relaxation of discipline, 'if meanwhile engineers in a few research departments invent, without the slightest evil intent, machines which reduce their souls and bodies to a state of exhaustion' (*The Need for Roots*, p. 54). Weil questions the point of the nationalisation of economic production if we are blind to the one conviction, which even in her latest writings she recognised as standing out with irresistible force in the works of Marx, namely that any change in the relationship between the classes 'must remain a pure illusion, if it is not accompanied by a transformation in technical processes, expressing itself in entirely new types of machinery' (*The Need for Roots*, p. 54).

Even though Rawls can readily admit that 'someone's plan of life will lack a certain attraction to him if it fails to call upon his natural capacities in an interesting fashion' (*A Theory of Justice*, p. 440), he tends to assume this is something individuals can control for themselves, especially if they have been guaranteed an equal liberty to pursue their own ends. If we have to learn to be realistic about our aspirations, this means acknowledging the qualities we have. A person with no musical ability does not strive to be a musician and so feels no shame for this lack. Rather, for Rawls, we feel ashamed because we have not achieved what we could have achieved in the exercise of our particular talents and abilities. We feel shame because we know we could have done otherwise. But if we can accept this about music, it is harder to accept this about manual skills. Marx was centrally concerned to show that working-class people are not free to choose the conditions and relations in which to exercise their skills. If we are to recognise the value of physical labour then, according to Weil,

> To take a youth who has a vocation for this kind of work and employ him at a conveyor belt as a piece-work machinist is no less a crime than to put out the eyes of the young Watteau and make him turn a grindstone. But the painter's vocation can be discerned and the other cannot. (*Selected Essays*, 'Human Personality', p. 17)

Weil puts this so starkly because she wants to challenge the blindness of a society that seems incapable of recognising the nature of the injustice being done to people. Nobody even considers the possibility of not injuring people in the flesh, since otherwise we would surely have found alternatives to the use of automatic drills worked by compressed air in the mines, 'which sends an uninterrupted series of shocks for eight hours through the body of the man manipulating it' (*The Need for Roots*, p. 54).

Simone Weil recognises that even Soviet propaganda has never claimed that Russia had discovered a radically new type of machine that was worthy of being handled by working people. Socialism as we have largely inherited it has seemed almost equally incapable of grasping the essential idea of 'posing in technical terms problems concerning the effects of machines upon the moral well-being of the workmen' (*The Need for Roots*, p. 55). Here we are thinking of respect not simply in terms of personal relations, but of social relations of production which acknowledge the dignity and human worth of people's capacities and skills. This raises the question of whether an assembly-line production that subordinates people's bodily movements to the movements of the line can be morally justified. It is one thing to recognise that the mind is essentially free and sovereign when it is really and truly exercised, but if this is only allowed to people a few exhausted hours a day when they are slaves to the machine for the rest of the day, as Weil has it, this 'is such an agonising spiritual quartering that it is almost impossible not to renounce' (*The Need for Roots*, p. 68). So we cannot even assume that people are free to have their own thoughts. We have to recognise a contradiction between what people need for themselves to sustain a sense of self-respect and the needs of production they have to conform to. If people cannot insist that their particular skills will always be exercised to the full, they can at least feel justified in claiming that the institutions recognise the virtue and moral worth of their capacities and abilities. Against this it can be said that in a capitalist economy only skills and abilities that have an exchange value on the market can be validated. It is also commonly said that when people work their time is not their own, but belongs to their boss. People should be ready to do whatever is asked of them, once they have made their initial choice to take a job.

Liberal theory often side-steps these questions by saying that we show our respect for people by recognising the value of whatever job or task they happen to do. Not only do we respect others regardless of the job they do or position they hold, but we also recognise that whether people are doctors or factory workers they are making a contribution to society which is roughly consonant with the abilities they have. The relationship between liberalism and a functionalist view of society has become very close. Both seem to excuse us from thinking about the chances people have within the prevailing organisation of work and domestic relations to exercise their capacities and abilities. Since property is generally regarded as a means through which individuals pursue their freely chosen ends, Rawls does not think of it as a 'common asset'. But nor does he think of the means of production as giving people *control* over the lives of others. It was exactly this kind of argument that tempted Kant into thinking that individuals have to be independent and self-sufficient, even if this means people have a right to a certain degree of individual property. This would mean, for a socialist tradition, a reworking of the meaning of collective ownership in terms of the effective control and autonomy this gives individuals over their lives. But this itself is a critique of forms of socialism as the concentration of control in a centralised state. It would involve a recovery of the libertarian tradition within Marxism.[13]

Injustice has to do with the way people are mistreated, not only in their personal relations, but also in the everyday material conditions of their lives. Working on an assembly-line can be an equal insult and injury to our dignity as human beings, however tactful a foreman is in approaching us. When Mill acknowledges that in proportion to the development of our individuality there is 'greater fullness of life' (*On Liberty*, p. 192) about our own existence, we recognise how this can mean so much more than Rawls's idea that a person's sense of his own value concerns 'his secure conviction that his conception of the good, his plan of life, is worth carrying out' (*A Theory of Justice*, p. 440). A recognition of the difficulties people face in developing their individuality was part of what propelled Mill towards socialism. Rather than the attenuated conception of the person which dentological liberalism inherits from Kant, we need a sense of the moral importance of people being able to express their capacities, powers and abilities in their everyday relationships. This also involves acknowledging, as I have continually argued, the individuality of our emotions, feelings and desires. But this has to be a conception of the self that is not limited to our personal egos and its desires. We have to be careful that Rawls's argument from arbitrariness, consistently applied, does not make the individual inviolable only by making him or her invisible. This calls into question the very dignity and autonomy that liberalism seeks above all to secure. A theory of justice has also to be concerned with illuminating the *vulnerability* of people to hurt and injury in our relations with others. But if we end up, as Nozick has claimed, attributing everything noteworthy about a person completely to certain sorts of 'external' factors we end up 'denigrating a person's autonomy and prime responsibility for his actions'. Nozick is right that this 'is a risky line to take for a theory that otherwise wishes to buttress the dignity and self-respect of autonomous beings' (*Anarchy, State and Utopia*, p. 214). In contrast, Nozick argues that people are entitled to their natural assets and the benefits that flow from them in a sense of entitlement antecedent to social institutions. The concept of entitlement is made to do the same work as desert, though he fails to acknowledge its lesser moral force. He also fails to spell out the conception of the self that could make entitlement equivalent to desert.

Sandel is well aware that

it is one thing to assert what is in some sense undeniable, that we are 'thick with particular traits', and quite another to show

this can be true in a way not subject to the rival incoherence
associated with a radically situated self, indefinitely
conditioned by its surroundings and constantly subject to
transformation by experience. (*Liberalism and the Limits of
Justice*, p. 101)

For Rawls the absence of individual desert creates a presumption
in favour of regarding the distribution of abilities and talents as a
common asset. Institutions are unconstrained by antecedent moral
claims in their pursuit of the primary virtue of justice. But this is
to *separate* our understanding of justice from the fulfilment of
human needs even if, according to Rawls, 'the principles of justice
manifest in the very basic structure of society men's desire to treat
one another not as means only but as ends in themselves' (*A Theory
of Justice*, p. 179). But if regarding natural talents as a common
asset is to avoid Nozick's criticism that it treats people's abilities
and talents as a resource for others, it has to press '*very* hard on
the distinction between men and their talents, assets, abilities and
special traits' (*Anarchy, State and Utopia*, p. 228). Sandel concedes
that here Nozick goes to the heart of Rawls's theory of the subject,
since Rawls does indeed press very hard on the distinction between
the self and its various possessions. But this is because Sandel
assumes Rawls is forced to reply that not persons, but only their
attributes, are being used as means to others' well-being. We would
be reminded, he thinks, not to confuse the self with its contingently
given and wholly inessential attributes to me being the particular
self I am. Sandel thinks that Nozick's objections to the difference
principle succeed since 'The notion that only *my assests* are being
used as a means, not me, threatens to underlie the plausibility, even
the coherence, of the very distinction it invokes.' (*Liberalism and
the Limits of Justice*, p. 79.)

Rawls is convinced that whether a society is just does not simply
depend upon whether many people have a desire to act justly, but
rather whether its 'basic structure' is of a certain kind. Plato's
Republic similarly argues that individuals cannot live just lives if
they lived in unjust society. Though he thought very differently, he
also wanted to settle the issue of the nature of a just society independently of a consideration of the needs, desires and emotions of
individuals. His was also a project set in the rationalist tradition.
If we are to avoid the problems of a radically situated self, we

205

require a sense of tension between what individuals need for themselves and the requirements and demands of a larger society. Both functionalist and structuralist theories have settled for a conception of the human subject who is socially and historically determined. In Althusser's hands this has impoverished our conception of socialism since it has inhibited the terms in which we could critique capitalist social relations. Socialism becomes a more 'advanced' or 'efficient' mode of production, not a more human and equal society.[14] But this is also an issue for the liberal theory of Rawls and Dworkin. The argument from arbitrariness works, as Sandel realises, only to undermine individual desert, not necessarily to legitimate a social conception in which the community as a whole has some pre-institutional status of desert. This is equally true when Dworkin's argument for affirmative action assumes that when merit is excluded, the collective ends of society as a whole should automatically prevail. The individual and society are set up as the fundamental framework of liberal theory.

Both Rawls and Dworkin tend to think of justice from the point of view of an impartial government, assumed to exist over and above the struggles within civil society. Rawls focuses upon the issue of a just distribution of resources. He tends to see our abilities and talents as if they are 'ends' which individuals freely choose to exercise. We feel shame if we are left thinking we could have more greatly developed our faculties and talents. Even if Rawls recognises that just institutions have to identify and foster particular talents, he assumes that is a matter of what talents are acknowledged as morally worthy. He assumes that our talents and abilities exist intact, being unable theoretically to grasp how they can be injured, damaged and denigrated within particular relations of power and subordination. Since our talents and abilities are individually identified, they tend to be grasped as desires and feelings with no essential connection to the realisation of the self. This makes it hard to recognise an injury to our capacities as an *injury to self*, rather than simply a limitation to our personality and its desires. A small child has to be taught boundaries by her parents as she learns to recognise that her parents also have needs and wishes they want to fulfil. This is something a small child might protest about, but it can help rather than block the development of a secure sense of self. This is different from the rejection a child can feel if she feels she is a nuisance every time she reaches out for her parents. This can teach her that she is not entitled to have needs at all. She learns not to reach out or to develop a false sense of self. She has learnt to distrust herself.

This is not simply an issue of the talents and abilities just institutions choose to value and reward. So, for instance, this is not an issue of schools learning to recognise and value other abilities beside a purely academic or sporting ability. Certainly the school can help foster the recognition of a much broader range of talents which can help more people to value themselves. In a traditional school setting children can be left feeling that if they are not clever, there is no way they can value themselves. It is not just that they are not as clever as others, but they cease to have any value at all. Children can learn to despise themselves and be left with a deep sense of inferiority that makes them think others cannot be expected to take them seriously since nothing they say can be of any value. I cannot forget a student describing his hurt years ago when a new teacher came into their small country school saying that other teachers pitied him for having to waste his energies on such a class of thickies. This didn't just scar his intelligence but it undermined his very trust in himself. Years later he would always begin speaking with an apology, as if he had no right to speak at all. This is a situation that can possibly be slowly and sensitively healed, but it is not within his rational control nor is it a matter of simply being told that he has an equal right and value with others, since this is not the reality for him. As his intelligence has been injured, so has his sense of self. An injustice has been done.

But nor can we think in Dworkin's terms of an equal concern and respect, as if this is always within our rational control. Somehow this has to be given expression within the actual workings of our institutions so that we are not simply talking about the official self-conception of a school, say, but of the *quality of experience* which individuals enjoy. But this involves a fuller recognition of the vulnerability of our sense of self, especially within relations of power and dependency. If we are powerless we can so easily be abused, or else we close off emotionally making ourselves invulnerable to the hurt and pain of others, but often at the cost of the reality of our experience. We will learn not to show ourselves in a classroom in which we fear we are likely to be humiliated by a teacher. We learn to protect ourselves. It is only when our self is injured that we no longer have *control* over these ways of defending ourselves, but find ourselves being incapable of openness and warmth towards others, even when we want to. We need to illuminate the connection between harm and injury done to the self and an injustice being done because we have treated people with a lack of respect. This often has to do with failing to treat someone with respect within an unequal relationship of power and subordination.

Simone Weil discovered that her relations with superiors were governed by the principle that she conceives

> human relations solely on the plane of equality; therefore, so
> soon as someone begins to treat me as an inferior, human
> relations between us becomes impossible in my eyes. So I treat
> him in turn as a superior. By which I mean that I endure his
> power as I endure the frost and the rain. (*Seventy Letters*, p. 34)

This is partly why she thinks, whether from pride or timidity, 'a glum silence is the general rule in a factory'. This was part of a more general lesson she drew from her experience of factory work, that humanity seemed to be divided into two categories – the people who count for something and the people who count for nothing. 'When one is in the second category one comes to find it quite natural to count for nothing – which is by no means to say that it isn't painful.' (*Seventy Letters*, p. 35.) As far as Weil is concerned everybody knows this present state of affairs is not acceptable 'but nobody on either side dares make the slightest allusion to it'. She was always concerned to discover whether, in the existing conditions, 'one can bring it about, within a factory, that the workers count, and have the feeling that they count'. But she knew that this called for something quite different than the manager learning to behave well to them, significant as this can sometimes be.

Though Weil lost her belief in revolutionary politics, she always retained a sharp sense that 'Nothing is more paralysing to thought than the sense of inferiority which is necessarily induced by the daily assault of poverty, subordination, and dependence.' (*Seventy Letters*, p. 24.) She always thought that 'The first thing to be done for them is to help them to recover or retain, as the case may be, their sense of dignity.' She knew from her own experience how difficult it is in the conditions of a factory to retain that sense and how precious any moral support can be. This was to become a central insight of the black movement and the movement for women and gay liberation in the 1960s and 1970s, though its significance for the revitalisation of socialist politics is still to be grasped fully. This is paradoxical, since for Weil it was directly connected to her understanding of class feeling. She says significantly about class feeling that

> In my opinion, it can hardly be stimulated by mere words, whether spoken or written. It is determined by actual conditions of life. What stimulates it is the infliction of humiliation and suffering, and the fact of subordination; but it is continually repressed by the inexorable daily pressure of need, and often to the point where, in the weaker characters, it turns into servility. (*Seventy Letters*, p. 24)

She had learnt to her surprise that oppression, beyond a certain degree of intensity, does not engender revolt, but often submission.

A moral tradition which thinks of respect as an attitude we freely take up towards others tends to think of justice either as an issue of distribution or else of personal relations. It becomes difficult to grasp that the actual *conditions of life* can humiliate and cause suffering. This can leave people with a deep sense of inferiority which is not lifted because people are assured equal political and legal rights in another sphere of life. If it is true, as Walzer insists, in *Spheres of Justice*, that we live in different spheres each with their own discrete criteria of justice which we have to learn to respect, we also need to recognise the power which relations of subordination at work continue to have in people's lives. We have to realise that our personal relations take place *within* material relations of power and subordination, so that, for instance, sexual relations between men and women are influenced by the relative power men and women enjoy in the larger society. We cannot meaningfully abstract our personal relations as if they take place in a space of their own, in the hope that issues of power have no place in relations of love and affection.

Dworkin assumes that when people are denied some liberty, say to form certain sexual relations, people suffer because their conception of a proper or desirable form of life is despised by others. This is tantamount to treating them as inferior or of less worth than others, or not deserving equal concern and respect. Dworkin thinks that every denial of freedom on the basis of external preferences implies that those denied are not entitled to equal concern and respect. This is part of Dworkin's attempt to derive liberal rights from the duty of governments to treat all its citizens with equal concern and respect. But the idea of equal concern and respect, even though it has the appearance of resting on something as un-controversial as 'a postulate of political morality' we are all 'presumed to accept', is too indeterminate to play the fundamental role they have in Dworkin's theory. In the end, Dworkin, like Rawls, wants to guarantee us a framework within which individuals are free to pursue their own visions of happiness. The liberal conception of equality requires governments to be neutral between their subjects' values or visions of the good life. But again this assumes, as Kant had, that individuals are essentially independent and self-sufficient, rather than locked into class, ethnic and sexual relations of power and dependence. Not only does Dworkin want to challenge the traditional liberal idea of a general right to liberty but he wants to show that specific liberties can be derived from a prior right to equal concern and respect.

This attempt is flawed if we think that the denial of freedom of worship, or homosexuals being denied freedom to form sexual relations, has to be challenged because of the role these liberties play in human life. I have argued that what is crucial is their connection to ideas of autonomy and independence, when this is not grasped simply in rationalist terms but has to do with actual conditions of life. Hart thinks these liberties are too precious to be put at the mercy of numbers even if in favourable circumstances they may win out. He thinks it fantastic to suppose that if people are denied these liberties what they 'chiefly have to complain about is not the restriction of their liberty with all its grave impact on personal life or development and happiness, but that they are not accorded *equal* concern and respect' (*The Idea of Freedom*, p. 97). The vice of the denial of such liberties is not its inequality or unequal impact. Hart emphasises that 'what is deplorable is the ill-treatment of the victims and not the relational matter of the unfairness of their treatment compared with others' (p. 97). But if this reveals difficulties with the liberal conception of equality, it also illuminates problems we have in explaining the 'grave impact' which a denial of specific liberties has upon 'personal life or development and happiness'. This is not simply an injury to the personality and its desires but reaches far deeper into the constitution of the self. It is only if we challenge the inherited assumptions of our rationalist moral traditions that we can grasp with full force Hart's idea that 'The evil is the denial of liberty or respect; not *equal* liberty or *equal* respect.' (*The Idea of Freedom*, p. 97.)

Somehow we have to connect our grasp of our liberties with our sense of what it means to exist as a person in our own right. This is not simply an individual quest, but as I have shown, can involve learning to reclaim not only our feelings, desires and bodily experience which our inherited moral culture would denigrate, but also class, ethnic and sexual identities which we have automatically learnt to disown in the struggle to assert ourselves within the terms of a possessive individualism. Crucially this involves a recognition of the contradictions in our moral experience as we need to challenge prevailing relations of power and dependency, if we are to realise a different sense of our individuality. But this can also involve a reassessment of the larger structures of power and the values they reproduce. For Marx this essentially meant a recognition in a capitalist society of the continuing importance of the sphere of material production in people's lives. It cannot be conceived as one sphere amongst others, though its relative significance has always to be grasped historically. He points out that 'In fact, the realm of freedom actually begins only where labour which is determined by necessity and mundane considerations ceases; thus in the very nature of things it lies beyond the sphere of material production.' (*Capital*, Vol. 3, p. 820.) The shortening of the working-day was a basic demand for Marx because it is only beyond the sphere of production that 'begins that development of human energy which is an end in itself, the true realm of freedom' (*Capital*, Vol. 3, p. 820). But Marx sometimes trapped himself in drawing too sharp and categorical a Kantian distinction between a realm of necessity and a realm of freedom, forgetting his crucial insights into the labour process which recognises workers would be continually struggling to enlarge their autonomy and control within production itself. This was the emphasis Weil wanted to explore in her attempts to sustain the dignity of workers' lives in conditions which could so easily undermine and crush it.

Within a liberal democratic society we generally assume that the existence of political liberties is sufficient guarantee of our independence and autonomy. I have argued that in a society characterised by structured relations of power and dependency, autonomy requires much more than explicit political liberties and protections. It also requires more personal ones as well. This is recognised by Cohen and Rogers when they argue that

> Free public deliberation follows upon and itself requires the exercise of individual self-governing capacities in arenas that are not commonly recognised as political. That exercise in turn depends on the protection of freedom of expression, speech, belief, and thought within those arenas. (*On Democracy*, p. 153)

While it is acknowledged that autonomy has to be mutual, so that individual exercise of such self-governing capacities should not constrain the autonomy of others, we still need to also consider the moral issue of dependency and subordination. This means recognising that social and economic inequalities cannot simply be arranged, as Rawls thinks, 'to the greatest benefit of the least advantaged' (*A Theory of Justice*, p. 302) without *also* exploring how they can also undermine a person's autonomy. Even though material inequalities are not inconsistent with a requirement of basic material satisfaction for all, we have to be concerned with the nature of the control people exercise over different parts of their lives. As feminism has stressed, for a woman to exist as a person in her own right she also needs a chance to explore and exercise her individual capacities, not simply an equal chance to fit into the prevailing order of work.

This is part of a challenge to ideas of fair opportunity which Rawls assumes along with the difference principle. Women have argued that it is not simply an issue of competing with men on more equal terms, but also of challenging *the terms* of this competition, so that more of their qualities can be acknowledged and validated. Women have sought to find their own voices, rather than be forced to silence themselves to be acceptable in the terms of a traditional masculine world. But this has been part of recognising that women have been generally subordinated in a world that had promised them much greater equality of opportunity. Often women have been forced to forsake or deny their qualities to get on in a world they had little power to remake in their own image. This showed itself sociologically, before feminism, in career women often unwittingly despising women who had settled for domestic lives. As they were encouraged into identifying with men in the world of work, they found that the price was the little space to validate and respect their experience as women. This was the price women had to pay for success in a man's world. But this involved a cost and hurt that was rendered invisible as people were assured a formal equality.

We grow up within a liberal moral culture to treasure the idea that we each have an equal opportunity to express fully our personalities. Simone Weil was wary of the idea, thinking that the right of the personality to what is called 'full expression' depends upon it being inflated by social prestige. She thinks the idea is absurd because the privilege upon which it is based is, by definition, inequality. Even if the everyday experience of subordination of working people makes them fully aware they do not enjoy an equal chance to express themselves, it is hard to reject an idea which is so institutionalised. As Weil says, 'To the dimmed understanding of our age there seems nothing odd in claiming an equal share of privilege for everybody – and equal share in things whose essence is privilege.' (*Selected Essays*, p. 22.) This promise is hidden in the very grammar of respect, when we use the same term to mark hierarchy as we do to express our sense of equality with others. But hopefully I have helped explain this, at least in its Kantian form, since the respect for ourselves is itself built upon the denigration of our natures. Since women have been regarded at least since the enlightenment as closer to nature, it has been a continuously erupting theme of feminism to reassert the value and dignity of our natures, as part of women learning to respect and value their own experience. This has involved a critique of the relationship of language to power and often a willingness to interpret Weil's sense of challenging inherited ideas in more gender specific terms than she intended, when she says

> the category of men who formulate claims and everything else, the men who have the monopoly of language, is a category of privileged people. They are not the ones to say that privilege is unworthy to be desired. They don't think so and, in any case, it would be indecent for them to say it. (*Selected Essays*, p. 22)

Kant had grasped in his reflections upon the relation between rich and poor that a relationship of dependency can compromise our equal capacity to live moral lives. As long as the poor are dependent on the rich for their very means of livelihood and have less than they need for themselves when the rich have more, an injustice is done. It is only when Kant can assume that individuals are independent and self-sufficient that he can sustain his confidence in our equality before the moral law. Nor, for a time, did he think we could abstract ourselves from the structured relations of power and dependency to show our respect for others as equal human beings. This could only be justified if the sources of wealth were transformed, so that if inequalities persisted, they did not leave the poor dependent for their very means of livelihood. The rich had to be prepared to give up their privileges and wealth to restore a more equal situation. The Christian vision, which informs the liberal inheritance to say that, whatever the structured relationship of power and subordination, we can show our respect in abstracting from these relations, could no longer be sustained. Morality had to engage with material and social inequalities once it was recognised they produced relations of dependency that threatened our autonomy and independence. This was important for Kant's process of preparing a compromise with social life. This is embodied in the liberal idea that we can show equal respect for the ends individuals have chosen for themselves. This assumes people are making a contribution to the larger society which is roughly consonant with their talents and abilities.

But it was also because Kant defined dependence in opposition to independence, that it was something to be feared. I have argued against this dualistic conception, showing how it is the identification of dependence with weakness which tacitly legitimates the subordination of women. Since emotions and feelings are a source of weakness, women need the external authority of men's reason to escape this form of dependency. It is the implicit rationalism that makes women's experience problematic but which also renders *invisible* difficulties men can have in emotional relationships.[15] Men are left feeling that they need to be sources of strength to help women deal with their stronger inclinations which would otherwise make it impossible for women to escape the grip of emotional dependencies. In the moral culture Kant helps prepare men become fearful of showing signs of weakness and vulnerability, since we are convinced that, in the competitive world, this would quickly be used against us. Since the ideals of independence and self-sufficiency are taken very much for granted within Kantian moral theory, men's difficulties in acknowledging needs of support and caring from others are hidden. So Kant helps sustain contemporary notions of masculinity, which in themselves are rendered invisible, since they are written into the very conceptions of morality, individuality and rationality we implicitly inherit. Alternative traditions of moral theory often share these deeper assumptions so that the differences we learn to identify leave them untouched.

Kant saves his conception of the autonomy of morality with an assumption that the poor can always escape a relationship of dependency. This makes it a sign of moral weakness which in the end prepares the ground for people feeling they only have themselves to blame. Our moral vision can be restored to its individualistic foundations and the issue of justice side-stepped. He falls back into thinking of both inner dependency on our inclinations and dependence on social relations of power in similar terms. They are both forms of unfreedom that we can supposedly escape through identifying with our intelligible selves. It is as if these can be rendered as different forms of the same basic struggle to act out of a sense of duty. As long as we can think of morality as an individual quest the boundaries between morality and social theory remain secure. But the fact that Kant was forced back into positions he had himself questioned shows the difficulties we inherit for thinking through the moral nature of relations of power and dependency. In this sense our Kantian inheritance limits our moral vision and constantly brings us back to focus upon the morality of individual action, as if this can be settled once and for all through giving universal reasons. It is as if we are powerless to think morally about the character of structured relations of power which connect our individual moral experience to our experience of social classes, races or sexes, but only about how individuals are supposed to behave within these given relations of power and subordination. For Kant it became an issue of how the rich and powerful are to learn tact and consideration so they do not needlessly compromise the self-respect of those who are powerless and subordinate.

But if our moral theory is to be renewed it has to be able to face the moral nature of structured relations of inequality. This should be clear since the very relation Kant most feared of the poor becoming dependent for their very means of livelihood has become a standard form of relation within a capitalist mode of production. It is the very interconnection of our lives within social relations of power that threatens an individualistic moral consciousness that has wanted to believe that individuals could always categorically discern the right thing to do. What is more this would supposedly be equally right for anyone else facing the same situation. It is this universalism that is also challenged, as we discover how our inherited sense of our equality before the moral law had implicitly depended upon an assumption of independence and self-sufficiency. This is not only true of Kant but also of liberal moral and political theory that has been shaped in his image.

Since the enlightenment we have cherished the idea that there is always a morally right thing to do which we can discover through our reasons alone. The differences have been around how individuals are to discern this and whether they have the moral qualities to enable them to do what they have discovered to be right. This is equally true of Kant and utilitarianism which have provided the twin pillars of a liberal moral culture. But Kant had the courage to show this tradition was threatened, as was its central idea of the autonomy of morality, when the poor are dependent for their means of livelihood and have less than they need when the rich have more than they need. An issue of justice threatens the idea that individuals can decide for themselves what is morally right, through the workings of reason alone. But now the universalism of this vision is challenged as the poor find their relationship to the moral law *mediated* by their subordination and powerless in relation to the rich and powerful. We can no longer think what others might do in a similar situation, without now locating our experience within particular relations of power and subordination. I have to learn to situate myself within the social world, rather than abstract myself from it, as I could more legitimately do when others could be assumed to be equally free to pursue their own ends. I can no longer situate myself outside the struggles of the social world looking for a point of impartiality and neutrality. I have to begin with discovering my identity and individual experience within these relations of power and subordination.

As soon as we question the universalism and rationalism of our Kantian inheritance, we are forced to realise the specific character of the historical relations we inherit. Working-class people enter a capitalist society in a different situation of wealth and power. Though individuals will handle this differently there is also a shared class experience that can be acknowledged and respected. This is an experience people can feel ashamed of, too, especially if they assume it indicates failure on the part of their parents. Individualism can provide an escape from these feelings of shame as it leaves young people feeling they can make their lives individually, according to their own abilities and talents. We will be tempted into thinking of class as a set of values, rather than as a relationship of power and dependency. Our moral traditions will also stress that what matters is not our backgrounds, since, for instance, there are good and bad people in different social classes, but what we can make of ourselves individually. I have continually acknowledged the strength of an individualistic moral tradition, especially when it illuminates issues of autonomy and independence, while acknowledging the costs of a tradition that cannot illuminate what have become, since Kant, quite central features of our moral experience. Even the issues of autonomy and independence have to be placed within a different setting, as we grapple with the moral realities of dependency, subordination, oppression and exploitation.

Our moral theory has to illuminate the contradictions in our moral experience in a society characterised by structured relations of power and dependency. Only when we are aware of how our inherited traditions *simplify* these moral realities will we reach for different conceptions. In particular, an individualistic tradition, while encouraging us to make individual efforts, can make it difficult to appreciate the *difficulties* we face. It can make us less aware and less sensitive of our class, ethnic or sexual formation, as we learn to think of this as purely contingent and incidental to who we are as individuals. This can *separate* us from our experience and leave us feeling *rootless* in a world we have to take on individually. We will continually be attempting to think of ourselves, within a tradition of possessive individualism, as individuals with an equal chance to succeed and only having ourselves to blame if we fail. Partly because of the impersonal character of the reason we inherit, we will be *estranged* from the significance of our class and sexual identities, thinking this can only cloud and interfere with the clarity of our moral vision. Against this it can be argued that our backgrounds only need be significant if we choose to make them so. But this is part of the voluntarism that needs challenging. There is an important sense that when we discount, say our class identities, our respect for ourselves is being injured. We do not choose our class background though we can do our best to hide it, especially if it brings back painful memories. But this is part of our inherited identity so that if we despise our class background, say, we are despising part of ourselves. We are making ourselves less than we can be.

To acknowledge our history and culture does not mean we have to be trapped by them, though it does mean an awareness of the particular issues it faces us with. So, for instance, a working-class child is often faced with the issue that if he makes it into a middle-class world he can be betraying the background he comes from. He can be acutely aware of the distance, even hostility, this can create between himself and his parents, even though they have supported his achievements in going to grammar school and then on to university. He is painfully aware that this is a choice his middle-class friends have not had to make. Looking back he might feel the loss of the closeness he had in his family, recognising how tense and uneasy he often feels with people now. Possibly he can see now how going to university was a critical moral issue for him, though he never appreciated it at the time. He is not so sure he made the right decision, in the sense that he could say what others should do. He can still feel the contradictions of the situation he was in, knowing that in some important sense there was no *right answer* and that he was going to lose something whatever he did. He knew it was not so straightforward an issue of individual success, as he had once thought. He sometimes felt angry when he thought that he had to make such a choice.

We inherit an impersonal conception of reasons, as if our reasons have to be impersonal and potentially universal for them to count as reasons at all. This has had a profound impact upon our conceptions of morality, as it has also helped foster a particular idea of personal identity. When it comes to morality it is only the impersonal reason we supposedly share with others that defines our moral identities. This can make it difficult to recognise the contradictions in our moral experience, as we treat our class, ethnic, or gender identities as if they are inevitably partial and so bound to cloud our moral vision. Since it is generally assumed, to pursue our education example, that any child would welcome the chance of going to a grammar school and then on to university, a person can be made to feel 'irrational' if he worries that this could be a betrayal of class background. Even if he is told his parents do not want to 'stand in his way' this does not always help. He can resent having to make the choice. He also knows it is not just an issue of being attached to his background, since he has learnt that class has to do with a relationship of power in his mining community. Even though he has been told he could put his skills and knowledge at the service of the wider labour movement, he doubts whether he will have the strength to see this through. This is a critical moral issue for him, though he recognises others might face it in quite different ways. Even other people at his school do not feel the same way. Middle-class children at the school find it extremely hard to understand the issue, knowing only that they would be grateful if they had the chance themselves. They do their best to be sympathetic, but the point is that they *are not* in the same situation, nor does it make sense any longer to say they should be able to put themselves in the same situation.

Kant appreciated that the rich and poor in a relationship of dependency cannot put themselves in the 'same situation'. This tacit assumption of our moral theory assumes that people are independent and self-sufficient. Similarly men and women are in a different situation, say, when it comes to the issue of abortion, since it is women who in the end carry the children. We might think of different men facing a similar issue of abortion in their relationships and they may well learn from each other, but it is important to realise that in this situation at least men and women do not stand in the same relation to the moral law, if we can so express the issue. The universalism of a Kantian tradition has assumed it is always possible meaningfully to imagine ourselves in the moral situation others face. This is taken to be an issue of imagination and empathy. Important as this is, it can blind us to the moral significance of recognising the differences and particularity of a person's situation, not least the moral relevance of relations of power and subordination. This assumption has served the interests of the powerful in society, often as a means of controlling the articulation of the injustice, misery and indignity suffered by the powerless and oppressed. The very assumption that we exist as free and equal rational beings, able to choose ends for ourselves, articulates as universal a situation enjoyed by relatively few on our planet. If it is an important part of our dream of freedom and justice, we also require a theory which starts with illuminating existing realities of injustice and oppression.

The tradition of universalism in our moral theory helps sustain a sense of our equality as moral agents. It helps foster a particular conception of individualism in which we can consider ourselves as equal to others, but at the crucial cost of making contingent our class, ethnic and sexual identities. In learning to respect ourselves as individuals we are made to distance ourselves from these partial identifications which supposedly limit our impartial and objective moral vision. We are set on a path which defines individual identity very much in opposition to shared social identities, that are often presented as so many different roles we can choose to play. We find it hard to learn that working out how these different identities have formed our experience and helped make us the individuals we are, can be part of learning to respect ourselves. Rather we find ourselves *disempowered* because we only seem able to exist *as individuals* to the extent that we renounce our class, ethnic or sexual identities. This can *silence us* about say, our working-class background or our jewishness, thinking that what is important is that we are individuals existing in our own right. But this can hide deeper feelings of shame in which we are often sustaining an identity that does not feel firmly rooted. This makes it hard to learn how respecting our history and culture can be an integral part of learning to respect ourselves.

This is hard to acknowledge within a liberal moral culture in which we learn to stress not what we have with others as a shared experience or common inheritance, but what we have made of ourselves individually. So, for instance, many people feel uncomfortable with a feminist stress upon the influence of gender relations in the formation of individuality. We commonly hear the claim that it does not matter whether we are men or women but what kind of people we are individually. This assumes we are free to make our own lives. It wants to ignore the power of social definitions of masculinity and femininity as well as relations of power both between and within the sexes. Even if we would wish to have grown up in a different kind of society in which individuals are free to pursue their own ends, this does not alter the different social and historical experiences we have had growing up as men or women in society. These influences remain to be discovered even if we insist in asserting that we exist as free and equal rational beings. Our moral theory should bring us closer, rather than distance us from an acknowledgment of important features in our moral experience. Once we recognise, say, how significant a shared experience of masculinity, for example in the way I was treated at home and school, has been in shaping my sense of self this does not have to make me any the less an individual. If anything it promises to enrich and deepen my individuality and sense of self respect, as it helps me discern what I have inherited and what I have shaped for myself. This can help illuminate certain tensions and contradictions in my experience in a shared experience of masculinity, which I had previously assumed were personal to me. This can help define my individuality in clearer ways, rather than, as we tend to think in the common sense of liberal individualism, submerging myself in a collective history and identity that inevitably takes me over and clouds my sense of my individual needs. But this is an exploration that cannot simply be presented intellectually. It promises to transform the predominantly rationalist sense we have of ourselves as we discover connections between our reason and our emotional lives we had never given attention to before. We learn that we can exist as individuals without having to forsake the significance of shared identities. This is part of an ongoing moral and emotional practice of redefining an individuality we can no longer assume in rationalist terms. This can involve the painful recognition of the injury and damage we have suffered and also done to ourselves. This is part of reassessing images and identities we have assumed for the approval of others in a competitive world in which we have rarely had the power to set the terms.

This universalism has also made it difficult to grasp the moral nature of relations of power and inequality. We have enshrined a misleading distinction between moral theory and social theory as we have learnt to treat power as a social category which is more or less unequally distributed. This established the issue of equality and justice as it has traditionally been defined within political philosophy. Then morality can centrally concern the choices individuals make within these given social relations. Social relations are thereby conceived as *externally* constraining moral relations which take place within their grasp, rather than as moral relations themselves which can affect the kind of power people have over the lives of others. Liberal moral theory can then assume that the structure of social relations do not have to constrain or restrict the nature of our individual moral relations. We are always free to relate to others as we choose. But this is ambiguous because Kant insisted that moral relations are universal and so has made it harder to identify a morality of personal relations and has also blinded us to the ways Kantian moral tradition has helped to depersonalise our moral experience and sense of self. I have tried to show this process at work, as it becomes hard to acknowledge the centrality of our relations with others and also the injury and hurt we can suffer in our personal relations. Within a Kantian tradition morality is fundamentally an individual quest in which we have to prove ourselves to be morally worthy. This is an anxious and uneasy process because at some unacknowledged level we are still plagued by a protestant vision of the evilness of our natures. This makes it extremely hard to accept fully an alternative vision of morality which depends upon ideas of self-acceptance and the moral significance of relations with others.

Since the enlightenment we have sought to use reason to gain control of our lives and to guarantee our freedom, self-determination and independence. As Marx learnt from Hegel, this moral vision made it harder to come to terms with structured relations of inequality and dependency. Kant's moral theory helped define a tradition which was formed in opposition to the very power of tradition, habit and convention in feudal Europe. People were to be given control over their lives through the freedom to use their own minds and an encouragement to question every form of traditional authority. People had to be convinced through the evidence of their own senses. All forms of dependency were seen as regressions to a state of unfreedom and childishness. This was imagined equally true of our emotional natures and desires which could so easily keep us in the grip of habits and traditions we had outgrown. But this freedom was internalised as it was assumed that it was only through the inner workings of our reason that we can discern a path of freedom and autonomy. So we end up displaced from our natural selves, as well as from the social and historical relations we inherit. We are free at the cost of being estranged. We are trapped into identifying progress with the domination of both inner and external nature. This has left us with a very limited vision of respect for ourselves and others, as well as for the planet we inhabit. We have yet to learn to work with nature, not against her. This involves redefining our moral traditions so that we can *begin* with identifying the moral nature of the injury we do to ourselves and others, as well as the injustice and suffering people endure. This will involve relearning what it means to respect others, as we deepen our understanding of what it means to respect ourselves.

Issues of injustice, inequality and dependence do not simply grow out of individual decisions, nor are they avoidable consequences of a lack of individual decisions, nor are they avoidable consequences of a lack of individual moral will. The issues are deeper and need to be brought into focus, even if this means challenging inherited moral traditions and bringing moral theory into closer relation with social theory. It also involves challenging the reductionism of an orthodox Marxist tradition which has been impatient with moral issues, wanting to replace them with issues about the distribution of property and power. I have also shown that these spheres cannot be so neatly separated. We can help restore the moral weight of Marx's writings if we realise Marx rejected bourgeois morality because it fosters a vision that society can be effectively challenged by showing its injustice and presenting an alternative ideal of a socialist society. But it is not enough, as Marx often realised, to declare that we can only expect equal respect in an unequal society. We also need to challenge inherited traditions to develop a moral theory which can illuminate the moral and political issues of how people are to live more equal, free and just lives within an unequal and unjust society. The notion of respect, however transformed, will continue to echo the dignity and worth of individual lives. But this will help illuminate a sense of individuality that has been enriched, since it is fully able to acknowledge a respect for our emotions and desires, as well as for our history and culture. It will also mean transforming prevailing relations of power and subordination when they seek to threaten our individual and collective autonomy.

NOTES

CHAPTER I: INTRODUCTION: RESPECT, EQUALITY AND THE AUTONOMY OF MORALITY

1 I invoke a notion of 'the autonomy of morality' to indicate a general conception that it is always possible for an individual to decide what is morally appropriate to do in a situation, without having to question the basis of the relationship he or she is in. This is to assume that individuals are always free to treat others in any way that they choose, regardless of the relationship of power and subordination. This is to assume a fundamental separation between morality and politics. After completing this study I discovered a related usage in an early article by Alasdair MacIntyre. He writes that:

> One of the root mistakes of the liberal belief in the autonomy of morality now stands out. The believer in the autonomy of morality attempts to treat his fundamental moral principles as without any basis. They are his because he has chosen them. They can have no further vindication. And that is to say among other things that neither moral utterances nor moral action can be vindicated by reference to desires or needs. ('Notes from the Moral Wilderness, Part 2', *The New Reasoner*, 8, Spring 1959, pp. 89–90)

2 'The Idea of Equality' was originally published in the Proceedings of the Aristotelian Society, LVI (1955-6), pp. 281 seq. and is republished in Bernard Williams, *Problems of the Self*, Philosophical Papers 1956–72 (Cambridge University Press, 1973, pp. 230–49). This article has had a central position in the thinking that has gone on in the analytical tradition about issues of equality. It is enormously suggestive.

3 See the Foreword but also the papers 'The Availability of Wittgenstein's Later Philosophy' and 'Austin at Criticism' in Stanley Cavell's *Must We Mean What We Say?* (Charles Scribners, New York, 1969; Cambridge University Press, 1976).

224

4 See particularly Antonio Gramsci's discussion in 'The Study of Philosophy' to be found on pp. 321–77 in *Selections from the Prison Notebooks of Antonio Gramsci*, trans. Quintin Hoare and Geoffrey Nowell Smith (Lawrence & Wishart, London, 1971).

5 See Max Weber's *The Protestant Ethic and The Spirit of Capitalism* (George Allen & Unwin, London, 1930).

6 I shall be focusing upon Immanuel Kant, *Foundations of the Metaphysics of Morals*, trans. Lewis White Beck (New York, Library of Liberal Arts, Bobbs-Merrill) to illustrate classical formulations of Kant's moral writings. Sometimes I shall also refer to H. J. Paton's translation to be found in his *The Moral Law* (Hutchinson, London, 1948) where the differences seem to be significant. I contrast these writings with Kant's later writings particularly *The Doctrine of Virtue*, trans. Mary J. Gregor, which is Part 2 of Kant's *The Metaphysics of Morals* (Harper & Row, New York and London, 1964) (Academy edn page numbers). I think we can be helped in our understanding of the development of Kant's moral writings by Keith Ward, *The Development of Kant's View of Ethics* (Basil Blackwell, Oxford, 1972). The fullest exploration of themes in *The Doctrine of Virtue* has been in Mary Gregor's *Laws of Freedom* (Oxford University Press, 1963). The other translation of *The Doctrine of Virtue* (Part 2, Tungendlehre of *The Metaphysics of Morals*) has been by James Ellington as *The Metaphysical Principles of Virtue* (Indianapolis, 1964).

CHAPTER II: RESPECT AND HUMAN NATURE

1 See the essay on 'Kant and Rousseau' in Ernst Cassirer, *Rousseau, Kant, Goethe* (Princeton University Press, 1945).

2 Immanuel Kant, *Religion within the Limits of Reason Alone* (Harper & Row, New York, 1960).

3 See Jean-Jacques Rousseau's *Discourse on the Sciences and Arts* published along with the *Discourse on the Origin and Foundations of Inequality* as *The First and Second Discourses*, ed. Roger D. Masters (St Martin's Press, New York, 1964).

4 See Kant's 'An Answer to the Question: What is Enlightenment?' in *Kant's Political Writings*, ed. Hans Reiss (Cambridge University Press, 1970, pp. 54–60).

5 See Ernst Cassirer's *Rousseau, Kant, Goethe*, p. 12, and the quotation which is drawn from Kant's early essay *Observations on the Feeling of the Beautiful and the Sublime*, trans. Goldthwait (University of California Press, 1965).

6 See the interesting discussion in Allen W. Wood, *Kant's Moral Religion* (Cornell University Press, 1970).

7 See, for instance, its influence within John Rawls, *A Theory of Justice* (Oxford University Press, 1971). See also the various discussions of Rawls's work which have been collected in *Reading Rawls*, ed. N. Daniels (Blackwell, Oxford, 1976).

8 See an interesting discussion of this in Heidegger's 'Letter on Humanism', published in David Farrell Krell's *Martin Heidegger: Basic Writings*, pp. 193-242 (Routledge & Kegan Paul, London, 1978).

CHAPTER III: RESPECT AND DIGNITY

1 I take this to be an integral aspect of a liberal moral culture. It is usually taken as a virtue of Kant's moral theory in contrast to the equally significant tradition of utilitarianism that he gives us a way of articulating the value and significance of individual lives. I raise doubts about his success in doing this because of the ways he is continually undermining a stronger sense of individuality in his fragmented and increasingly attenuated conception of individuality.

2 It is because Kant thinks that people inevitably do things for profit or gain in the social world that he looks towards a different realm to define his sense of dignity. At one stroke it becomes unnecessary for him to consider differences in the kinds of lives which could be lived in societies organised in different ways.

3 In Chapter VIII I show the implications this carries for Kant's conception of citizenship. This bears directly upon Kant's sense of people being able to live free and independent lives.

4 This discussion can be usefully set against Georg Lukács's discussion in *History and Class Consciousness* in his chapter on 'Reification and the Consciousness of the Proletariat', especially part 2, 'The Antinomies of Bourgeois Thought', pp. 110-34 (London, Merlin Press, 1971).

5 This is a source for what I have called a stronger sense of individuality in Kant's writings. It is something he never fully develops. I try to explain why it is so difficult for him to develop this insight.

6 Kant tends to think within an opposition between 'inner' and 'outer' whence the 'outer' is taken to be a realm of determination and control, while the 'inner' is a realm of choice and freedom. This is so deeply embedded in his thinking that it is difficult to do more in this study than to notice different ways it can lead our understanding astray.

7 I suggest that we are often implicitly drawing upon an everyday sense of respecting others which involves a fuller confirmation and validation of the experience of others, including our emotions and feelings. I argue how this is connected to our sense of respecting someone as involving a recognition that someone is a person in their own right with wants and desires of their own. In this study I largely hint at this alternative conception through showing the limits of Kant's conceptions. I argue against the implicit rationalism and individualism of his account showing how respecting others can involve validating different aspects of people's experience as well as recognising the importance of relationships with others.

8 See Karl Marx's *Economic and Philosophical Manuscripts* of 1844 which have been reprinted in many places including *Marx and Engels: Selected Writings* (Lawrence & Wishart, London, 1952). See also a useful

discussion of 'The Concept of Estrangement in Marx' in John O'Neil, *Sociology as a Skin Trade* (Heinemann, London, 1972).
9 Immanuel Kant, *Critique of Practical Reason*, trans. Lewis White Beck (The Liberal Arts Press, Bobbs-Merrill, Indianapolis and New York, 1959). See also Lewis White Beck's *A Commentary on Kant's Critique of Practical Reason* (Chicago, 1960).

CHAPTER IV: RESPECT, IMPARTIALITY AND THE MORAL LAW

1 See 'The Incentives of Pure Practical Reason' which is Chapter 3 of Book 1 of Kant's *Critique of Practical Reason*, pp. 74–92, trans. Lewis White Beck (The Liberal Arts Press, Bobbs-Merrill, Indianapolis and New York, 1959).
2 See Theodor Adorno's discussion 'On the Metacritique of Practical Reason' which forms Chapter 1 of Part 3 entitled 'Freedom' in his *Negative Dialectics*, trans. E. B. Ashton (Routledge & Kegan Paul, London, 1973, pp. 221–99).
3 Relatively little use has been made in the analytical literature of Max Scheler's interesting discussion of Kantian ethics to be found in his *Formalism in Ethics and a Non-Formal Ethics of Values*, trans. Manfred Frings and Roger Funk (Northwestern University Press, Evanston, 1973). There seems to be much to learn from this text, even if you do not agree with the ways that Scheler uses his discussion to develop his own version of ethical personalism. It seems to me as if the tradition of thought that Scheler was a part of deserves much more serious attention.
4 An introduction to this tradition of moral theory is given in J. N. Findlay, *Axiological Ethics* (Macmillan, London, 1970).
5 See the interesting discussion in C. B. MacPherson, *The Political Theory of Possessive Individualism* (Oxford University Press, 1962) and his *Democratic Theory* (Oxford University Press, 1973).
6 See Jean-Paul Sartre's discussion in *Anti-Semite and Jew* (Schocken Books, New York, 1965).
7 See *Letter to a Teacher* by the School of Barbiana (Penguin Books, Harmondsworth, 1970).
8 This raises important questions about human equality that we cannot do justice to here. It is enough for us to realise the kind of challenge they present to the ways we so often think and feel about equality.
9 See, for instance, works which would otherwise be clearly opposed to each other such as Georg Lukács, *History and Class Consciousness* (Merlin Press, London, 1971) and Louis Althusser, *For Marx* and *Reading Capital* (New Left Books, London, 1977).

CHAPTER V: RESPECT, INDEPENDENCE AND SELF-SUFFICIENCY

1 In this chapter I draw heavily upon Kant's discussion in Part 2 of *The Doctrine of Virtue* entitled 'On Duties of Virtue to Others', pp. 115–39, trans. Mary Gregor (Harper & Row, New York, 1964).

2 See the interesting discussion in Chapters 2 and 4 of Allen W. Wood, *Kant's Moral Religion* (Cornell University Press, 1970).

3 I am saying little about the process of secularisation though I would want to argue that a religious morality in which we have to prove ourselves worthy in the eyes of God prepares the ground for the social relations of individual achievement and competitiveness which are so central to the nature of morality in capitalist society. It is the strength of Max Weber's *The Protestant Ethic and the Spirit of Capitalism* that he can help us think about these connections, even if we think that the version of historical materialism that he took himself to be challenging was the economic determinism that was influential in the Germany of his period.

4 This has been influentially discussed in Isaiah Berlin's 'Two Concepts of Liberty' reprinted in his *Four Essays on Liberty* (Oxford University Press, 1969).

5 This is thought about in an interesting way in Bernard Williams's *Morality* (Cambridge University Press, 1972).

6 See a related discussion in Isaiah Berlin's 'John Stuart Mill and the Ends of Life' reprinted in his *Four Essays on Liberty*, *op. cit*. See also Robert Paul Wolff, *The Poverty of Liberalism* (Beacon Press, Boston, 1968), Chapter 1.

CHAPTER VI: OBLIGATION AND INEQUALITY

1 In this chapter I focus upon issues raised in Part 2 of *The Doctrine of Virtue* which focus 'On Duties of Love in Particular and On the Duty of Beneficence', pp. 117–22, trans. Mary Gregor (New York, Harper & Row, 1964).

2 See Sheila Rowbotham's article 'Women's Liberation and the New Politics' which has been reprinted in *The Body Politic* (Stage One, London, 1972), Lee Comer, *Wedlocked Women* (Feminist Press, Leeds, 1974) and Adrienne Rich, *Of Women Born* (Virago, London, 1977).

3 Kant's discussion of the relationship between the sexes is to be found in Part 2 of *Anthropology from a Pragmatic Point of View* in a section entitled 'On the Character of the Sexes', trans. Mary J. Gregor (Martinus Nijhoff, The Hague, 1974).

4 It has been an enduring tendency within social theory to present class relations of power in terms of different classes having different values and beliefs. This mystifies the relationships of power that exist between different classes. This is related to the issue of the treatment of 'values and beliefs' in sociology more generally. A useful book that can help

counter this influence, even if it does not explore the issues theoreti-
cally, is Richard Sennett and Jonathan Cobb, *The Hidden Injuries of
Class* (Cambridge University Press, 1973). See also Melvin L. Kohn,
Class and Conformity: A Study in Values (Dorsey Press, Homewood,
Illinois, 1969).

5 See *Property: Its Duties and Rights*, edited by Charles Gore (Macmillan, London, 1913). It is important to explain why there has been such
relatively little philosophical discussion of these critical issues.

6 Alexis de Tocqueville, *Democracy in America* (Vintage, New York,
1952). This offers an interesting discussion about the meaning and
conditions of equality contrasting what Tocqueville thinks of as 'aristocratic' societies with 'democratic' societies. He also anticipated the im-
mense significance of the development of manufacturing industry. This
has been discussed in Irving Zeitlin, *Liberty, Equality and Revolution in
Alexis de Tocqueville* (Little, Brown & Company, Boston, 1971).

CHAPTER VII: LIBERALISM, INEQUALITY AND SOCIAL DEPENDENCE

1 Kant assumes that if he could show that this could usually be done
then relations of inequality would not have to generate moral issues. It
leaves it as an issue of the duties of individuals.

2 The discussion of gratitude is drawn from Kant's discussion 'On the
Duty of Gratitude' in Part 2 of *The Doctrine of Virtue*, pp. 123–31.

3 See my discussion of this in 'Trusting Ourselves: Marxism, Human
Needs and Sexual Politics' in Clarke *et al.*, *One Dimensional Marxism*
(Allison & Busby, London, 1980).

4 These writings draw upon the more developed social and political writings of Hayek, for instance, *The Constitution of Liberty* (London, 1960)
and *Studies in Philosophy, Politics and Economics* (London, 1967).
Some of these views have been usefully surveyed in 'The Political Ideas
of Neo-Liberalism', *American Political Science Review*, 49 (1955), pp.
509–25. For an interesting contemporary discussion of the significance
of these views in the 1980s see Andrew Gamble's 'The Free Economy
and the Strong State: The Rise of the Social Market Economy' in the
Socialist Register 1979 (Merlin Press, London, 1979).

5 Alvin Gouldner's essays 'Anti-Minotaur: The Myth of a Value-free
Sociology' and his 'The Politics of the Mind', which both appear in his
collection *For Sociology* (Allen Lane, London, 1973) can help us think
about these issues.

6 See C. B. MacPherson, *The Political Theory of Possessive Individualism*
(Oxford University Press, 1962).

7 There is an enormous literature which can illustrate these themes.
Richard Hoggart, *The Uses of Literacy* (Penguin Books, London, 1959)
is an important example. For a background historical understanding
see E. P. Thompson's *The Making of the English Working Class* (Penguin Books, 1970).

8 See Kant's *Metaphysics of Morals*, Part 1. The relevant introduction to *The Metaphysics of Morals* and the Preface to *The Doctrine of Law* can be found in the opening sections of Mary Gregor's translation of *The Doctrine of Virtue*.

9 See Galvano della Volpe's discussion in his *Rousseau and Marx*, trans. John Fraser (Lawrence & Wishart, London, 1978). See in particular the 'Critique of Rousseau's Abstract Man' (1957) and the 'Clarifications' in which he discusses Kant's moral writings more specifically.

10 *The Metaphysical Elements of Justice* (Part 1, Rechtslehre, of *The Metaphysics of Morals*), trans. John Ladd (Indianapolis, 1965). Not a complete translation. See also John Ladd, 'Kant's View on the Relation of Law to Morality', *Journal of Philosophy*, 1960.

11 Denial of rights of citizenship to dependents was a stock attitude right into this century. In 1914 they still questioned whether those in receipt of poor relief should be allowed to vote.

CHAPTER VIII: LIBERALISM AND THE AUTONOMY OF MORALITY

1 This is drawn from H. L. A. Hart's very useful paper 'Between Utility and Rights', p. 77 in Alan Ryan (ed.), *The Idea of Freedom* (Oxford University Press, 1979).

2 These useful ideas are raised but never fully developed in Bernard Williams's article 'Persons, Character and Morality' reprinted in his collection *Moral Luck*. The difficulties we face in developing these ideas often bring into question critical assumptions in our prevailing moral theory.

3 Dworkin's ideas are discussed in *Taking Rights Seriously*. The paper entitled 'What Rights Do We Have?' is of particular significance in placing his idea of an equality of concern and respect. Another useful starting point is his paper 'Liberalism' in *Public and Private Morality*, ed. Stuart Hampshire.

4 Sandel's stimulating discussion in *Liberalism and the Limits of Justice* does a great deal to illuminate the different ways individuals can relate to their ends, though this itself proves a limiting framework within which moral issues of power and subordination can be raised.

5 Iris Murdoch's *The Sovereignty of Good* makes us aware of alternative traditions of moral thought and feeling which can help us question an essentially utilitarian conception of the good.

6 The question of human needs still requires careful exploration, especially if we are aware of an instrumentalism towards people that can characterise both liberal and Marxist theory. Stimulating discussions can be found in Simone Weil's *The Need for Roots* and in Agnes Heller's *The Theory of Need in Marx*.

7 This is part of a crucial recognition that contradictions exist in our lives, not simply in our consciousness. This insight was part of Gramsci's attempt at a moral renewal of Marxism in his *Prison Notebooks*.

8 Simone Weil's deliberations are particularly relevant since she is often at one and the same time deeply influenced by Kant and struggling against his inheritance to be able to illuminate the moral realities of her experience of factory work.

9 Carol Gilligan's evidence helps question the assumed universalism of a Kantian tradition, though it stops short of thinking through how we are to relate it to the gender differences. Somehow this seems to connect to its apparent disconnection from relations of power and subordination.

10 The identification of reason with masculinity has been so culturally embedded that it has only rarely been questioned within liberal or Marxist theory. Feminists have raised these issues but men have rarely theorised this complicated relation between language and masculine experience.

11 This has been helpfully illuminated in Susan Griffin's *Pornography and Silence* which can help bring our moral theory of respect and equality into closer touch with historical reality.

12 See, for instance, Freud's discussion in *Civilisation and Its Discontents*.

13 These issues have been central to discussions of socialist feminism. See, for instance, Sheila Rowbotham's *Dreams and Dilemmas*.

14 See E. P. Thompson's discussion in *The Poverty of Theory* as well as the articles in S. Clarke *et al.*, *One Dimensional Marxism*.

15 I have tried to clarify this further in my article 'Fear and Intimacy' to be found in *The Sexuality of Men*, ed Humphries and Metcalf.

BIBLIOGRAPHY

This is a bibliography of texts that I have either referred to directly or which have influenced the thinking that has gone into this study.

ADORNO, Theodor, *Negative Dialectics*, trans. E. B. Ashton, Routledge & Kegan Paul, London, 1973.

BECK, L. W., *A Commentary on Kant's Critique of Practical Reason*, University of Chicago Press, 1960.

BERLIN, Isaiah, *Four Essays on Liberty*, Oxford University Press, 1969.

BERLIN, Isaiah, *Vico and Herder*, Hogarth Press, London, 1976.

BLUM, Lawrence, *Friendship, Altruism and Morality*, Routledge & Kegan Paul, London, 1980.

CASSIRER, Ernst, *Rousseau, Kant, Goethe*, Princeton University Press, 1945.

CAVELL, Stanley, *Must We Mean What We Say?*, Charles Scribners, New York, 1969; Cambridge University Press, 1976.

CAVELL, Stanley, *The Claim of Reason: Wittgenstein, Skepticism, Morality and Tragedy*, Oxford University Press, 1979.

COHEN, J. and ROGERS, J., *On Democracy*, Penguin Books, New York, 1983.

DOWNIE, R. S. and TELFER, E., *Respect for Persons*, Allen & Unwin, London, 1969.

DWORKIN, R., *Taking Rights Seriously*, Duckworth, London, 1977.

FALK, W. D., 'Morality, Self and Others', in G. Dworkin and J. Thompson (eds), *Ethics*, Harper & Row, New York, 1968.

FEINBERG, Joel, *Doing and Deserving: Essays in the Theory of Responsibility*, Princeton University Press, 1970.

FOOT, Philippa, *Virtues and Vices*, Basil Blackwell, Oxford, 1977.

FREUD, Sigmund, *Introductory Lectures on Psycho-Analysis*, George Allen & Unwin, London, 1929.

FREUD, S. *Civilisation and its Discontents*, standard edn, Vol. 21, pp. 54–145, The Hogarth Press, London, 1930.

Bibliography

FRIED, Charles, *Anatomy of Values*, Harvard University Press, Cambridge, Mass., 1970.

FRIED, Charles, *Right and Wrong*, Harvard University Press, Cambridge, Mass., 1978.

FROMM, Erich, *Fear of Freedom*, Routledge & Kegan Paul, London, 1960.

FROMM, Erich, *Greatness and Limitations of Freud's Thought*, Jonathan Cape, London, 1980.

GILLIGAN, Carol, *In a Different Voice*, Harvard University Press, 1982.

GOLDMANN, Lucien, *Immanuel Kant*, trans. Robert Black, New Left Books, London, 1971.

GOLDMANN, Lucien, *Lukács and Heidegger*, Routledge & Kegan Paul, London, 1978.

GORE, Charles, *Property: Its Duties and Rights*, Macmillan, London, 1913.

GOULDNER, Alvin, *The Coming Crisis of Western Sociology*, Heinemann, London, 1971.

GOULDNER, Alvin, *For Sociology*, Penguin Books, Harmondsworth, 1976.

GRAHAM, Keith, *Contemporary Political Philosophy*, Cambridge University Press, 1982.

GRAMSCI, Antonio, 'The Study of Philosophy' in Quintin Hoare and Geoffrey Nowell Smith (eds), *Selections from the Prison Notebooks of Antonio Gramsci*, Lawrence & Wishart, London, 1971.

GREGOR, Mary, *Laws of Freedom*, Basil Blackwell, Oxford, 1963.

GRIFFIN, Susan, *Pornography and Silence*, The Women's Press, London, 1982.

GUTMAN, Amy, *Liberal Equality*, Cambridge University Press, 1980.

HAMPSHIRE, Stuart, *Public and Private Morality*, Cambridge University Press, 1978.

HARE, R. M., *The Language of Morals*, Oxford University Press, 1952.

HARRIS, Errol, 'Respect for Persons' in Richard T. de George (ed.), *Ethics and Society*, Doubleday, New York, 1966.

HART, H. L. A., 'Between Utility and Rights' in Alan Ryan (ed.), *The Idea of Freedom*, Oxford University Press, 1979.

HEIDEGGER, Martin, 'Letter on Humanism' in David Farrell Krell, *Martin Heidegger: Basic Writings*, Routledge & Kegan Paul, London, 1978.

HELLER, Agnes, *The Theory of Need in Marx*, Allison & Busby, 1976.

HIRSCHMANN, Albert, *The Passions and the Interests*, Princeton University Press, 1977.

HOGGART, Richard, *The Uses of Literacy*, Penguin, Harmondsworth, 1959.

HONDERICH, Ted, 'The Problem of Well-Being and the Principle of Equality', *Mind*, 1981.

JONES, Hardy, *Kant's Principle of Personality*, University of Wisconsin Press, Madison, 1971.

Bibliography

JONES, W. T., *Morality and Freedom in the Philosophy of Kant*, Oxford University Press, 1940.

KANT, Immanuel, *The Moral Law*, trans. H. J. Paton, Hutchinson, London, 1948.

KANT, Immanuel, *Critique of Practical Reason*, trans. Lewis White Beck, Bobbs-Merrill, Indianapolis and New York, 1956.

KANT, Immanuel, *Foundations of the Metaphysic of Morals*, trans. Lewis White Beck, Bobbs-Merrill, New York, 1959.

KANT, Immanuel, *Religion Within the Limits of Reason Alone*, trans. Greene and Hudson, Harper & Row, New York, 1960.

KANT, Immanuel, *Lectures on Ethics*, trans. L. Infield, Harper & Row, New York, 1963.

KANT, Immanuel, *The Doctrine of Virtue*, trans. Mary J. Gregor, Harper & Row, New York, 1964 – also James Ellington, Bobbs-Merrill, Indianapolis, 1964.

KANT, Immanuel, *Observations on the Feeling of the Beautiful and the Sublime*, trans. Goldthwait, University of California Press, Berkeley, 1965.

KANT, Immanuel, *The Metaphysical Elements of Justice*, Part 1 of *The Metaphysics of Morals*, trans. John Ladd, Bobbs-Merrill, Indianapolis, 1965.

KANT, Immanuel, 'What is Enlightenment?' in Hans Reiss (ed.), *Kant's Political Writings*, Cambridge University Press, 1970.

KANT, Immanuel, *Anthropology from a Pragmatic Point of View*, trans. Mary Gregor, Martinus Nijhoff, The Hague, 1974.

KIERKEGAARD, Soren, *The Concept of Dread*, Princeton University Press, 1955.

KIERKEGAARD, Soren, *Works of Love*, trans. Howard and Edna Hong, Harper & Row, New York, 1962.

LUKÁCS, Georg, *History and Class Consciousness*, Merlin Press, London, 1971.

LUKÁCS, Georg, *The Young Hegel*, Merlin Press, London, 1975.

LUKES, Steven, *Individualism*, Basil Blackwell, Oxford, 1973.

MacINTYRE, Alasdair, *A Short History of Ethics*, Macmillan, New York, 1966.

MacINTYRE, Alasdair, *After Virtue*, Duckworths, London, 1983.

MacLAGAN, W. G., 'Respect for Persons as a Moral Principle', *Philosophy* 35, No. 134 (July 1960), pp. 139–217), and No. 135 (October 1960), pp. 289–305.

MacMURRAY, JOHN, *The Self as Agent*, Faber & Faber, London, 1957.

MacPHERSON, C. B., *The Political Theory of Possessive Individualism*, Oxford University Press, 1962.

MARCUSE, H., *Reason and Revolution*, Routledge & Kegan Paul, London, 1949.

MARX, Karl, *Capital*, Vol. 1, Vol. 3, Lawrence & Wishart, London, 1970.

MARX, Karl, *Early Texts*, trans. David McLellan, Basil Blackwell, Oxford, 1971.

Bibliography

MARX, Karl, *Theories of Surplus Value*, Moscow, 1968 and 1971.

MELDON, A.I., *Essays in Moral Philosophy*, University of Washington Press, Seattle, 1958.

MELDON, A. I., *Rights and Persons*, Basil Blackwell, Oxford, 1977.

MILLER, Jean Baker, *Towards a New Psychology of Women*, Penguin Books, Harmondsworth, 1978.

MURDOCH, Iris, 'Vision and Choice in Morality', *Proceedings of the Aristotelian Society*, 1956.

MURDOCH, Iris, *The Sovereignty of Good*, Routledge & Kegan Paul, London, 1970.

MURPHY, Jeffrie, *Kant: The Philosophy of Right*, Macmillan; St Martin's Press, London, 1970.

NOZICK, Robert, *Anarchy, State and Utopia*, Basic Books, New York, 1974.

PITKIN, Hanna, *Wittgenstein and Justice*, University of California Press, Berkeley, 1972.

RAWLS, John, 'Two Concepts of Rules' in Philippa Foot (ed.), *Theories of Ethics*, Oxford University Press, 1967.

RAWLS, John, 'The Sense of Justice' in Joel Feinberg, (ed.), *Moral Concepts*, Oxford University Press, 1969.

RAWLS, John, *A Theory of Justice*, Harvard University Press and Oxford University Press, 1971.

REICH, Wilhelm, *Sex-Pol, Essays 1924-1934*, ed. Lee Baxandall, Vintage, New York, 1972.

RHEES, Rush, *Without Answers*, Routledge & Kegan Paul, London, 1971.

ROUSSEAU, J.-J., *The First and Second Discourses*, ed. Roger D. Masters, St Martin's Press, New York, 1964.

ROWBOTHAM, Sheila, *Woman's Consciousness, Man's World*, Penguin, Harmondsworth, 1973.

ROWBOTHAM, Sheila, *Dreams and Dilemmas*, Virago, London, 1983.

SANDEL, Michael, *Liberalism and the Limits of Justice*, Cambridge University Press, 1982.

SARTRE, J.-P., *The Portrait of an Anti-Semite*, trans. F. de Mauny, Secker & Warburg, London, 1948.

SCHELER, Max, *The Nature of Sympathy*, trans. Werner Stark, Routledge & Kegan Paul, London, 1965.

SCHELER, Max, *Formalism in Ethics and a Non-Formal Ethics of Values*, trans. Manfred Frings and Roger Funk, Northwestern University Press, Evanston, 1973.

SCHOPENHAUER, Arthur, *On the Basis of Morality*, trans. E. F. Poyne, Bobbs-Merrill, New York, 1965.

SEIDLER, Victor J., 'Trusting Ourselves: Marxism, Human Needs and Sexual Politics' in Clarke *et al.*, *One Dimensional Marxism*, Allison & Busby, London, 1980.

SEIDLER, Victor J., 'Fear and Intimacy' in M. Humphries and A. Metcalf (eds), *The Sexuality of Men*, Pluto Press, London, 1985.

SENNETT, Richard and COBB, Jonathan, *The Hidden Injuries of Class*, Cambridge University Press, 1973.

Bibliography

SIMMONS, A. John, *Moral Principles and Political Obligation*, Princeton University Press, 1979.

SKILLEN, Anthony, *Ruling Illusions*, Harvester Press, Sussex, 1977.

SLATER, Philip, *The Pursuit of Loneliness*, Beacon Press, Boston, 1971.

SMART, J. J. C. and WILLIAMS, B., *Utilitarianism, For and Against*, Cambridge University Press, 1973.

TAYLOR, Charles, *Hegel*, Cambridge University Press, 1977.

TAYLOR, Charles, *Hegel and Modern Society*, Cambridge University Press, 1978.

THOMPSON, Edward, *The Poverty of Theory*, Merlin Press, London, 1979.

TOCQUEVILLE, Alexis de, *Democracy in America*, Vintage, New York, 1952.

VLASTOS, Gregory, 'Human Worth, Merit and Equality' in Joel Feinberg (ed.), *Moral Concepts*, Oxford University Press, 1969.

VOLPE, Galvano della, *Rousseau and Marx*, trans. John Fraser, Lawrence & Wishart, London, 1978.

WALACE, James, *Virtues and Vices*, Cornell University Press, Ithaca, 1978.

WALZER, Michael, *Spheres of Justice*, Basil Blackwell, Oxford, 1983.

WARD, Keith, *The Development of Kant's View of Ethics*, Basil Blackwell, Oxford, 1972.

WEBER, Max, *The Protestant Ethic and the Spirit of Capitalism*, George Allen & Unwin, London, 1930.

WEIL, Simone, *The Need for Roots*, Routledge & Kegan Paul, London, 1952.

WEIL, Simone, *Oppression and Liberty*, Routledge & Kegan Paul, London, 1958.

WEIL, Simone, *Selected Essays 1934-43*, trans. Richard Rees, Oxford University Press, 1962.

WEIL, Simone, *Seventy Letters*, Oxford University Press, 1965.

WEIL, Simone, *Lectures on Philosophy*, Cambridge University Press, 1978.

WILLIAMS, Bernard, *Morality: An Introduction to Ethics*, Cambridge University Press, 1972.

WILLIAMS, Bernard, *Problems of the Self*, Cambridge University Press, 1973.

WILLIAMS, Bernard, 'Persons, Character and Morality', in Amelie Rorty (ed.), *The Identities of Persons*, University of California Press, Berkeley, 1976, reprinted in *Moral Luck*, Cambridge University Press, 1981.

WINCH, Peter, *Ethics and Action*, Routledge & Kegan Paul, London, 1972.

WITTGENSTEIN, Ludwig, *Philosophical Investigations*, trans. G. E. M. Anscombe, Basil Blackwell, Oxford, 1963.

WOLIN, S., *Politics and Vision*, Allen & Unwin, London, 1961.

WOLFF, R.P., *Kant: A Collection of Critical Essays*, Doubleday, New York, 1967.

WOLFF, R. P., *The Poverty of Liberalism*, Beacon Press, Boston, 1968.

Bibliography

WOOD, Allen, *Kant's Moral Religion*, Cornell University Press, Ithaca, 1970.

ZEITLIN, Irving, *Liberty; Equality and Revolution in Alexis de Tocqueville*, Little, Brown & Company, Boston, 1971.

INDEX

abortion, 152-3, 219
action, rational: maxims for, 59-61; moral worth of, 133, 134; side constraints on, 187-8; *see also* labour; talents
activities, expression through, 8, 25-9, 31-3, 37-8, 42, 191-5
Adorno, Theodor, 47
affliction *see* humiliation; suffering
Althusser, Louis, 55, 206
animal nature, 20, 29-30, 35, 38-42, 61; *see also* feelings
Aristotle, 134
autonomy: and dependence, 113-17, 119-54, 159-62; and dignity, 33-4; ends and means, 154-90; and feelings, 140-5; injustice and respect, 190-223; of morality, 1, 6-7, 9-14, 224; of the will, 21-3

babies, 165
beneficence, 75-84; generosity, 69, 74, 78; kindness, 28, 106-7
Bentham, Jeremy, 172, 189
Berlin, Isaiah, 228
bondsman and master, 86-7, 91-4

capitalist society: and dependence, 11, 93-4, 96-102, 104-5, 107-8, 157, 161-2, 179, 186-7, 196
Cassirer, Ernst, 16, 19

character, 37, 199-200; of men/women, 72-4, 90, 214; *see also* individuality; personality
charity, 69, 78-80, 85; *see also* beneficence
children: relationships with, 142-3, 165-6, 177, 206-7
choice, 130; of career, 37-8, 65-7, 140, 166; of ends, 124-5, 128-35, 163, 195-8; freedom of, 23, 123-4, 134, 186; of subordination, 89-93
Christianity, 2, 4, 20, 24, 56-7; and property relations, 84-5
citizenship, 108-14, 119-20, 156
class, social: community of, 107-8, individuality and, 51-5, 216-20; power relations and, 96-105, 228-9
coercion, 186-7; *see also* control; oppression
Cohen, J., 212
conduct, codes of, 195
consciousness, moral, 103-4; formation of, 2-3, 5-6
contract, 125, 130, 194-5
control, 143-9, 175, 178-9, 186-7, 190, 192-3, 203; of lives, 175, 190, 192-3, 203; self-, 143-4, 178-9; *see also* autonomy; dependence; power, relations of

oppression, 159, 178, 181–3, 187, 209
optimism, 17

parents: expectations by, 37–8, 64, 65–7, 140; relations with children, 142–3, 165, 177, 180, 206–7
people, treated as ends *see* ends in ourselves, people as
person and personality: fragmented conception of, 25–35, 35–8, 44, 48–50, 120–3, 127–30, 154–5, 170–1, 191–4, 197; man as, 25–6, 29–37, 155; moral, 25–6, 37, 125–8, 191–4, 218–21; *see also* individuality
personal relations, 102, 150–1, 156–7; and subordination, 209; *see also* children, relationships with; love; sexes, relations between the; social relations
Plato, 205
political morality, 118–20, 156, 172–5, 188–9, 210–12
politics: and morality, 9; revolutionary, 208–9; *see also* citizenship; governments
poor, the: dependency of, 7, 95–7, 101–2, 109–14, 130–1, 134, 157, 168–9, 188, 213–16; obligation to help, 68–82; and sources of wealth, 82–94
power, relations of, 7, 9–11, 13–14, 68, 95, 112–16, 139, 157–62, 190, 192–3; bondsman and master, 86–7, 91–4; class, 96–105, 228–9; and moral philosophy, 119, 134–6; and respect, 208–23; *see also* control; dependence, relations of; factory work; oppression; poor, the; women, subordination
price, 26–7, 30–2, 155
principles, 144–5, 164–5
private realm, 109
production, relations of, 99–101, 201–4, 206, 208–9, 211; *see also* capitalist society

property relations, 82–94, 190, 192, 196, 203; *see also* poor, the, dependency of
psychology, 147–8, 170, 173–4, 177–9
public realm, 109

race, 53–5, 133
rationalism, 18, 39, 44, 51, 116, 138–40
rationality and reason, 5, 222; and feelings, 122–7, 138–45, 147–54, 155, 162–4; and individuality, 47–50, 51, 116, 120–4; and masculinity, 140, 141–3, 149–53, 160–1, 164, 214–15, 231; and nature, 125–31
Rawls, John, 13, 125–6, 127–40, 142, 144, 149, 167, 168, 172, 178, 179, 180–2, 191–206
relationships, 25–9, 31, 33–5, 38, 40–2, 94, 102; morality of, 179–80; morality of responsibility, 151–3; *see also* personal relations; power, relations of; production, relations of; social relations
respect, 1–2, 6–10; and autonomy, 169–79; and dignity, 25–43; and human nature, 15–24; and impartiality, 51–5; and injustice, 190–223; and the moral law, 44–50; and non-interference, 56–62; of others' ends, 130–8; and self-sufficiency, 62–7; *see also* ends in ourselves, people as; self-respect
responsibility, 145–6; individual or social, 158–60, 169; morality of, 151–3; for subordination, 98–9; of women, 145, 150–3, 173; *see also* autonomy
Reynaud-Guerithault, Anne, 183
rich, the: beneficence of, 78–82; obligation of, 68–78; sources of wealth, 82–94; *see also* poor, the, dependency of
right, the, and the good, 122–8, 130–5, 183–5, 200; *see also* justice

International Library of Philosophy

Editor: Ted Honderich

(Demy 8vo)